Project Procurement Management

Contracting, Subcontracting, Teaming

Quentin W. Fleming

FMC PRESS

Editorial and Sales Offices: FMC Press
14001 Howland Way, Tustin, California 92780

Publisher's Cataloging-in-Publication
(Provided by Quality Books, Inc.)

Fleming, Quentin W.
    Project procurement management-- contracting,
subcontracting, teaming / Quentin W. Fleming.
    p. cm.
    Includes bibliographical references.
    LCCN 2003095371
    ISBN 0-9743912-0-4

    1. Project management. 2. Industrial procurement.
I. Title

HD69.P75F555 2003   658.4'04
                                     QBI03-200614

10
First Edition

Cover and interior design by Lightbourne, Inc.

Manufactured in the United States of America

Contents

Introduction

This book was intended to cover the subject of project procurement management. As way of background, a decade ago my son and I wrote a book on this same subject which was then entitled *Subcontract Project Management: Subcontract Planning and Organization.* Our book covered the subject of project procurement management, but it was targeted specifically to the aerospace and defense industry, to those companies which had prime government contracts and were subcontracting large segments of their work to other firms for performance. By contrast this new book was intended to provide a more general treatment on the subject, with an application to any project, of any size, in any industry which buys some of their project scope from another firm.

However, there were sections in our earlier book which applied nicely to projects in general. In particular the sections on teaming arrangements, types of contracts in use, risk management, seller oversight and possibly others. These sections continue to be valid today. Therefore, I incorporated some concepts from our earlier work as it pertained to the broader issue of buying project scope.

As an author and management consultant, I have collected many books on my favorite subject of project management. In my home I have assembled a rather extensive library of books on project management. Before starting with this endeavor I conducted my own "non-scientific" survey of books on project management. The one thing that became obvious to me was that all of these books, without exception, had one thing in common: they did not address the subject of buying scope from another company. It was as if most projects did all of their work themselves, with their own employees, within their own organizations. We know that is not the case with many projects. Success is often determined by how well we procure scope.

Typically, the more complex, the more challenging the project, the more work will be sent outside of the company for performance. Yet there is a lack of coverage of project procurement management. Even the big five project management books (the big sellers) do not address procurement management or even "make or buy" analysis. Question: how could we adequately define the scope of work on a new project without also doing a make or buy analysis? The answer: not very well.

Fact: it is common today for companies to procure major portions of their projects from other companies. Some projects today buy as much as 80% of their project scope from other companies. And to compound the issue further, often the items which are bought from other companies are the high-risk segments of the project. After it's over, when management assesses what went wrong with their project performance, they often will find that it was the work which was contracted or subcontracted to another company which adversely impacted their overall project performance. My conclusion: how well we manage other firm's performance to our projects will often determine how well, or how poorly we do on our projects.

One of my pet concerns with how well procurement management works on projects centers on the delicate relationship of the project manager to the procurement people, typically called buyers. We must always keep in mind that it is the project manager who has the ultimate responsibility for the project's technical performance, including the cost and schedule results. By contrast those individuals who have their company's delegated procurement authority, the buyers, too often fail to recognize that their mission in life . . . is to support their company's projects. They buy things for projects within their established purchasing policies. Often on the major complex procurements the project manager will elect to appoint a technical specialist to manage critical components, functioning as a team leader in an integrated project team environment. In such cases the assigned buyer must become a subordinate, a critical deputy to the designated project team leader.

The point that many of these professional individuals fail to realize is that they exist to support the projects, not to interfere in the management of the project. Managing the project is the responsibility of the person carrying the title of project manager. It is often only an attitudinal issue, but one which can impede the maximum performance on projects.

One additional important point. In our 1994 book, my son and I subdivided the project procurement activities into three simple but distinct processes: "<u>planning</u>," "<u>procurement</u>," and "<u>performance</u>." This subdivision of work made sense to us at the time. And it still does.

However, since that time the Project Management Institute (PMI) issued their 1996, 2000, and 2004 Editions to *<u>A Guide to the Project Management Body of Knowledge-PMBOK ® Guide</u>*. In this landmark document which has since become the de facto world standard for project management, they elected to subdivide the project procurement effort into six distinct processes:

What we had called "<u>planning</u>" the *PMBOK ® Guide* broke into two processes described as "<u>Procurement Planning</u>" and "<u>Solicitation Planning</u>."

What we had called "<u>procurement</u>" the *PMBOK ® Guide* divided into "<u>Solicitation</u>" and "<u>Source Selection</u>."

And finally, what we had referred to as "<u>performance</u>" the *PMBOK ® Guide* used the terms "<u>Contract Administration</u>" and "<u>Contract Closeout</u>."

I felt very comfortable with the finer subdivision of project procurement management into these six distinct processes, as described in the *PMBOK ® Guide*. Thus, in this book I initially followed the model of the *PMBOK ® Guide* and described project procurement management as having six distinct processes. As I look back on my industrial career, every major subcontract I worked followed these six distinct processes.

One additional point on the PMI *PMBOK ® Guide*. It was my distinct privilege to serve on the eight person core team which updated this document for the year 2000 edition. I was assigned responsibility by our project manager Ms. Cynthia A. Berg, PMP, for all "earned value management" content in the document, and for Chapter 12 covering Project Procurement Management.

Then in 2007 and 2008 I was again given the honor of serving as a volunteer for the Fourth Edition update to the *PMBOK ® Guide*. This time our project manager was a colleague of mine from the University of California Irvine: Ms. Cyndi Snyder-Stackpole, PMP. Cyndi asked that I be responsible for managing two of the nine PMI knowledge area chapters: 7. Project Cost Management (which included earned value) and 12. Project Procurement Management.

Part way through the update I got a call from Cyndi. She asked if I felt it would be beneficial if we reduced the number of procurement processes from six to four, thereby making the procurement section more compatible to a greater number of projects. I welcomed the idea. We then agreed on four procurement processes: Plan Procurements; Conduct Procurements; Administer Procurements; and Close Procurements. Based on the favorable response from those PMI members who reviewed the 2008 *PMBOK ® Guide*, this was a positive move.

One final matter. I have decided not to rewrite this book as a result of going from six to four procurement processes in the PMBOK ® Guide. My reasoning is simple: nothing has really changed. The work of procuring project scope is the same. Only the convenient grouping of processes has been redefined. See Figure 1.4 in Chapter 1. It will illustrate the evolution of procurement coverage within the *PMBOK ® Guide*.

Quentin W. Fleming

Acknowledgements

Beginning in 1995 I started a long-term relationship with the University of California at Irvine to assist them to deliver a series of courses to the public and corporations to help them better perform on their projects. It has been a successful series and has reached thousands of individuals, literally around the world. The UCI director of this series has been **Lori Munoz-Reiland**, and her work has been outstanding.

One of the two courses I developed for UCI is entitled: *Project Procurement Management-Contracting, Subcontracting, and Teaming.* We have qualified six instructors to deliver this course. Each of these individuals took time from their busy schedules to read my draft manuscript and provide their comments, concerns, and suggestions.

We need to give them a "special thanks" for their help.

- **Jan Birkelbach**, PMP,
- **Ed Fern**, PMP,
- **David Jacob**,
- **Janice Preston**, PMP,
- **Fred Samelian**, PMP,
- **Cyndi Snyder**, PMP

Lastly, my son **Sheldon J. Fleming** is a practicing attorney here in California and he reviewed the materials on the legal aspects of procurement. Thanks Shel.

Quentin W. Fleming

List of Figures

CHAPTER 1

What is Project Procurement Management

Project Procurement Management includes the processes required to acquire goods and services, to attain project scope, from outside the performing organization.

—A Guide to the Project Management Body of Knowledge (PMBOK Guide), Year 2000 Edition[1]

Subcontracting, a way of life. MCI reaps the benefits of over 9,000 research and development engineers not on its payroll.

. . . in an industry where new products routinely become obsolete in a year, MCI claims that it's more efficient to spend time looking for innovative subcontractors than developing its own technology.

—Dick Liebhaber, MCI, from the Tom Peters book *Liberation Management*[2]

There are many reasons why it is a sound business practice to buy some part of a project's scope from another firm. MCI's Dick Liebhaber cites one of the more important reasons to buy scope: to quickly expand the intellectual base at his company. MCI finds that it is easier to obtain technical brainpower from other companies, than to attempt to recruit and add permanent employees. And there is also the opposite advantage: to be able to quickly downsize the company should that unpleasant task become a necessity. Companies can cancel contracts much easier than to layoff a workforce. But there are also other valid reasons for companies to follow such a policy.

In addition to adding to its intellectual base, firms often find that relationships with suppliers will bring them resources, facilities,

---

1. Project Management Institute, Newtown Square, Pennsylvania, 2000, page 147.
2. Alfred A. Knopf, Inc., New York, NY, 1992, pages 306-307.

investments and equipment, which would not otherwise be available to a project utilizing its own limited company assets. The addition of suppliers to a project will often reduce the risks of a new venture by sharing the costs of the venture, and enhancing their chances of success.

This book is about project management. However, its primary focus is on that portion of the project which will be performed by another company. It deals with the project work which is contractually procured and performed by people working for another company. Such transactions are sometimes called contracts, sometimes subcontracts, and sometimes teaming agreements. The key distinguishing ingredient: they are all procured under some type of a legal relationship.

The purpose of this book is to describe the project procurement process in a meaningful way so as to help the project managers and their teams to better manage this critical work. As our projects become increasingly more complex, more and more we will be finding that we must rely on people from other companies to help us perform our project work. How much project scope do we buy from other companies: estimates range from as little as zero to as high as 90%.

The procurement of project scope whether it be done through teaming arrangements, contracting or subcontracting, will be progressively taking a larger share of our business. Thus, we must perform this management process well, if we are to be successful on our projects.

A basic premise of this book: Contracts or Subcontracts (the procurements) exist to support successful project management. Any contract or a subcontract (a procurement) placed on a project is merely a subproject of the total project. Any contract or subcontract manager can best be thought of as being a surrogate extension of the project manager.

This book will emphasize the importance of managing project procurements well. It will not describe in great detail the legal or contractual issues, the terms and conditions, general or specific contractual provisions, except in a broad strategic way to keep the project team from making avoidable errors. In most cases the project team will be supported by a procurement professional, a person loaned into the project team by an organization which exists under the title of purchasing, procurement, material, materiel, supply management, etc.

The main mission of these professionals is to support and improve the management of the project.

The Project = the "Make" content + the "Buy" content

There are numerous definitions of what constitutes a project. Such definitions have multiplied profusely with the expanded interest in project management which came into vogue in the 1990s. One such definition somewhat different from the others is as follows:

> *A project is a special kind of activity. It involves something that is both unique and important and thereby requires unusual attention. It also has boundaries with other activities so that its extent is defined. And it has a beginning and an end and objectives whose accomplishment signal the end.* [3]

This definition of a project is consistent with others, but it also emphasizes in particular the outer limits of a project.

Still another way to look at a project is to focus on who will be performing the actual work. One could easily separate a project into two distinct parts: that portion which will be done with your own company employees, and that portion which will be sent outside of your company for performance. It is the external work (from one's own company) which is the theme of this book: the buy content. This approach to subdividing a project into two generic parts is illustrated in Figure 1.1.

Here the project is simply separated into two parts: the "Make" work and the "Buy" work. What is the importance of this distinction? Simply put, the "Make" work will be authorized by the project manager with use of non-legal documents typically called work authorizations or budgets. Most companies have internal procedures which cover this kind of activity.

Question: what happens when the internal "Make" work effort

---

3. Dr. Arnold M. Ruskin and Mr. W. Eugene Estes, *What Every Engineer Should Know About Project Management,* (New York: Marcel Dekker, Inc., 1995) page 3.

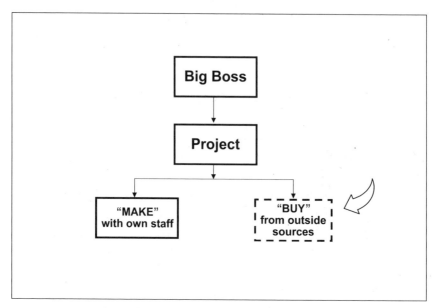

Figure 1.1 *Project Procurement Management: Buying Project Scope*

starts to experience problems, as is sometimes the case. Likely such difficulties will be discovered in the periodic project status reviews that takes place within most companies. When the "big boss" identifies such problems often they will gently urge the lagging areas to get back on performance with some benevolent comments such as: *I don't care what it takes I want you back on track even if it means working all night!* And not surprisingly, most problems are quickly corrected by responding to the recommendations by the "big boss." Point: the big boss has influence over what happens . . . within the company.

However, let's now discuss what happens whenever the "buy" work fails to perform up to our expectations. What influence does our "big boss" have over the work we sent to another company for performance. Answer: virtually nothing. Unless there is a special personal relationship between the big boss and the performing company, the work sent outside of the company will be governed strictly by the legal document the buyer has issued called the contract, or subcontract, or purchase order. If we failed to specify precisely what we wanted the other company to do for us, the big boss will be little help getting the other company to improve performance. The safety wall for other companies is the precise language of our contractual document. The contract language has to be right.

This is the key distinction between the make work versus the buy work. Senior management can and will often intercede with the internal make work. They will use their clout, and cause an improvement in performance. But the buy work is a legal and binding formal relationship. In effect, the buy work is a "non-forgiving" relationship. If we made a mistake in defining what we wanted from the seller, an adjustment can be made . . . but often for an exorbitant price. The process of adjusting such work is called an "equitable adjustment", sometimes also called seller "claims."

Project Managers will act both as a Buyer and as a Seller of Scope

Project Managers are somewhat like a Coach of an athletic team. They are responsible for everything that happens to their team, the good and of course the bad. It doesn't matter whether they can control these issues. Someone has to be held accountable and it is typically the Coach or the Project Manager who holds that position.

Project Managers, in addition to overseeing everything that happens on their projects, are also ultimately responsible for what happens with two external company relationships, one (upward) with their customer(s), and the other (downward) with their suppliers. These two external company project relationships are depicted in Figure 1.2.

Shown on the left side of the figure is the relationship between the project manager and the customer(s). Often during the period of project performance the initial agreed to scope of work will need to be changed, for whatever reason. It is critical that whenever the original scope of work changes, that the project's commitment to management also be changed, that it be expanded or decreased as may be the case.

Often when the scope of work is altered there must be an adjustment in the authorized budget, or in the schedule commitment, or both. What constitutes a customer can be internal company management on a

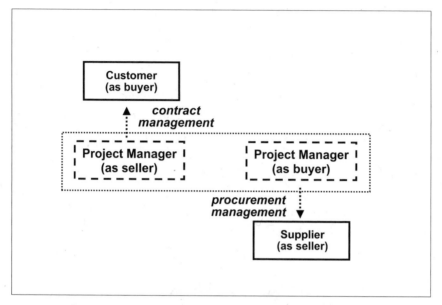

Figure 1.2 *Two Critical Project Relationships: as Buyer or Seller*

funded project, or some external buyer when the project consists of a contract from an external source, like another company or perhaps the government. Many projects start out with a single customer from one source, but will later find that other entities become interested in their project. Thus it is not uncommon for the Project Manager to put other interested candidates on contract, to also sell them scope, most often with another separate contract. In this role the Project Manager can be thought of as being the "seller" of project scope, and often this work is best described as that of contract management.

Conversely, as shown on the right side of the figure, the Project Manager also assumes the role of the "buyer" of scope, from an external source. The Project Manager is essentially acquiring the performance of project scope from another firm. This book will focus exclusively on the Project Manager as the buyer of project scope. However, it must be understood that the other role, that of the seller of project scope, is also an important duty for any Project Manager.

Who exactly has the Procurement Delegation of Authority (DOA)
or
Centralized versus Decentralized Procurement

With a new, start-up company, virtually anyone can do anything and it is typically alright. There are no formal rules, no procedures, no precedents to follow. However, as a new firm starts to mature, certain rules and restrictions begin to take over. Tasks previously allowed for employees are systematically declared to be off-limits by management. One of the first things to be curtailed by a maturing company is the ability to "buy" things on behalf of the firm.

It isn't necessarily that there is distrust in employees. It is simply a fact, that one of the most judiciously guarded functions in any company is the ability to place orders (legal agreements) to buy something. This practice is called a procurement "delegation of authority" to buy, and such procurement DOAs come straight from the top person of any company.

The top person in most organizations will go by various titles. In the United States they are typically called the general manager. In Europe they are often call the managing director. Without being told, we instinctively know who they are, because they have the best office and the best parking spot in the organization.

General managers are very careful about who is authorized to buy things on behalf of their company. They will carefully execute a memo giving a specific delegation of authority to buy things on behalf of their company. Such delegations will typically go to someone carrying the title of vice president of procurement, or purchasing, or supply management, or perhaps the Chief Procurement Officer (CPO), etc. An important point: such authorities to buy will rarely ever be given to the project manager. Fact: project managers rarely have a delegated authority to buy on behalf of their companies. This revelation sometimes comes as a shock and a disappointment to project managers.

However, if the procurement process is working well, and it generally does work well, it really doesn't matter. The vice president of procurement will assign someone (a buyer or a subcontract manager) to the project manager to support the project effort. The assigned buyer will do anything and everything the project manager asks them to do, <u>but</u>, always working within the formal procurement policies and procedures of the company. A professional buyer will not violate purchasing policy, even if directed to do so by a more senior project manager.

The buyer (subcontract manager) will be required by policy to insist on (for example) a competition, if appropriate, and insist that everyone in the competition be treated equally. These are reasonable requirements to impose on any project. One of the main purposes of company procurement policies and procedures is to prevent any project manager from taking short-cuts, perhaps in the best interests of the project, but not in the best long-term interests of the company and its relationship to the supplier base. Companies have a strategic need for maintaining a viable supplier base to support the company over the long-term. Projects, because of their short term nature, will sometimes overlook the long-term needs of the company.

This issue being described here is called "centralized" versus "decentralized" purchasing, and is illustrated in Figure 1.3. On the top of the figure is shown "centralized" purchasing (procurement). The authority to execute procurements on behalf of the company goes from the general manager, to the director or vice president of purchasing, who then assigns someone to support project buys. By contrast, shown at the bottom is "decentralized" purchasing, often commonplace with new start-up companies. Here the project manager is either given specific procurement authority, or perhaps most often, simply executes such legal purchase agreements without having a specific delegation. Since most new companies often lack internal controls policies and procedures, the project manager gets away with it, for the time being.

Most mature companies do not give procurement authority to their project managers. Why, perhaps the chief executive of a major design construction management firm expressed it well when he was asked this very question: "do your project managers have procurement authority?" His answer:

"Centralized" Purchasing:
A functional person (Director/VP) has
delegated procurement authority…and
assigns a buyer to support the project.

General Manager

Purchasing Director/VP

"Decentralized" Purchasing:
The project manager has authority to
execute contracts directly with another
Company…to buy something.

General Manager

Project Manager

Figure 1.3   *"Centralized" versus "Decentralized" Purchasing Authority*

"I would never give procurement authority to a project manager. There is just too much at stake, too many non-technical matters to know, which most project managers are typically not prepared to handle. Procurement authority must be restricted to people who are familiar with contracting terms, procurement regulations, funding and contractual compliance issues. We delegate procurement authority to only procurement people, but who are assigned to support the project manager." [4]

Most firms follow this same approach, project managers are rarely given the authority to execute contracts on behalf of their companies. They operate in an environment referred to as "Centralized" purchasing or procurement. The role of the project manager is to define precisely the needs of the project, typically taking the form of a formal

---

4. Mr. Zoltan Stacho, President of Holmes & Narver, Inc., quoted with his permission from remarks he made at a meeting of the Orange County Chapter of the Project Management Institute on August 9, 1994.

document called a "Purchase Requisition" which the assigned buyer uses as authority to execute the formal contract, subcontract, or purchase order with another company. In most cases this process works well, as long as both the project manager and the assigned buyer have mutual respect for the other's position.

Even the United States Government follows the practice of requiring a distinct separation of project responsibility from those individuals having procurement authority. The Government will assign a project manager to all projects, typically carrying the title of Program Director, Program Manager, Project Manager, etc. However, these individuals, no matter what their rank may hold, will not possess the authority to execute contracts. The role of executing contracts is done on their behalf by a separate organization, by individuals who carry the title of Procurement Contracting Officer, Administrative Contracting Officer, etc. This process works well with the United States Government.

Before we leave this subject, one point needs to be mentioned. Most firms today, even the government, are finding it beneficial to issue personal credit cards to selected employees to allow them to efficiently buy routine, low-cost items. Generally, these items are consumable supplies, used to support an organization or a project within the company. There is typically a set limitation in value of perhaps $1,000 to $2,500 on such purchases. Credit card purchases by selected employees, are not the same as buying project scope from another company. They are typically limited to acquiring routine shelf commodities.

The major Project Procurement Processes . . . as defined by the *PMI PMBOK® Guide*

The Project Management Institute's A Guide to the Project Management Body of Knowledge (PMBOK® Guide) is one of the most respected sources of knowledge on the subject of project management in the world. Chapter 12 to this document covers the subject of this book: Project Procurement Management.

Initially the PMBOK ® Guide broke the procurement area into six distinct processes. These six processes acted as the overall outline for this book.

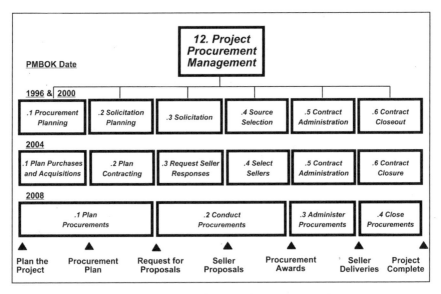

Figure 1.4   The PMBOK ® Guide Procurement Processes

In the fourth edition to the PMBOK ® Guide a decision was made to reduce the number of procurement processes from six to four. The impact on this change in process grouping is illustrated in Figure 1.4. An important point to understand: the work of project procurement did not change with the reduction in the number of processes. It was done simply to make the document more relatable to a greater number of projects.

The four PMBOK ® Guide procurement processes are:

12.1 Plan Procurements
(previously called 12.1 Plan Purchases and Acquisitions and 12.2 Plan Contracting)
This process begins at the start of a new project, includes the make or buy analysis, the identification of potential sellers, and the development

of a Procurement Management Plan. It ends with a definition of items or work or services to be procured, sometimes taking the form of a formal document often called a Request for Proposal(s) (RFP).

12.2 Conduct Procurements
(previously called 12.3 Request Seller Responses and 12.4 Select Sellers)
Takes the RFP and requests formal proposals from sellers, evaluates seller proposals, and ends with the issuance of a procurement contract award to a seller.

12.3 Administer Procurements
(previously called 12.5 Contract Administration)
Monitors seller(s) performance, and manages changes to seller authorized scope.

12.4 Close Procurements
(previously called 12.6 Contract Closeout):
Settles all open contractual issues, closes out each procurement, preserves the records. Assesses lessons learned to benefit future projects.

CHAPTER 2

Placing Procurements into Generic Categories

Not all project procurements are created equal. Some purchases are big, others small. Some are complex, while most are routine. Some procurements carry high risks, while others have only minimal or perhaps no risks at all. Some procurements require a major long-term commitment from both the buyer and the seller, while other commodities are immediately available for purchase in the open market, including on-line or e-commerce buys.

Question: why might it be a good practice to place all procurements into generic categories? Answer: because you manage project procurements differently, according to their complexity, their risks, their unique characteristics. Sometimes you must form project teams to manage the critical buys.

Many project buys are routine and simply require that someone track the orders to make sure that the commodities arrive in time to support the project schedule, and are inspected to make sure that they work, and meet all quality standards. However, some procurements, because of their characteristics, require the management oversight of a full team of specialists representing multi-functional disciplines. With these types of procurements, which are always critical to the success of any project, no one individual can adequately manage them because they are too complex. Between these extremes lie generic categories of procurements, most being routine, but some by their nature requiring special treatment.

In order to properly manage the procured items, some firms have found it beneficial to categorize their project procurements into broad but distinct "generic families." This helps management better focus their attention on the unique problems and issues peculiar to each category of procurement.

One such grouping of project procurements would create three generic categories, plus two special relationships as follows:

1. Major (high risk) complexity procurements, the purchase of something which does not exist, tailored to the project's unique specification. These would be considered critical sub-projects.

2. Minor (low risk) complexity procurements, will often represent large monetary values, but the commodities exist and will conform to the seller's existing product specification.

   (Note: Minor product tailoring such as unique name tags or special color schemes would not add risks to the procurement, and thus would not change their classification. However, major alterations to an seller's existing product, perhaps requiring a product re-design and perhaps new product testing, would likely place them buy into a Category (1) procurement).

3. Routine buys of COTS (Commercial Off-The Shelf) commodities or purchased services.

4. Special procurements: done under corporate teaming arrangements.

5. Special procurements: to other segments of the project's company, typically called interdivisional work.

We will discuss each type of procurement in greater detail below.

(1) Major (high-risk) Complexity Procurements . . . to the Buyer's Specification

These procurements are the most challenging buys for any project to manage. By their nature, they typically represent high risks to the project's technical, quality, costs, and schedule. They often require the creation of something new by a seller, something that doesn't already exist. In order to be managed properly these items require that the project specify precisely what it needs, typically taking the form of specifications, drawings, and often includes a comprehensive statement of work.

Sometimes, these new items may actually push the "state of the technical art" in the creation of the new product, as with perhaps a new advanced radar system, or a new computer software program. Other times they may be technically routine, but have never been done before, as with the design or the construction of a new high-rise office building. Sometimes they require that an existing product undergo a major redesign and development to essentially create a new product, requiring re-testing, re-certification, etc.

Such procurements will often result in a long-term relationship being created between a company (project buyer) and a supplier (seller) where significant developmental and capital expenses may have to be incurred by the company or the supplier or both. With these procurements there will be strong economic and perhaps emotional resistance to any changes of supplier sources without compelling and overriding justification. Both the project's buyer and seller will have made a major financial commitment to the project, and pity the poor individual who ever suggests bringing in a new supplier simply to save a few dollars! Once the relationship is set between buyer and seller, further competition is often waived as long as the quality remains high and the seller's pricing seems reasonable to the participants.

Typical characteristics for purchased items in this category might be: a new product or a system, a major new component, a major structural element, a design to a performance requirement, project interface documents, high risks to the overall project, and often, significant senior management and even customer oversight. Often these types of procurements will experience a phenomena typically called "scope creep" which are simply changes that seep into a nebulous product specification. Thus this category of procurements will normally carry high risks to any project.

Such procurements must be managed well for the good of the overall project, and are best thought of as being critical sub-projects to the total project. Firms employing the "integrated project team" approach will likely create a separate team for each of the procurements which fall into this category. Each team will be managed separately for the project by a designated team leader, often a technical person acting on behalf of the project manager, with a buyer acting as a deputy.

Early identification of these procurements will be critical to any project in order to adequately plan and organize for them. These procurements must be managed well for the success of the project.

Some examples of these kinds of procurements would be:
- The architectural design of a new commercial center.
- The construction of a new production factory.
- The outsourcing of information technology services.
- The creation of a new software package.
- The development of a new computer.
- The development of a new airplane.
- The development of a new radar system, or any critical project component.

(2) Minor (low-risk) Complexity Procurements . . . to the Seller's Product Specification

These procurements are for items which exist in some form with a given seller, and are defined by the seller's own product specification. They are commercially available from the seller, either in the seller's inventory or sometimes assembled after an order is received. Some articles may have a long lead-time delivery requirement due to scarce critical components. These items will often carry a high monetary value, sometimes exceeding the major complexity buys described above. Such buys are always critical to the success of a project, but do not require the creation of something new by the seller.

These articles are generally bought without modifications to the seller's product, or perhaps with only minimal modifications, for example the painting of a company logo on a procured bus. In terms of risks to the project, these items will normally carry a lower risk, as long as they arrive in time to support the project master schedule, and of course they work. Often these articles are bought as a result of long-term relationships between the buyer (project) and seller (supplier). However, comparable performance items may sometimes be substituted as long as they satisfy the same requirements of the project.

Early identification of these buys is important in order to properly schedule lead-times for each item and to budget the necessary funds for them. Some examples of these procurements might be:

- The purchase of existing automobiles, buses, transportation vehicles or perhaps aircraft.
- The purchase of an existing radar system, or large electrical generators.
- The purchase of existing, but high value software.
- The purchase of existing computers, and other developed, but high value components.

(3) Routine buys of Commercial-Off-The-Shelf (COTS) items or purchased services

It should be recognized that many projects will have considerable quantity of procurements to execute, but perhaps none which fit into the above two categories of major complex, or non-complex buys. Some projects may actually purchase substantial amounts of materials, but such procurements are often commercially available as "off-the-shelf" articles, or routine services. In these cases, the fundamental principles of basic purchasing will be more applicable than a requirement to manage complicated contracts or subcontracts as critical subprojects.

The early identification of these procurements is typically not vital to the success of the project, that is, they can be identified in later phases and generally not cause difficulties to the project. These commodities will often have interchangeable (substitute) components. Some examples of these procurements might be:

- Purchased labor, which will brought in plant and supervised by the project's staff.
- Purchased services, or testing, of a routine nature.
- Raw materials: nuts, bolts, fasteners, sheet metal, paints, solvents, etc.
- Pencils, paper, office supplies.
- Existing computers, printers, scanners, etc.
- Packaged commercial software.
- Outsourced complete but routine services, for example, cafeteria, accounting, security, etc.

(4) Special Procurements: performed under strategic company teaming agreements

These are project procurements which are executed strictly in accordance with an overriding corporate legal contract typically called a teaming agreement or alliance or arrangement, etc. Here, the executives of one company and another company (or companies) agree to combine their assets, facilities, people, shared risks, etc., and go after a new segment of work, typically in the form of some new project.

Teaming arrangements are normally strategic high dollar value accords between corporate executives whereby a major project or a new system is essentially divided into two or more parts, each part assigned to a separate company for performance. All subsequent resulting procurements must be executed in accordance with the overriding corporate agreement. The corporate teaming arrangement is the supreme governing document.

Teaming agreements are typically created to enhance a firm's competitive posture, and usually will have high visibility with the ultimate buying customer. Such arrangements can divide the new project by creating a "prime contractor-subcontractor" relationship, whereby the designated prime company will receive the contract. Or, sometimes they cover an "associate" type of relationship based on some percentage value allocated to each firm, whereby a single prime contract will have shared corporate performance responsibilities.

Teaming arrangements are somewhat analogous to "arranged marriages" between families in certain ancient societies. The parents (the corporate executives) make a decision and their respective children (the projects) have no say in the matter. The role of the children (the projects) is to make the relationship a successful one . . . period, end of all discussion. Most often these arranged relationships do work out very well. The role of the project is to implement what the corporate executives have decided in their agreement.

Early identification of these procurements is critical in order to adequately plan for them and to set up a project management oversight team. Procurements under Teaming Agreements will typically cover Category (1) or (2) buys as defined above, but could also include Category (3) items bought under a long-term relationship.

(5) Special Procurements: to other components of the project's company, interdivisional work

The significance of interdivisional work, sometimes also called intracompany work, is that such procurements should be the easiest arrangement to manage, after all "we are one happy family." But too often interdivisional arrangements turn out to be the most painful for any project to manage. Why would such be the case? Likely such results are caused by the organizational relationships within the company, the alignment of the project to the performing division. Far too often, projects do not get the "respect" they deserve within their own company. Amazing.

Interdivisional work are the procurements made within a single company by one operating unit (the project) with another operating unit (the performing organization). These procurements sometimes result from having a unique capability within the company which will enhance the performance of a project. However, at other times, the project manager may have little say in the matter and senior executives insist on the project work being kept within the company, even when a better price or better product might be available from an outside supplier. Sometimes, the most compelling justification for interdivisional work is simply the "availability" of a company workforce, or facilities, or capability, etc. The project managers are called on by executives to help with "our company problem."

Controlling interdivisional work can be a nightmare for the project. Why? Because the internal procedures covering interdivisional cost transfers are typically created by the company accountants who are primarily concerned with the orderly allocation and the recovery of all incurred costs. Contrast these goals with the project manager who invariably wants value added for all dollars spent. However, the accountants will always win this issue, and project dollars will be transferred without regard to the value of the work performed. Project managers often have difficulty shutting off interdivisional costs.

One problem with interdivisional work is the organizational relationship of the project to the performing group. The project manager's most senior executive are typically at the same corporate organizational level as the most senior executive with the organization performing the work. Neither executive has much clout over the other executive, and neither executive wants to do battle with the other because next month that same person "could be my boss!" Interdivisional procurements rarely enjoy the senior executive support that are given to critical procurements under teaming arrangements, where the senior executives will demand harmony and cooperation . . . or else!

Another problem for the projects can be the United States Government's attitude toward interdivisional work. In somewhat of a self-serving way, the Government may treat such work as either as "make" work or as "buy" work, depending on the point they are stressing. On the one hand the Government will insist on all interdivisional work being classified as "make" work, no matter where in the company such effort is assigned. In this scenario, the Government considers everything done in one company as make work. It doesn't matter if the project or the performing division are on the opposite sides of the world, have never worked together, it is all one company and thus "make" work.

However, the Government also expects that interdivisional procurements be conducted as if each were done under an "arms-length" arrangement, following all of the same purchasing procedures as with any external "buy." The Government wants to pay the lowest price for all work done under their contracts and will often insist on a formal solicitation, formal evaluation, source selection, and a documented competitive procurement process. They will often insist that external competition be held.

When things go <u>right</u> at the performing division, as they sometimes do, that division wants its fair share of the project's profits. After all it did perform the job in a responsible way, as any other outside supplier would have performed that same work. However, when things go <u>wrong</u>, as they sometimes do, perhaps experiencing cost overruns, schedule slips, poor workmanship, etc., that same performing division now expects to be treated not as an outside supplier, but as part of "our big family".

The early identification of many of interdivisional procurements is typically not critical for the project, unless such work involves the creation of something new, a Category (1) major complex buy. In these cases such procurements need to be identified early to start the planning effort. Interdivisional work, if complex, will often encounter the same challenges as with any outside supplier.

Interdivisional work can take many forms depending on the capability which exists in the other company units. They can be any of the three procurement categories mentioned above. Some examples of these procurements might be:

- The development of some new component or product.
- The manufacture of parts.
- The procurement of parts for the project.
- Design and testing services.
- Purchased labor.

Understanding the anatomy of the project "procured" work.

In order to better understand and to properly manage that portion of a project which will be purchased from another company or another company organization, the case for placing all buy work into three generic categories and two special relationships has been suggested. These generic categories and special relationships are displayed in Figure 2.1.

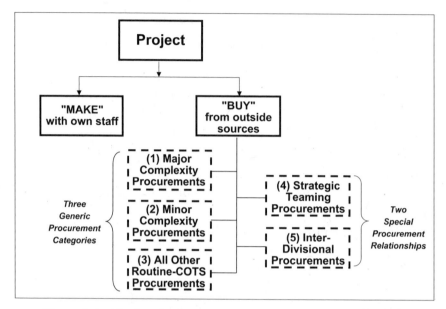

Figure 2.1 *Placing Procurements Into Five Generic Categories*

There are at least three distinct generic families of project procurements, as are shown with Items (1), (2), and (3). Category (1) buys are for newly developed items, and will always represent high-risks to any project. Category (2) buys are also critical to the project, and often represent high monetary values. Category (3) buys represent commodities which are considered routine, but nevertheless must arrive in time to support the project's schedule. Most Category (3) procurements are now being performed by highly efficient Internet or Electronic e-Commerce type buys.

Each category of procurement must be managed well for the success of the project. Thus, some firms have found it to be advisable to place their procurements into specific generic categories as discussed above.

In addition, there are two unique procurement relationships which must be recognized: (4) the Corporate Teaming Arrangements and the (5) Inter-divisional work. Both these special categories have been found to represent unique management challenges in the successful completion of any project.

CHAPTER 3

Plan Procurements
(1 of 2)

(PMBOK ® - Third Edition 2004: 12.1 Plan Purchases and Acquisitions)

The process of planning for the procurement of project scope from an outside organization is perhaps the most critical of all the work done in procurement management. If not performed properly the project will likely suffer the consequences for the duration of the project.

Earlier in Figure 1.4 the six procurement processes were displayed.[1] The following chapters will cover the first process which requires the planning for the work of procurement management.

This process will begin with the initiation of any new project and requires that the scope of the project be defined and decomposed to the extent possible. In order for any project to be fully defined, such definition must also include the "make or buy" choices, a decision as to who will perform the work. At the point where a project has taken a position with respect to the scope of the effort to be performed, such definitions should also include an understanding of what major critical elements of the project will be sent to another company or organization for performance.

The procurement planning process should culminate with the release of a formal document called a *Procurement Management Plan.* This plan should have been coordinated and endorsed by all key functions supporting the project. Ideally, each major organizational function impacted by the procurement will have contributed to the creation of this document.

---

1. Project Management Institute, Newtown Square, Pennsylvania, 2000, page 147

Defining Project Scope

In the management of projects there is likely nothing more critical to the success of a project than to begin with an adequate definition of the scope of work, and then to gain the acceptance of the definition by the customer. Project managers must define what they plan to do, and most important, must set the outer limits of what they are committed to do. Without a scope definition "firewall" in place, projects will be in the unenviable position of constantly accepting additional work, referred to as "scope creep" throughout the life of their existence. The only way to put finality into a project is to define the scope of work, and then to avoid the inadvertent acceptance of "minor refinements":

> *Large changes in scope are easily identified. It is the "minor refinements" that eventually build to be major scope changes that can cause problems. These small refinements are known in the field as scope creep.* [2]

One of the most unenviable positions any project manager can experience is to have an executive define a new project for them . . . in broad general terms . . . and then to refuse to accept a definition of the scope by saying: *"I have complete confidence that you will do the right things."* Respectfully, this project manager is being set-up, because the project effort will never end, because the project was never contained in the first place. Rule number one in project management: define your project scope and get your customer to agree on the definition . . . before the project begins.

A critical part of the process of completely understanding the work to be done for any project is to determine who will be performing the various segments of the project, particularly that work which will be purchased from outside the company. Why is this issue so important: because purchased work is done under legal relationships,

---

2. Gray, Clifford F., and Larson, Erik W., *Project Management-The Managerial Process*, (New York: McGraw-Hill, 2000) page 382.

called contracts. Such arrangements must be done with great care, must be precisely defined, because project procurements are "non-forgiving" in the sense that all changes in direction to a seller will of course be accommodated . . . but for a price.

It is likely that most projects today employ a technique to help define their projects called the Work Breakdown Structure (WBS). The WBS is to the project manager what the organization chart is to the company executive: it defines their universe. The WBS is a graphical portrayal of the project. Two authorities in project management have provided us with a solid definition of a WBS:

The work breakdown structure acts as a vehicle for breaking the work down into smaller elements, thus providing a greater probability that every major and minor activity will be accounted for. [3]

Displayed in Figure 3.1 is an example of a Work Breakdown Structure for a new project: a Transportation Vehicle. Level 1 of the WBS represents the total project, everything the project manager has agreed to do. Level 2 of the WBS provides a reflection of the management approach, the major chunks of effort, the critical subprojects.

Here the project has chosen to manage this new job by subdividing it into four major level 2 elements: vehicle structure, vehicle testing, data, and finally project management. The subordinate Level 3 and lower levels simply reflect a further decomposition of defined work into progressively smaller segments. Level 2 is likely the most critical subdivision for any project because it reflects the management approach.

The WBS diagram provides an excellent device for not only defining the work to be done on a new project, but also to assign the defined work to a specific individual and organization for performance. Sometimes a project can be done entirely within the project's own organization. This is sometimes the case on smaller projects. But most other times, for reasons which will be discussed below, some

---

3. Cleland, David I., and Kerzner, Harold, *A Project Management Dictionary of Terms*, (New York: Van Nortrand Reinhold Company, 1985) page 271.

work will need to be sent outside of the project's immediate organization, that is, it must be procured from another company. The WBS
provides an excellent device to assist in such work assignments.

For example, using Figure 3.1, the WBS at level 2 contains four
major elements, all considered to be in-house work from the level 2
vantage. However, when we go down into level 3 of the WBS we can
start to see the further subdivision of work into those tasks which will
be done in-house, as contrasted with those elements which will be sent
to other companies for performance.

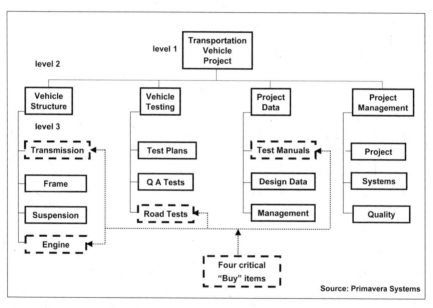

Figure 3.1   Scope definition must include "make" or "buy" choices

Under Vehicle Structure at level 2, we have four major subdivisions
of work: two of which will be performed in-house (the Frame and
Suspension), and the other two will be procured from outside the company (the Transmission and Engine). The critical distinction is that the
Frame and Suspension work will be authorized by simply issuing an
internal budget. However, the Transmission and Engines must be formally contracted, procured, using functional resources outside of the
project's immediate organization, for example, purchasing, legal, and

other key functions. It is fairly simple to place work within ones own organization. It gets complicated when one goes outside.

Addressing the other two buy items, under Vehicle Testing the project has chosen to procure the Road Testing of the vehicle from another company. Also, under Project Data, management has elected to procure Test Manual services from another firm.

With the use of the WBS to define and decompose a new project, the project manager, the project team, executive management, and most important the paying customer, can all immediately visualize the definition of the job and the assignment of all project elements. The WBS is the graphical portrayal, the detailed roadmap for any project to follow.

Deciding who will perform the work: "Make" or "Buy" Analysis

The public will sometimes observe "make or buy" choices being made and may not be aware of it. For example, it is not uncommon to see firms doing a self assessment in an effort to focus management attention on the "core competencies" of a company. The central issue: why are we in business? What are the key ingredients which put us where we are today? Often these same firms will then strategically decide to concentrate solely on their central core strengths, the unique activities which put them in business in the first place, and to reassign everything else.

Executive management will often take segments of their organizations and sell selected assets, often involving both equipment and people, and then buy back these same assets and the services they provide under a long term contractual arrangement. This process is called "outsourcing", and outsourcing is nothing more than a management "make to buy" decision.

Outsourcing is being done on a number of company services considered to be non-core to a firm, for example plant security, food services, routine accounting, etc. Virtually any service activity can be considered a candidate, but we are particularly seeing the outsourcing of information technology (IT) activities. Perhaps the IT departments are most vulnerable because they are complicated, expensive, have a reputation of being non-responsive, and often senior management doesn't have a clue as to what they do! Such services can be sold quickly and immediately bring in new cash to the firm.

Whenever management elects to sell their computers and transfer IT employees to another company, and then enter into a long-term contract to procure these same services back from the other company, management has effectively made a strategic make to buy choice. The outsourcing of information technology services, so common today, has enabled certain major firms like IBM, EDS, and CSC to grow at a phenomenal pace.

For new projects, the process of performing the make or buy analysis is one which will evolve from proposal to implementation. At the start of a new project the make or buy choices are often only tentatively set, as is displayed in Figure 3.2, on the left side of the chart. The initial position for a new project will have three categories of planned work: "must make" work, "must buy" work, and the as yet

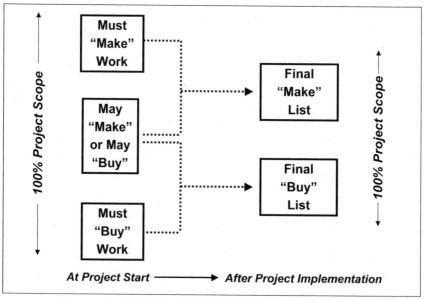

Figure 3.2   The project "make" or "buy" decision process

undetermined area of work in the middle labeled as "may make" or "may buy" items.

The "must make" work are the easy choices to be made because some tasks will want to be kept in-house for a number of reasons. We may have a proprietary position in a certain technology and therefore we will want to perform this effort with our own people to protect our competitive position. Also, we may have surplus staff immediately available to do this work. Pressures to make work on any project will include idle plant capacity, an idle work force, and sometimes the attitude of some that internal work is easier to control than purchased work.

Some other choices are also easy to decide as when we may have no capability in our company to do certain types of work. These will be the "must buy" tasks. Also, sometimes we have no other choice but to go outside for performance simply because the company people who could perform the work are already committed to doing other work during the same time frame they are needed.

The third category of work, the one displayed in the center of the left side of Figure 3.2 is where we will need to make some hard choices. This category is called "may make" or "may buy." Here based on all the factors available we must decide who will do the work: our internal company work force or another company. If we elect to send such work outside of the company for performance we will need to prepare a formal procurement package, solicit bids and make a final procurement choice.

After the project has made their final determinations of who will perform all the project work, the result will be just two final categories: that effort which we will perform in-house (make) and that which we will obtain (buy) from an outside company, as displayed on the right side of Figure 3.2.

In order to minimize the risks associated with the procurement of those items which will be performed outside of the company, a complete listing of the critical procurements (new developments) must be completed early in the scope definition phase. A complete definition of project scope must always include the identification of the major critical buys. Stated another way, the late identification of major critical procurements will vastly increase the risks to the project. Why? Because in order to procure anything from the outside, we must be in a position to define precisely what we want from another firm. Late definitions, vague definitions, changing requirements only increase the risks to the project.

Some time ago there was a study conducted entitled: *"Make or Buy: Factors Affecting Executive Decisions."* This study addressed the make or buy process in the United States and reached the following conclusions:

1. *Management tends to ignore the make-or-buy problem.*

2. *Many make-or-buy analyses are based on invalid cost comparisons, due to the excessive use of historical data when estimates of future costs should be used.*

3. *American businesses lose more money in making things that should be bought than in buying things that should be made.*

4. *Nevertheless, millions of dollars are lost annually by buying items that could be more economically made.* [4]

As we look around in industry today we may want to ask ourselves: have we come very far in improving the "make or buy" process over the last half century? Perhaps not.

However, in the management of our projects, adequately defining the make work versus the procured work is critical for the successful implementation of any new project.

Matching Project Requirements with Market Availability: Locating Potential Sellers

In the marketplace today there is virtually everything available to us . . . somewhere. Typically, the availability of goods to purchase does not present a major constraint to the project. The one exception to this

---

4. Lamar Lee, Jr., and Donald W. Dobler, *Purchasing and Materials Management*, (New York: McGraw-Hill Book Company, 1965), page 308.

general condition might be when there is but a sole source or a single source for a given commodity. In these cases the commodities will be available to the project, but often at an exorbitant price, and from suppliers who have an attitude! You stand in line to buy their goods.

However, another sometimes more serious exception might be where the required commodity does not presently exist, perhaps it has never been developed. New developmental items add technical risks to projects. The risks are that the commodity can't be developed . . . period, or perhaps not developed in time to support the project's need date. Either can add serious risks to any project.

With the availability of the internet and e-commerce many buyers supporting projects do not have to leave their offices to satisfy the procurement needs of the project. Most established firms will have a cadre of professional buyers (purchasing agents, supply-chain specialists) available to support the requirements of a project. Quite often the buying or purchasing organization will be organized along commodity lines, so there are product specialists to support the project.

Also, most of the established purchasing or supply-chain organizations will have developed a supplier historical database, which will allow the matching of the needs of the project with what is available in the open market. Such databases will typically incorporate actual performance history from these sellers: did they deliver prior products on time, did they stay within their original price, how was the quality of their final delivered product, etc.?

However, in those instances where the procured commodities have never been built before, and perhaps may be pushing the state of the technical art, there will be only a limited number of firms to provide these articles. In such cases the very best source for suggestions as to potential suppliers will often be the technical specialists, the expert opinions from those individuals who are designing the new system, or specifying the requirements. The engineers and scientists will have recommendations as to potential sellers, and typically their suggestions are quite valid.

What is available to buy in the market place typically does not present a major hurdle to any project, with the exceptions of single sources, sole sources, and newly created state-of-the-art items.

Full Funding Considerations . . . the Impact of Procurements

It is most efficient for any project to be completely defined, and then for management to allocate all of the funds needed to completely perform the work. However, as many of us may have experienced, this does not always happen. Often projects find themselves in the position of being funded piecemeal. Piecemeal funding is expensive anytime, but particularly with procurements.

It is inefficient to start internal (the make) work and then to stop or slow down the effort. But internal work is fairly easy to control. Not so with the outside (the buy) effort. To start and then slow down a procurement is always a painful and an expensive experience. There is probably no rational explanation for this phenomena except that when you slow down procurements, reduce the available funding, sellers view this as their "opportunity" to get back everything they may have lost in a tough negotiation, or under a highly competitive bid situation.

As a practical matter, try not to adjust the full funding of procurements. But if you must change the funding of the procured work, be prepared to pay a premium cost for such decisions.

Scope definition must include the early identification of all critical procurements

It is important for any project to begin with a complete definition of what it intends to accomplish and then to get the customer to agree with this definition. This is called the scope definition process. One of the most important outputs from the scope definition process will be a tentative listing of the procurements for the project, particularly all the high-risk major critical buys.

Make or buy choices should be a direct result from the definition of the project with use of the Work Breakdown Structure (WBS). Of greatest importance to the project will be the early identification of all of the Category (1) "Major Complexity" procurements. These are the high-risk developments of things which do not exist, or if they exist, must be modified to such a degree that they are essentially new components. There are risks related to procuring these items, and management must take decisive action to mitigate such risks down to acceptable levels. Having only a vague definition of the new critical commodity is one of the most common risks facing any project.

Many projects in an effort to reduce the risks of the procured items have found it advisable to develop a matrix of their anticipated procurements, as is illustrated with Figure 3.3. The project will prepare a listing of the articles it expects to procure, then classify these items according to their complexity. To facilitate this process a listing of all buys items should be prepared as displayed in Figure 3.3. An electronic spreadsheet or database helps nicely with this effort.

The first step in this process is to compile a complete listing of all buy items, sometimes referred to as the engineering Bill of Materials. This listing of procurements will evolve as the project definition evolves. The listing should be sorted into some type of generic classification, as with the five procurement categories as were described earlier in Chapter 2. It is imperative that all the Category (1) major complexity items be identified early, followed next by the Category (2) major non-complexity items. The routine Category (3) COTS items can be identified later and likely not adversely impact the project' schedule.

Once the listing of key procurements is identified the next important step must be taken: the assignment of individual responsibility for all major critical buy items. There are typically three individuals who must be identified: 1) a project team leader, 2) a responsible engineer, the technical person (to start preparation of the technical procurement specification), and 3) the responsible buyer (who will execute the actual purchase order). Sometimes the team leader and the responsible engineer may be the same individual. The key issue is that the appropriate people must be identified and assigned responsibility to manage each critical procurement . . . early.

The risks associated with project procurements can be reduced in direct proportion to the early identification and assignment of responsibilities for all major critical buys. Potential sellers must also be identified as more details becomes known about these key procurements.

Once the critical procured items have been identified and responsibilities set, the next critical work will be to relate the timing of each buy with the need dates of the project. The project's master schedule should indicate the dates required for all critical procured components. It will be the responsibility of the team leaders working closely with the technical person and the assigned buyer to make sure that all procured items are available in time to support the need dates of the project.

The matrix of procured items, as is illustrated in Figure 3.3, is an important first step in defining that project scope which will be procured from outside of the project organization. This matrix is also an important initial step toward creating the Project's *Procurement Management Plan*, which will be covered in detail in a subsequent chapter.

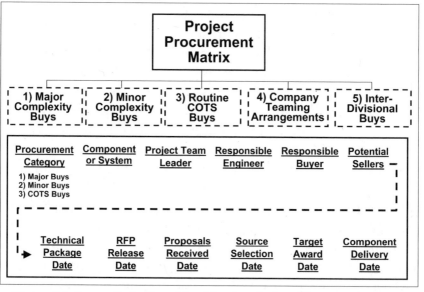

Figure 3.3 Scope Definition: identification & classification of all buys

CHAPTER 4

Project Procurements with: Corporate Teaming Agreements/Alliances/ Arrangements

Teaming agreements between corporations are a lot like "arranged marriages" within certain cultures of the world. The parents (mostly the fathers) get together and decide that my son will marry your daughter . . . period . . . end of all discussion. The parents then meet (mostly the fathers) and introduce the two young participants who have no say in the matter. It is a done-deal.

Likewise with many corporate teaming arrangements, one executive will meet with another executive and they will decide that my firm will join with your firm on a new project . . . period . . . end of all discussion. The executives then meet to introduce the project participants who have no say in the matter. It is also a done-deal.

The funny thing is that arranged marriages between previous strangers most often work. Even funnier, perhaps, such arrangements between corporations and their projects also seem to work. Perhaps we in industry have learned something from the ancient cultures.

Now that the United States Department of Justice and the European Community are starting to vigorously object to the permanent consolidations (acquisitions and mergers) between one company and another company, we are starting to hear more about the formation of strategic teaming arrangements between what are otherwise competing firms. Hardly a week goes by that we read about major competitors forming some type of an alliance, a strategic relationship, to go after a certain new project. And strangely, such arrangements seem to be working well.

We see this phenomena happening across all industries, but perhaps most particularly in the information technology (IT) outsourcing segment where new multi-year contracts are being awarded on a monthly basis. These huge mega-deals are often beyond the capability of any single firm to perform. But two or three or more companies acting together seem to work nicely. An example:

> *Electronic Data Systems Corp. was awarded a far-reaching contract valued at as much as $6.9 billion over eight years to revamp the U.S. Navy and Marine Corps' computer system. Its key partners in the contract include WorldCom Inc. and Raytheon Co.* [1]

What's the fascination with teaming arrangements? Why are so many being formed? When one firm commits to joining forces with another firm what does that really mean? And finally, what might be the best model for firms to take when structuring a new teaming alliance?

What are Corporate Teaming Agreements/Alliances/Arrangements

As a starting point we need to understand the concept itself. Teaming agreements in a nutshell are simply legal contracts between two or more companies. Firms agree to do something, or to refrain from doing something. Such agreements obviously need to be for a legal purpose and meet all legal requirements in order to be enforceable. These arrangements can be called whatever the participants want to call them: agreements, alliances, arrangements. Sometimes the word "strategic" is also inserted in the title.

Teaming agreements between one company and another means that two or more companies will join forces to go after a new segment

---

1. Marcelo Prince and Pat Maio, "EDS Wins Huge Contract To Revamp Military Computers," *The Wall Street Journal*, October 6, 2000.

of work, often a particular new project. Each company will commit something unique to their arrangement: financial resources, their key people, company assets, technology, etc., and each will expect to share in the risks and rewards of the endeavor. Perhaps a couple of specific definitions will help us to understand the concept.

Two leading authors in the field of project management have defined such arrangements in the following manner:

> ***Teaming Arrangement.*** *An agreement of two or more firms to form a partnership or joint venture to act as a potential prime contractor; or an agreement by a potential prime contractor to act as a subcontractor under a specified acquisition program; or an agreement for a joint proposal resulting from a normal prime contractor-subcontractor, licensee-licensor, or leader-company relationship.* [2]

Still another definition of the same subject may better reinforce our understanding. Since many of us work on contracts funded by the United States Government, perhaps we should understand their perspective of such arrangements:

> ***Teaming Arrangement****. An arrangement between two or more companies, either as a partnership or joint venture, to perform on a specific contract. The team itself may be designated to act as the prime contractor; or one of the team members may be designated to act as the prime contractor, and the other member(s) designated to act as subcontractors. When the characteristics of joint control (i.e., joint property, joint liability for losses and expenses, and joint participation in profits) are evident, then the teaming arrangement is a joint venture. When these characteristics are not present then the arrangement may more closely resemble that of a prime contractor/subcontractor.* [3]

2. Dr. David I. Cleland and Dr. Harold Kerzner, *A Project Management Dictionary of Terms,* (New York, USA: Van Nostrand Reinhold Company, 1985) page 253.

3. Defense Contract Audit Agency (DCAA) *Contract Audit Manual,* part 7-1802, c, January, 1996.

One of the features common to both of these definitions is that both suggest that such agreements will form either a "joint venture" or a "partnership" between the parties. Thus, we should also understand two additional definitions to fully grasp the concept.

> **Partnership.** *An ordinary partnership occurs when two or more entities (persons) combine capital and/or services to carry on a business for profit. From a legal standpoint, it is a group of separate persons.* [4]

In the world of purchasing or supply chain management they sometimes will use the term "partner" to describe what this book would consider as a teaming agreement:

> *A 'partner' is defined as a firm with whom your company has an ongoing buyer-seller relationship, involving a commitment over an extended time-period, a mutual sharing of information and a sharing of risks and rewards resulting from the relationship.* [5]

A good definition of a teaming agreement. Perhaps of interest is the fact that this definition came from two academic researchers who found in their study that while only 1% of buyer-suppliers relationships were covered by such partner agreements, but that the 1% accounted for some 12% of the purchasing volume of these firms. Thus, such relationships were very important to the strategic viability of the firms employing them.

Now let's understand the other common thread in the above definitions of teaming agreements, that of the joint venture:

> **Joint Venture.** *An enterprise owned and operated by two or more businesses or individuals as a separate entity (not a subsidiary) for*

---

4. Defense Contract Audit Agency (DCAA) *Contract Audit Manual*, part 7-1802, (d), January 1992.
5. Arjan J. van Weele, *Purchasing and Supply Chain Management*, (London: Thompson Learning, 2002), page 165, based on research by Ellram and Hendrick (1993).

the mutual benefit of the members of the group. Joint ventures possess the characteristics of joint control; e.g., joint property, joint liability for losses and expenses, and joint participation in profits. Joint ventures can be either incorporated or unincorporated. [6]

It would seem from this definition that a joint venture between two or more companies can take extreme forms. They can be a formal arrangement, whereby the parties assign certain assets to legally form a new enterprise. Or, they can be as simple an arrangement as merely participating in the joint processes of perhaps providing purchasing, marketing, research activities, etc.

However, some companies when forming a teaming arrangement flatly reject the notion that their agreement must form either a "joint venture" or a "partnership." Some companies suggest that a corporate agreement to form a teaming arrangement can be whatever the parties want their relationship to be. Some examples: (1) a joint venture; (2) a partnership; (3) a prime contractor-subcontractor relationship; (4) a licensee-licensor relationship; (5) a leader-follower company relationship; or (6) any other type of relationship as defined and intended by the parties to the agreement.

There are many who support this last position, that teaming agreements can be whatever companies want them to be. Whenever two or more parties announce that they have formed a teaming alliance, the specific details of who is responsible for what are typically known only to the teaming participants, and possibly sometimes their customer. Teaming arrangements are the unique product of the parties involved:

The strategic alliance is the parties' own creation. There are few laws constraining the teams to which the parties can agree . . . Parties to a strategic alliance agreement, therefore, need to be careful to state fully the terms of their alliance. [7]

---

6. Defense Contract Audit Agency (DCAA) *Contract Audit Manual*, part 7-1802, (b), January 1992.

7. Stuart B. Nibley, Esq., and Joseph J. Dyer, "Forming Strategic Alliances," *Contract Management Magazine*, December, 2001, page 9.

Good, bad or otherwise, a teaming arrangement between one company and another company or companies creates a unique arrangement. Great care must therefore be taken to ensure that the strategic arrangement represents the intent and the best interests of the parties involved.

Various Models are Employed for Teaming Agreements

One interesting thing about corporate teaming agreements is that there is no single model used by all firms when forming such alliances. Rather, companies have elected to employ a variety of approaches when creating these arrangements. The funny thing: most of these arrangements seem to work out, to varying degrees of success. We will discuss a couple of the more common models, and will offer some commentary on each approach.

Model # 1: Teaming arrangements creating a "superior-subordinate" relationship.

The first model for discussion creates a "superior-subordinate" relationship between the parties. This approach is illustrated in Figure 4.1. The figure portrays a recent United States Air Force contract for the Aerospace Center Support work at their Arnold Air Force Base in Tennessee. All parties to the agreement, including the buying customer and the two subcontractors, know precisely who is responsible for the project: the Computer Sciences Corporation (CSC). Responsibility, authority and accountability are clearly outlined in this teaming agreement.

This teaming model requires that CSC buy certain previously defined scope of work from its two major teaming members for the duration of the agreement period, in this case three years. Typically under such arrangements competition will be perpetually waived, and the principals involved must continue to buy (or sell) from (or to) the same source until the performance period is ended. However, some teaming agreements do allow for either a pricing update or a competition to be held at a given future point in time. Others find this provision unnecessary.

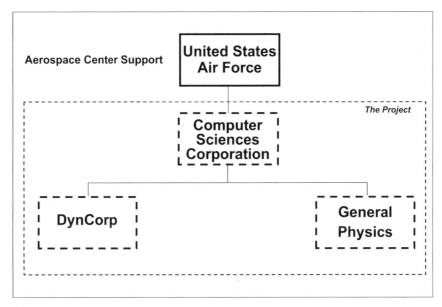

Figure 4.1 Teaming with a Superior-Subordinate Relationship

In this model everyone clearly knows who to hold responsible for the results. When things go right or possibly wrong, the buying customer, the USAF, knows exactly who to hold accountable. The USAF has a direct privity of contract with only one company, CSC, and CSC in turn has a direct contractual relationship (privity) with both DynCorp and General Physics.

It should be mentioned that under any superior-subordinate type teaming arrangement abuses can sometimes impede the process, but typically such problems are only temporary. People working on the projects from subordinate companies know that that the prime contractor has no choice but to buy their products for the duration of the agreement. However, teaming arrangements do have a self-correcting mechanism: the same corporate executives who formulated the arrangement.

Should there be any indication that the subordinate firm's employees are taking advantage of their legal agreement by not cooperating fully, by not providing reasonable prices or adequate services, an effective recourse is available for the superior company to simply elevate the issue back up to the executives who created their deal in the first place.

In most cases the continuing rapport between the executives who formed the initial agreement will be sufficient to bring cooperation and harmony back into the relationship. Much like the fathers in the ancient cultures, senior corporate executives expect, they will demand, that their teaming agreements work. Many an employee has been "reassigned" because they have failed to grasp the fact that teaming arrangements are expected to work . . . period . . . end of all discussion.

■   ■   ■

Sometimes the principal companies will subsequently trade places. As is shown in Figure 4.1 there is one company in charge of the teaming relationship, in this case the Computer Sciences Corporation (CSC). However, it is not an unusual practice under teaming arrangements for the roles of the participants to be changed, to be reversed in later agreements. The switching of primary roles is often driven by a simple marketing decision: which of us is in the best position to lead the effort to capture this new project. That firm will typically take the lead.

The scenario of changing roles is illustrated in Figure 4.2, whereby two otherwise competing companies will sometimes switch their respective roles in order to increase their chances of capturing the new project. On the left side of the figure McDonnell Douglas took the superior role, then years later they took the subordinate role as is shown on the right side of the figure.

In 1975, the Northrop Corporation found themselves in the position of having a fine new aircraft (their F-17) but without a buyer. They had just lost a competition for the new United States Air Force fighter aircraft. A competitor's F-16 had won the USAF competition.

When it later came time for the United States Navy to procure a new aircraft the executives at Northrop realized they had a great airplane, but little actual experience with the Navy customer. However, a competitor of theirs, the McDonnell Douglas Corporation, did have years of experience working with the Navy customer. So the Northrop Corporation teamed with McDonnell Douglas, and allowed them to lead their strategic arrangement. Together the McDonnell Douglas-Northrop team won the Navy's new F/A-18 contract.

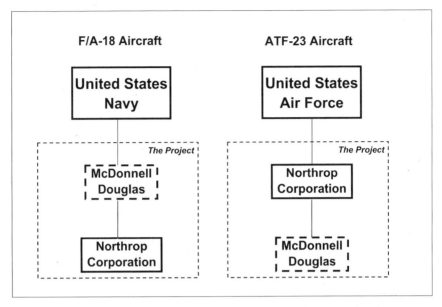

Figure 4.2 Superior-Subordinate: sometimes firms trade places

The interesting part is that years later, these same two competing companies again teamed to go after a new Air Force contract, but this time their respective roles were reversed, with Northrop now taking the lead position, and McDonnell Douglas became the principal subcontractor.

Under the superior-subordinate teaming arrangement it really doesn't matter who is in charge, as long as someone is given that responsibility, and all parties understand that point and abide by it. The superior-subordinate teaming arrangement is clean, clear, and it typically works.

Model # 2: Teaming agreements creating "partners."

The second teaming model we will review is sometimes used by industry. A corporate teaming arrangement will be created by two or more firms, then a single contract will be issued by a customer to either a joint venture, or directly to each of the various firms participating in the arrangement. This approach is illustrated in Figure 4.3.

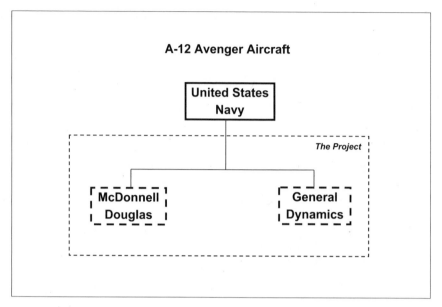

Figure 4.3 Teaming Arrangement with Equal Partners

In this case the United States Navy issued a single prime contract to two otherwise competing companies, McDonnell Douglas and General Dynamics. Each firm was expected to perform 50% of the project scope in accordance with their previously defined teaming agreement.

The expected benefits to be gained from employing this type of teaming arrangement is not obvious to this author. While at first glance the Navy may have believed that they would have less administrative effort involved because there would be only one contract to manage, the interface relationship between the two equal partners had to be cumbersome for each of them. Will the real boss please stand up! Who is in charge of this project? Who is ultimately responsible for total project performance, good or bad?

In the case of the Navy's A-12 Aircraft, a contract was initially let in 1988, then later cancelled for alleged default in 1991 by the then Secretary of Defense Dick Cheney. The relationship of the contractors versus the Navy has been in continuous litigation ever since, for over a decade. The two private contractors versus the Navy are arguing over an alleged over-payment of $1.35 billion dollars, which by 2001 has grown to $2.6 billion with accruing interest. In 2001 the contractors appealed the court's latest decision, and in 2003 the case went back to the lower courts. The saga continues.

Without suggesting that the contractual arrangement had anything to do with the subsequent litigation, the point must be made that the ambiguity in the roles and relationships between the two equal partners would <u>not</u> seem to be an ideal business model for anyone to follow. Whether the agreement calls for a 50/50 split, or some other sharing arrangement, the mere fact that neither party had a superior or subordinate position would seem to invite problems, in the opinion of this author.

Model # 3: Performance on a single project but "without" a teaming agreement

In the third model to be discussed there will be no teaming arrangement covering the multi-company performance on a single project. Rather, the project's buyer simply expects that the chosen companies will work together in a cooperative, harmonious way, under their direction. Sometimes this arrangement works well. Other times?

We will use as an illustration the outsourcing of Information Technology (IT) services which was done by British Petroleum Exploration (BPX) beginning in 1993. BPX executives planned to outsource all of their IT operations in an attempt to reduce their overall operating costs.

Initially BPX conducted a survey of how other IT companies had implemented their outsourcing services. They decided against using a single source supplier as many of the other firms had elected to do. Rather BPX planned to engage multiple contractors and insist that all selected companies work in concert to provide the needed IT services. The company sent out a Request for Information (RFI) packet to 100 potential candidates indicating an intent to issue multiple contracts covering all their IT work. They received some 65 responses to their RFI.

After a series of face to face interviews, BPX reduced their short-list of viable candidates down to just 6 firms. Week long sessions were held with these 6 final companies, resulting in the receipt of five compliant proposals. From these five proposals, BPX made a final selection of three firms to provide all IT services. BPX subsequently awarded three separate contracts to the selected companies, the details of each contract were known only to BPX and each respective company.

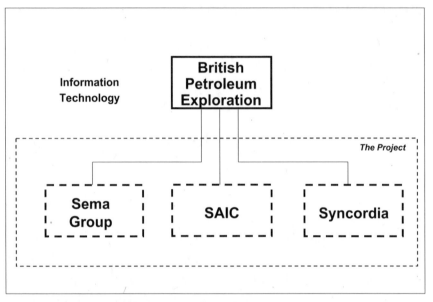

Figure 4.4 An umbrella contract for one project-without teaming

This approach is illustrated in Figure 4.4. There was a single overall IT project, with three separate contracts, requiring each contractor to work with the other two contractors to provide "seamless" IT services to BPX. The stated intent of BPX was to let the three contracted companies work out their own detailed interfaces, and to minimize the BPX management responsibilities:

> *They wanted them to work together as a consortium—to present a united interface to the company, and deal with any issues amongst themselves, thereby minimizing BPX involvement.* [8]

---

8. Dr. Mary C. Lacity and Dr. Leslie P. Wilcocks, *Global Information Technology Outsourcing*, (Chichester, England, John Wiley & Sons, 2001) page 225.

How did this BPX contractual approach work? It would appear to be adequate, the needed services were delivered . . . but not without experiencing certain problems:

> *The contracts were drawn up in ways that did not encourage cooperation between vendors. This left BPX a range of inter-contract problems arising from what was described as 'the cracks' between vendors. BPX ended up with the considerable task of having to manage not only each individual sub-contactor but also the relationship and interfaces between them.* [9]

At the end of their five year contracts, all three of the same companies were again retained by BPX, although in some cases the respective roles of each of these contractor was changed. But most significant perhaps, the vendor alliance concept was dropped at BPX. As one of the BPX managers later remarked:

> *It's very difficult to get multi-vendors to work in alliance . . . We decided to go for the one-supplier option.* [10]

So much for cooperation and harmony from multiple suppliers.

An Observation: Which of these arrangements seems to work best?

In the game of American football there's a play that is called the "Hail Mary Pass." This pass is used whenever a team is in desperate straights, and they have no other course of action. The Quarterback gets the ball, steps back, and throws a pass as far as he can in the direction of a cluster of players. Some of the players in the cluster are from his team, and some are from the other team. His silent prayer calls for someone <u>on his team</u> to somehow catch the ball. Sometimes it works.

---

9. Dr. Mary C. Lacity and Dr. Leslie P. Wilcocks, *Global Information Technology Outsourcing*, (Chichester, England, John Wiley & Sons, 2001) page 224.

10. Dr. Mary C. Lacity and Dr. Leslie P. Wilcocks, *Global Information Technology Outsourcing*, (Chichester, England, John Wiley & Sons, 2001) page 231.

Most of the time it does not. It is truly a desperate measure.

There are two conditions calling for the use of the Hail Mary pass: (1) sheer desperation, and (2) no definitive plan of action. It would seem to this author that the use of Model 3 described above, the out-sourcing of Information Technology work without establishing clear lines of authority, responsibility and accountability can be compared to the "Hail Mary pass" in American football.

Two other models of teaming arrangements were also presented. In the first model the relationship called for a teaming arrangement by creating a superior-subordinate relationship. The roles and relation-ships of all parties were clearly established. There was someone specif-ically in charge, and all other participants were subordinate to that company. In the second model, the relationships between participants were not precisely defined, and each entity was left to work out their role and relationship on their own.

Some will argue that the superior-subordinate model is unduly costly because the superior will often be given some value (a fee) for managing their subordinates. This may be the case, the prime con-tractor typically does get a small (negotiable) fee for managing the subcontractors. But it would appear to be a value well spent. You always know exactly who is in change, who is responsible for the pro-ject. You also know the total project costs at the outset.

However, whenever you do not set clear lines of responsibility with your suppliers, someone has to manage the "cracks" and the "overlaps" which will always emerge. Such management costs are often hidden, but they are nevertheless real, and will be contained within the buyer's organization. When quantified, such supplier management costs will typically exceed the costs of a small management fee paid to a prime contractor to manage the entire effort. Not placing clear lines of responsibility with suppliers in order to save a small management fee is simply a false economy.

Others have suggested that by not specifically defining the roles of suppliers with great precision, that synergies between the sellers will somehow emerge from their relationship, and each organization will excel with their respective contributions. This approach would seem to be unduly optimistic, perhaps even naive.

Model 1 would appear to this author to be most appropriate: the use of a definitive teaming agreement with clearly established roles. In any business relationship, it is mandatory that we know precisely who to praise when things go well, and who to hold accountable when things do not go as planned. There is nothing inherently wrong with teaming agreements, as long as the project buyers are made aware of the teaming arrangement, and there is a competition held with other firms, or other teams.

Model 2 has also been demonstrated to be effective, although the precise lines of authority may be mixed, overlapping, and cumbersome for the individual parties to work out.

Model 3, a project without defined roles for everyone, would appear to be fundamentally flawed, in the opinion of this author. As the BPX outsourcing experience later demonstrated:

> *Our outsourcing strategy has not always worked smoothly, we have encountered some bumps . . . While senior managers at BP and the three suppliers clearly understood the vision of seamless service captured in the framework agreements, their respective operations did not.* [11]

Perhaps we should again look to the ancient ways of arranged marriages between families. In the Old World the families (mostly the fathers) would agree on the matching of one boy and one girl. But after the marriage, who was responsible for what was left up to the two participants, although there were certainly family precedents to follow.

What the author is suggesting is that companies should follow the ancient ways and let the parents (the corporate executives) decide which projects should be joined by other companies. However, such corporate relationships should not be left open to chance, for the parties to work out.

In all cases, the same executives who arrange for the formation of the strategic alliances should also insist on such agreements being

---

11. John Cross, *IT Outsourcing: British Petroleum's Competitive Approach*, Harvard Business Review, May-June, 1995 page 100.

reinforced in great detail, defining precisely who is responsible for what, covering among other things the possibility of an early breakup, a dissolution of their arrangement, and a way to reasonably settle any disputed issues. In the modern World we often refer to these document as "prenuptial agreements."

Thus, in the opinion of this author, a combination of the Old World with the modern World makes the best form of a strategic teaming arrangement. All teaming agreements should be created by the families (the corporate executives), and the precise details of their arrangement should be specifically spelled out: who does what, who is responsible for what, how do we get out of this arrangement, taking the form of a corporate "prenuptial agreement", i.e., a teaming agreement.

Antitrust Law Implications on the Use of Teaming Arrangements

Anyone who has spent time observing business practices in the United States knows well that there are certain basic "truths" concerning commerce and the public. One such truth is that competition among business firms is normally considered to be in the best interests of the public. Another related truth is that any restraints on open and free trade would be felt to be not in the public's best interest.

Thus, when two or more otherwise competing companies form a corporate teaming agreement for the express purpose of collectively pursuing a specific new project, don't their actions in fact reduce competition and place unreasonable restraints on free trade? Possibly, but not necessarily. While contractor teaming agreements are perfectly legal and are recognized by the government, such arrangements are nevertheless subject to the antitrust laws of this nation.

Therefore, we should touch on this delicate issue briefly and discuss the two major antitrust laws, if for no other reason than to avoid the pitfall of being classified as a business trust.

First, we need to understand the specific term "trust" because it appears to somewhat resemble what some would refer to as teaming agreements. When forming a teaming arrangement we seem to be walking a delicate line.

Black's law dictionary provides the following definition of a trust for us:

> **Trust**: *An association or organization of persons or corporations having the intention and power, or the tendency, to create a monopoly, control production, interfere with the free course of trade or transportation, or to fix and regulate the supply and the price of commodities. In the history of economic development, the "trust" was originally a device by which several corporations engaged in the same general line of business might combine for their mutual advantage, in the direction of eliminating destructive competition, controlling the output of their commodity, and regulating and maintaining its price, but at the same time, preserving their separate individual existence, without any consolidation or merger.* [12]

We must take care in structuring our teaming agreements so as to not be in violation of any laws prohibiting such actions.

The provisions of the two legislative acts which cover trusts are also pertinent to this discussion. These two laws are the Sherman Act, passed July 2, 1890, and the Clayton Act, passed October 15, 1914. While these acts are admittedly quite old, they have been continually updated by the United States Congress, and must be considered whenever contemplating a teaming arrangement with another firm. No firm would willingly want to infringe on these two established antitrust laws. The penalties are just too great.

Quoting from the language of the Sherman Antitrust Act, section 1, which deals with restraints of trade taking the form of business trusts, and section 2, which covers the establishment of business monopolies:

> *§ 1. Trusts, etc., in restraint of trade illegal; penalty*
> *Every contract, combination in the form of trust or otherwise, or conspiracy, in restraint of trade or commerce among the several*

---

12. *Black's Law Dictionary*, (St. Paul, Minnesota: West Publishing Company).

States, or with foreign nations, is declared to be illegal. Every person who shall make any contract or engage in any combination or conspiracy hereby declared to be illegal shall be deemed guilty of a felony, and, on conviction thereof, shall be punished by fine not exceeding $10,000,000 if a corporation, or, if any other person, $350,000, or by imprisonment not exceeding three years, or by both said punishments, in the discretion of the court. [13]

§ 2. Monopolizing trade a felony; penalty
Every person who shall monopolize, or attempt to monopolize, or combine or conspire with any other person or persons, to monopolize any part of the trade or commerce among the several States, or with foreign nations, shall be deemed guilty of a felony, and, on conviction thereof, shall be punished by fine not exceeding $10,000,000 if a corporation, or, if any other person, $350,000, or by imprisonment not exceeding three years, or by both said punishments, in the discretion of the court. [14]

Now, citing the language from the other major law, the Clayton Antitrust Act, section 7 deals with the pooling of corporate assets to substantially lessen competition:

§ 18. Acquisition by one corporation of stock of another
No person engaged in commerce or in any activity affecting commerce shall acquire, directly or indirectly, the whole or any part of the stock or other share capital and no person subject to the jurisdiction of the Federal Trade Commission shall acquire the whole or any part of the assets of another person engaged also in commerce or in any activity affecting commerce, where in any line of commerce or in any activity affecting commerce in any section of the country, the effect of such acquisition may be substantially to lessen competition, or to tend to create a monopoly. [15]

---

13. Title 15 United States Code § 1, (2001).
14. Title 15 United States Code § 2, (2001).
15. Title 15 United States Code § 18, (2001).

These are the two principal laws which corporate legal counsels must consider when reviewing the language of any prospective teaming arrangement being proposed by the managements of firms contemplating such alliances.

Specifically in this discussion we will focus on some of the more narrow issues that are peculiar to the area of contracting and subcontract management, particularly the topics of pricing and data rights. As you read this section, remember that a complete discussion of antitrust issues would fill an entire book. It is the case law interpretation of these statutes that defines the parameters of antitrust violations, and the rulings on these cases are still evolving. Again, only an experienced antitrust attorney can answer specific questions in this area.

A good place to begin is to try to classify the nature of the teaming arrangement based upon the nature of the relationship: Is it a "vertical" or a "horizontal" union of two or more companies? These two business variations should be understood.

A *vertical* agreement is one in which two or more otherwise competing companies, with the same relative economic capability, agree that one firm will act exclusively as the prime contractor, and the other(s) will act exclusively as subcontractor(s) to the selected prime on a particular endeavor. The subcontractor or subcontractors in this case are often referred to as being the "principal subcontractor(s)." This relationship creates a hierarchical-type structure, where the company winning the prime contract, and ultimately responsible for producing the end product, combines with other subcontractors who produce the necessary sub-components going into the end-item. This has the effect of collecting the manufacturing processes used to produce the end item under the prime contractor's control. Model #1 described above would appear to fit the definition of a vertical agreement.

A *horizontal* agreement is one in which two or more otherwise competing companies, with the same relative economic capability, will combine their assets to form a single unit in pursuit of a particular endeavor. The single unit will sometimes form a partnership or a joint venture. In this situation, the team members act more like "peers," with the differing members combining to form a team to help strengthen each others' areas of perceived weakness. Model # 2 described above would also seem to fit this description.

Vertical teaming arrangements give rise to some unique issues: the pricing of the subcontracts, and the data rights of the parties involved. Both issues are related, and both come into play whenever any teaming arrangement essentially guarantees that a particular component or portion of work effort will be directed to a supplier (subcontractor) for the life of a given program or project.

One of the main concerns that arises whenever a particular subcontractor is assured of an award for the life of a program — which could last anywhere from years to decades — is that there may be little incentive provided for the subordinate supplier to reduce its costs during the life of the product. This is the issue of subcontractor pricing. As we will also illustrate, the issue of the data rights of the parties can have an impact on the prices charged by these subcontractors.

One of the unique aspects of U.S. government contracting is that the government has an assortment of options at its disposal to deal with potential abuses from suppliers. For example, if the government feels it is being overcharged by a second or lower tier supplier, it may use its authority to "break-out" or even to "re-procure" such articles — or merely threaten to do so — which will typically have the effect of reducing the price of the product. In order to do so, however, the government must have unlimited data rights over the articles in question (i.e., it must own the design and/or technology of the subcontracted items).

One of the reasons why the U.S. Government is so insistent about obtaining unlimited data rights whenever it invests funding in a particular new project is to have the means to go elsewhere whenever it feels a supplier is showing little incentive to lower the costs of a component. Whenever the government owns the unlimited data rights, and usually the tooling and special test equipment required to produce the item, it has the ability to counter abuses in the long-term vertical pricing of teaming agreements if it so chooses.

Finally, to reiterate one of the most important messages of this section: the issues involving the legality or possible violation of antitrust laws are not a simple matter. Professional legal counsel can sometimes have difficulty with the subject. We have merely raised a few issues to try to illustrate some of the problems, the pitfalls, but will not pretend that this provides an in-depth coverage of the topic. The balancing of business interests in conjunction with sound legal counsel is a must when structuring a new teaming arrangement.

What does the future hold for teaming arrangements? How much government interference can firms expect? It is not only the United States that can object to agreements and/or mergers being formed between companies. Recently we found that the European Community is beginning to flex its muscles as was evidenced when they objected to the merger of two American mega firms:

> *Europe vetoed General Electric Co.'s $41 billion purchase of Honeywell International, Inc. The decision marked the first time a proposed merger between two U.S. companies has been blocked solely by European regulators.* [16]

This is likely the first of many such objections which may come from the World community. Always keep in mind that there are no substitutes for the professional antitrust and teaming lawyers who must be brought into the teaming process early, to guide us carefully through the pitfalls.

In Summary

When making that critical corporate decision of whether to team or not to team, certain basic guidelines are recommended for the management of any private contractor. First, make certain that the purpose of the teaming arrangement is both proper and legal. Such arrangements are often conceived by the technical line executives hoping to capture that next critical project, and these executives may not be sensitive to all the potential ramifications which can exist when such contracts are legally executed. Get the full spectrum of corporate management involved early in the process, particularly the

---

16. Alan Clendenning, "EU rejects Honeywell-GE merger," Associated Press, July 4, 2001.

lawyers, finance, and business management, to mention only a few. Balance the final decision to team or not to team with both technical and business practitioners.

Second, always make sure that the company's prized technical "jewels" — the proprietary data rights — are adequately protected. The particular wording (or lack of wording) used in the agreement, or the acceptance of only a few dollars of government funding, may inadvertently cost you the competitive advantage that you have over other competing firms.

Third, get your customer involved. Let them know what you are planning when forming an alliance. This is true in the private sector, and particularly when dealing with the U.S. Government.

Finally, always know the "hard" issues to demand when forming a teaming arrangement. Likely one of the most astute negotiators of corporate teaming agreements has to be Microsoft's founder Bill Gates. In 1980, he and his inexperienced young colleagues took on one of the most powerful and savvy corporations in the world: IBM. With all their professional executives and legal staff, Big Blue still did not grasp what was important to keep, and what could be conceded. IBM gave away the most important of the crown jewels, the computer operating system source code:

> . . . the roots of IBM's decline began when it failed to demand the source code for DOS from Gates. Thus, each new upgrade had to be purchased from Microsoft, which maintained control of the most critical piece of software in the PC industry. [17]

A lesson to be learned. When sitting down to negotiate your next corporate teaming arrangement, sit back and ask yourself: what would Bill Gates do in this situation? You might just discover the "hard issues" to demand from your partner.

■   ■   ■

17. James Wallace, *Overdrive-Bill Gates and the Race to Control Cyberspace*, (New York: John Wiley & Sons, Inc. 1997) page 21.

The concept of teaming arrangements between companies is exciting. Companies team with one another for a number of reasons. By pooling their intellectual talents and resources, and sharing the risks of a new endeavor, they likely increase their chances to capture new business. The old adage "two heads are better than one . . . " certainly applies to strategic alliances. Most often we see these arrangements formalized based on long-term relationships between companies.

As a way of providing guidance to the formation of such arrangements, four examples of teaming arrangements are included as an Appendix to this book. These examples are:

A. A model teaming arrangement, provided by a lawyer who specializes in this field.

B. A teaming agreement questionnaire, also provided by a lawyer in the field.

C. Guidelines for teaming agreements, from lawyers who work in this area.

D. A model outline of a teaming arrangement, from an anonymous source.

CHAPTER 5

The Management of Project Procurement Risks

> *Risk management . . . is the art and science of identifying, analyzing and responding to risk factors throughout the life of a project and in the best interests of its objectives.*
>
> Project Management Body of Knowledge (PMBOK), 1987. [1]

This next subject is one which is essential to the successful management of all projects: the containment of project risks. However, an important point needs to be stressed: risk management must relate to the total project. While the focus of this book is confined to the procured items for a project, as contrasted with the internal make items, one cannot simply focus on the procured work and expect to control a project's risks. The management of project risks is all encompassing, and must include both the make work and the buy work.

The reason: during the course of a project's life-cycle the same tasks may be assigned to different organizations for performance: including going from make to buy, or from buy to make work. The inherent risks associated with these tasks may well be unaffected by a change with the designated performance responsibility. A risk is a risk, no matter whether the work is to be made or to be bought.

Also, quite often the make or buy determinations will be conducted as a project's risk mitigation strategy. For example, a high risk internal task may additionally be procured from an outside firm, as a hedge on the possible risks of failure with the internal work. Sometimes critical high risk tasks will be deliberately duplicated, both

---

1. D.V. Pym and R. Max Wideman, *Project Management Body of Knowledge (PMBOK)*, (Drexel Hill, Pennsylvania: Project Management Institute, 1987) page E-2.

made and bought, or procured from duplicate sellers, hoping that at least one source will be successful. Risk mitigation strategies typically require initial early investments. Redundancy is often employed as a risk mitigation approach, with both make <u>and</u> buy used as a deliberate strategy.

Prior to getting into the details of this subject, it might be appropriate for us to stand back and discuss the risk management concept, what it entails, and a few definitions of specific risk terms we will be using.

What is Risk Management

The matter of risk, the possibility that something may go wrong, or may not happen as planned, is an essential part of effective project management. It is unrealistic to assume that project performance will happen without the possibility (or the distinct likelihood) that something will not work. Risk management attempts to deal with adverse threats in an organized and systematic manner. Therefore risk management can be thought of as the disciplined process of assessing, quantifying, analyzing, and planning for the abatement (the closure) of risks, or at least bringing such risks down to levels which are acceptable to the project. Sometimes, the identified project risks cannot be eliminated completely, but they nevertheless can be addressed.

Now for a few of the more significant definitions we will be using in this chapter:

> **Risk**: *Possibility of loss or injury, a dangerous element or factor, the chance of loss, the degree of probability of such loss.* [2]

> **Risk Identification:** *The process of systematically identifying all possible risk events which may impact a project . . . Not all risks will impact all projects, but the cumulative effect of several risk*

---

2. *Webster's New Collegiate Dictionary*, (Springfield, Massachusetts: Merriam-Webster, Inc., 1981).

events occurring in conjunction may well be more severe than examination of individual risk events might suggest. [3]

Risk Assessment*: The process of subjectively determining the probability that a specific interplay of performance, schedule, and cost, as an objective, will or will not be attained along the planned course of action.* [4]

Risk Management *is the systematic process of identifying, analyzing, and responding to risk. It includes maximizing the probability and consequences of positive events and minimizing the probability and consequences of adverse events to project objectives.* [5]

Risk management can hence be reduced into a simple three step process: (1) the identification of potential project risks; (2) the assessment of the probability of a risk's occurrence as well as the determination of the impact/consequences should the risk materialize, and lastly (3) the development of a risk closure plan to bring all identified dangers down to acceptable levels, but not necessarily eliminating them altogether. In some cases project risks cannot be completely eliminated, but they can be identified, monitored and managed.

The risks associated with a project such as the internal development or the external procurement of a critical component may be divided into the three traditional areas of project management, often referred to as the project's triple constraint:

The Risks associated with Technical, Quality, or Performance: The possibility that the item being developed or procured will not perform to the levels needed by the project. Without question, technical risks are paramount to the success of any project. If a

---

3. R. Max Wideman, *Project and Program RISK MANAGEMENT*, (Drexel Hill, Pennsylvania, Project Management Institute, 1992), page E-3.
4. David I. Cleland and Harold Kerzner, *A Project Management Dictionary of Terms*, (New York: Van Nostrand Reinhold Company, 1985), page 220.
5. *A Guide to the Project Management Body of Knowledge (PMBOK Guide)*, (Newtown Square, Pennsylvania: Project Management Institute, 2000) page 127.

critical component does not work it will have an adverse impact on the success of any project. Technical risks are most often "show stoppers" and they must be corrected.

The Risks with Schedule Performance: The possibility that a critical item needed by the project will not be available in the time-frame needed, and/or that the technical risks will cause an adverse impact on the project schedule. Depending upon the circumstances, schedule risks can be merely an annoyance, or possibly have a catastrophic impact on the project. Schedule risks are second in criticality, right next to technical performance.

The Risks with Cost Performance: The possibility that the costs of the critical items will exceed that which is has been estimated, budgeted, or even available to the project, and that the technical and/or the schedule risks will have an adverse impact on the costs of the subproject. Of the three categories, cost risks are typically the least serious. Owners of projects will likely disagree with this assessment . . . but it is nevertheless true. The risks of cost growth are a distant third in the triple constraint.

All three of these risk categories are interrelated such that unfavorable results in any one of these three risk areas will likely have a resulting adverse effect in one or the other two. Technical performance will unquestionably be the primary concern over both schedule and cost risks. However, too tight a budget, or too ambitious a schedule, can also have a detrimental effect on the technical and or quality performance factors.

The project management practitioners in England have always taken the subject of risk management very seriously. However, they also recognize that the management of project risks need not be complicated:

At its most fundamental level risk management is extremely simple. The risks are identified, a prediction is made of how probable they are and how serious they might become, decisions are taken on what to do about them, and then the decisions are implemented. [6]

Project procurements, because of their critical nature to most projects, must also play an important role in any risk management strategy.

The Identification of Project Risks

Risk management begins with the identification of project risks, the listing of all the known or potential risks. Once identified, the risks can then be assessed, and a strategy devised to eliminate them, or at least to formulate a plan to contain them within acceptable bounds. The very worst strategy for any project to follow would be to proceed with their plans under the assumption that risks will be addressed at the time they surface. Such a strategy could prove fatal to any project.

Also, since risk mitigation often requires the allocation of early funding, the earlier all risks are identified and analyzed, the more likely that such hazards can be contained. Risk mitigation will typically require the investment of up-front monies, which is normally a good investment for any project to make.

Some of the more accepted approaches to risk identification will be discussed below.

The Project Work Breakdown Structure (WBS)

Likely there is no device better suited to display and to analyze the anatomy of a project than with use of the Project's Work Breakdown Structure (WBS). The preferred graphical display would be the WBS diagram, not simply an indented listing of WBS elements. A WBS diagram was shown earlier in Figure 3.1, which also displayed the make versus buy elements.

By definition the WBS identifies all of the project effort, and then systematically decomposes it level by level down to manageable pieces,

---

6. The Association for Project Management, *Project Risk Analysis and Management Guide (PRAM)*, (Norwich Norfolk, England, 1997) page 11.

exposing the critical subprojects within each WBS element. Thus in the identification and analysis of project risks, the use of a WBS can be a vital tool. In order to address the project procurements it would therefore be necessary to decompose the WBS elements down to the point where the "make versus buy" choices become apparent, exposing all of the major critical procurements.

Brainstorming

Brainstorming is likely the most popular and perhaps the most useful method for identifying project risks. The initial goal of the Brainstorming approach is to develop a comprehensive listing of all possible risks facing the new project, but not necessarily to immediately resolve them. Possible solutions will be addressed later. Quantity of the risk threats facing a project is the objective of Brainstorming. Once identified, the project team can subsequently devise a strategy to deal with them.

There are three participants in the Brainstorming process: (1) the impartial project facilitator; (2) the official scribe; and (3) the team members. Each has a critical role to play.

The facilitator must be a good listener and keep the session moving. The role of the facilitator is to encourage the free flowing (suggestions) of lots of ideas, some of which may have no particular value in themselves, except that they may stimulate new ideas from others. The more new ideas suggested, the better. A good facilitator will not allow the pre-judging of new ideas. No criticism, no blame, no pressure can be allowed in the Brainstorming session. One person's wild silly idea may allow others to hitch-hike on the same idea and make something worthwhile out of it.

The role of the scribe is to record every new idea on a board or flip-chart as they are generated. Note: One person cannot adequately perform both as a facilitator and a scribe at the same time. The output from the scribe is sometimes called the Project's Risk Register.

Team members are selected from the project itself. Typically they are people who are responsible for performance on a particular segment of the project, a particular WBS element, a sub-project, a project team, a critical procurement, etc. It is advisable in Brainstorming to include members who have approximately the same organizational standing, otherwise the free flowing of ideas may be suppressed. Senior organizational personnel, and dominant personalities, will often have the tendency to inhibit the free flowing of new ideas.

Some experts on the subject of Brainstorming suggest that the ideal team size will be between five members minimum and ten members maximum. However, many successful sessions are often held with larger groups. The flow of information and new ideas (risks) runs from one team member to another team member, and each is encouraged to add and expand on other's thoughts. This approach is presented in Figure 5.1, the new ideas run from member to member.

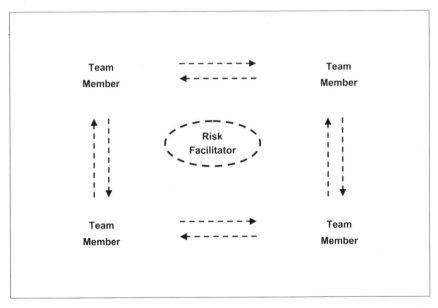

Figure 5.1 Information flow using "The Brainstorming Technique"

Typically, Brainstorming takes place within a prescribed time limit of perhaps one to two hours. Ground rules for Brainstorming would typically include: all new ideas are welcomed; creativity of suggestions is encouraged; quantity of suggestions within a specific time period is preferred; each team member gets an opportunity to make a suggestion;

teams members should take other member's suggestions and build on them, no matter how wild they may seem. Lastly, there is no such a thing as a "bad idea" in a Brainstorming session.

The Delphi Technique

This next approach to the forecasting of future events was originated in the late 1960s by the Rand Corporation for the United States Air Force. Here we will discuss the Delphi Technique as a process to identify the risks associated with projects, and possibly later to assess these risks as to their probability of occurrence and impact or consequences on a project should they materialize.

Delphi is a structured, interactive method used to gain a consensus position from a group of experts on any given subject. Here they may be experts on the project itself, actual team members, or possibly experts in risk management.

The key to the process is the selection of an impartial facilitator who will work with the panel of experts to formulate their group position. Provocative questions will be prepared on the desired subject and then responses solicited by the facilitator from the panel of experts, asking each expert to provide an anonymous response to the proposed questions. Responses from individual experts are only known to the facilitator, not to the other experts.

There will be no interaction between the various experts, the individual team members with Delphi. Any questions of clarification will be directed to the facilitator alone. Thus by isolating the inputs from various team members, the dominance of a strong personality or a senior staff member will be prevented from influencing the final collective results. The process is repeated several times, until the facilitators feels they have formed a collective position. This approach to risk identification is illustrated in Figure 5.2. Inputs flow from team experts only to the facilitator, not to other experts.

The Delphi process will often take the following steps:

1. A risk facilitator will be selected. This is typically a person who is an expert in research data collection, but not necessarily in the project itself;

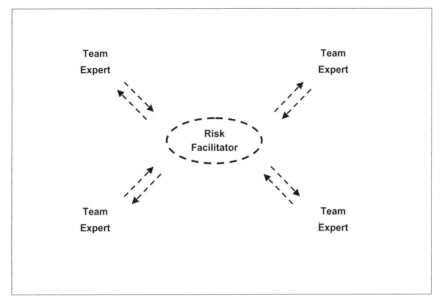

Figure 5.2 Information flow using "The Delphi Technique"

2. A panel of experts on the project itself will be selected. Often this group will be comprised of the key project team members, with possibly the addition of a few outside experts in the area;

3. A preliminary listing of risk criteria will be formulated by the facilitator in conjunction with the project manager to start the back and forth process. Such criteria will consist of a compilation of some of the more obvious challenges facing the new project;

4. The facilitator will transmit the risk criteria to each of the designated panel of experts (by mail, telephone, facsimile, or most likely today by email) and ask them to anonymously rank and return the preliminary risk criteria according to some designation such as: (1) a very critical risk, (2) a somewhat critical risk, or (3) not a critical risk issue. At this time each member is encouraged to introduce new criteria as they feel may be needed;

5. The facilitator will compile the inputs, come up with a new listing of risks, and continuously repeat the process until a group consensus of these experts is reached.

Interviewing

In this process risk identification is directed to specific individuals who are considered to be experts in a particular project, or perhaps the technology of the project. They have been there before, and have valuable experiences to share. They do not necessarily have to be working on the project. Sometimes the paying customer will be included in the process. Such interviews can happen face to face, or solicited by telephone, email, etc.

The interviewing process can be performed to both identify new risks, and also to assess the risks identified earlier using Brainstorming or the Delphi Technique.

■ ■ ■

The output of the risk identification process consists of a listing of potential project risks. What comes next? Perhaps it is the right time to now assess each of the identified risks, and to rank them according to their potential severity. This process is typically referred to as Qualitative Risk Analysis.

The Assessment of Project Risks

Once the project has compiled a listing of the potential risks ahead the next logical step would be to determine the likelihood of the risks materializing, and the impact (consequences) to the project should they happen. As an example, most of the newer commercial jet airliners today have only two engines, as contrasted with most having four engines only a few years back. This was a deliberate design change because of the reliability demonstrated by jet engine performance.

The likelihood of one jet engine failing has become very-very low, and the likelihood of both engines failing at the same time is considered to be extremely low. Thus, the consequences of having only one engine available to the aircraft is now considered acceptable, the planes have enough power with a single engine to land safely. Of course loosing both engines at the same time is . . . still potentially a catastrophic event! But there are two separate risk issues to consider: probability and consequences.

Somehow the project must take their raw listing of all the potential project risks and decide what to do about them. They need to set priorities, and the ranking of project risks. These two independent risk variables need to be assessed to adequately rank the project risks.

The first variable is the likelihood or probability that the identified risk will in fact happen. The second variable is the consequences or impact should the risk happen. These two variables can be combined to establish a range of potential risks, often referred to as a probability-consequences matrix.

Employing a Risk Probability (likelihood) times the Consequences (impact) Matrix

One of the most effective techniques for distilling a random listing of risks into a ranked listing is by creating a matrix which reflects both the degree to which a risk may come to fruition, times the degree to which the risk will have an impact a project, should it happen. Continuing with a Brainstorming, or a Delphi, or expert interviews process, the risk facilitator will next ask the team to set independent values for each of the identified risks.

The process is typically starts with a focus on the probability that the risk will occur. After determining the probability or likelihood of occurrence, the second independent round will address the consequences or impact of each risk, should they actually occur. This process is shown in Figure 5.3, assigning a probability times consequences point value for each of the identified risks.

In the Figure 5.3 a linear scale is presented, going progressively from a low probability of 0.1, to an almost certainty of 1.0. However, the subjective assigned scales could be skewed in either direction to reflect a higher or lesser degree of expected results. Typically, the project team and experts in risk management will determine the appropriate values to be used in this process.

The results of this process would be the creation of a list of potential risks facing the project, as is displayed in Figure 5.4. All identified

Project Risks—determining a Risk Scope

Probability of Risk		Consequences of Risk
Very Low (0.1 to 0.2)	X	Very Low (0.1 to 0.2)
Low (0.3 to 0.4)	X	Low (0.3 to 0.4)
Moderate (0.5 to 0.6)	X	Moderate (0.5 to 0.6)
High (0.7 to 0.8)	X	High (0.7 to 0.8)
Very High (0.9 to 1.0)	X	Very High (0.9 to 1.0)

Figure 5.3 Qualitative Risk Analysis: probability times consequences

Project Risks—listed in descending order

WBS Element or Procurement	Probability of Risk		Consequences of Risk		Compounded Risk Score
1).....................	....	X	....	=	....
2).....................	....	X	....	=	....
3).....................	....	X	....	=	....
4).....................	....	X	....	=	....
5).....................	....	X	....	=	....

Figure 5.4 Qualitative Risk Analysis: the ranking of project risks

project risks will be listed, in descending order, with those risks felt to represent the highest risks listed first. An obvious listing would be by Project WBS element, and, or, simply by critical procurements.

By systematically going through this process, the project can spread their raw listing of all identified risks into a display which can isolate the "Top Five" or "Top Ten" Project risks. Such risks can be tracked by the project team until successfully eliminated. By establishing a manageable listing of the highest five or ten risks, the team is then ready to take the next step: planning for risk closure.

Risk Management and Closure Planning

By systematically preparing a ranked listing of all known risks the project will be off to a good start in the management of their risks. The next step would be to determine a plan to close on each of the identified risks. There are essentially four strategies which work well in the management and control of project risks. We need to understand each approach.

Avoid the Risks

Projects can sometimes eliminate identified risks through a reexamination of the requirements which may have caused the risk. It is often a good practice to discuss the identified risks with one's customer, who sometimes may have inadvertently over-prescribed requirements when initially defining the project. The buying customer may have unconsciously specified an approach, a sequence of testing, certain components, which add nothing to the goal of the project, but may have added unnecessary risks. Sometimes a customer will modify scope, if doing so will increase chances of project success.

Often projects in their initial planning will prescribe an approach which pushes the technical state-of-the-art. On a closer re-examination they may find proven methods, commercial components, packaged software, which are adequate and will eliminate the defined risks.

The use of highly experienced people, demonstrated processes, reliable expertise, may add costs up-front, but increase the overall chances of success of the project the first time. Redundancy is often used to avoid project risks, but redundancy does cost money. Duplicate components having the same purpose, perhaps developed both by an in-house effort as well as a procured item, will reduce the chances of failure. Redundancy is costly, but sometimes necessary.

In the area of procurement, many firms have adapted a policy of using only experienced, dependable, proven sellers, in lieu of holding an open public competition and awarding an order to the lowest price. The lowest bid price may not be the best price if the award goes to a seller who has no demonstrated expertise in a given area.

Another risk avoidance technique is to use only pre-qualified sellers, using a two-step procurement practice. Step one pre-qualifies the prospective sellers according to established criteria, and eliminates the unqualified suppliers. Step two solicits bids from only qualified sources. A competition held between both qualified and unqualified sellers . . . is no competition at all.

Some companies, in an effort to reduce the risks on highly complex procurements, will take two deliberate steps before issuing their Request for Proposal (RFP) to selective sellers. First, they will take the RFP package and conduct an in-house "bid-ability review." This process will assign an experienced team to examine the solicitation package and determine whether or not anyone can make sense of it. Often this results in a re-write of the draft RFP. If prospective sellers cannot discern what is wanted in the RFP, the risks of suppliers adding useless contingencies will increase.

Another practice with complex procurements is to take the RFP package and perform an "independent cost estimate" for the new job. The estimate gives the project an independent benchmark against which the seller's cost proposals may be compared.

Transfer the Risks

A second approach to risk management is to transfer or share in the risks, should they happen. Many companies in an attempt to reduce their risk exposure will form strategic joint ventures, sometimes called teaming arrangements, with other firms to spread the impact of risks should they occur. Generally such arrangements will specifically pre-scribe the extent to which each firm will share in the upside profits, or in the downside risks.

Some projects, once the potential risks have been identified, will go back to their customer and request relief from the identified risks in the form of a renegotiated contract, a change in scope. Such prac-tices simply transfer the risks back to the buying customer.

With complex procurements many projects will deliberately select a type of contract with their sellers to shift the risks in one direction or the other. A firm fixed price arrangement will transfer all risks of performance to the sellers, if, the project can define precisely what it wants to buy, and if the likelihood of design changes is minimal. If however, the project cannot precisely define the scope for the seller, and or if the project needs flexibility in changing requirements, some type of cost contract may in fact result in lesser risks to the project.

Other approaches for handling complex procurements may include inserting a liquidated damages provision into the contract, to transfer the risks back to the seller's performance. Other techniques include buy-ing performance insurance, bonding, guarantees, and warranties.

Mitigate the Risks

Many projects attempt to mitigate risks by reducing the likelihood of the occurrence of the risks, and or the impact should they happen. Working to a precise risk closure plan will help in this approach. Adding additional product testing, proofing, prototyping, are all risk mitigation strategies.

Employing only experienced personnel, using only proven suppli-ers, will mitigate risks. Inserting incentive performance provisions into contracts with sellers can sometimes help.

Accept the Risks

This last approach is the one taken when all else fails. Sometimes risks cannot be eliminated altogether. The only option for the project is to live with the condition. Risk contingency plans will be made, but the identified risks cannot be eliminated completely. In such cases the status of known risks becomes a critical part of the routine review process.

One approach some project managers have taken when facing risks which cannot be eliminated is to aggressively "scrub" all project scope, every budget, every schedule date, and then take away all hidden contingency monies, schedule float, unnecessary work tasks, and only authorize the use of these reserves on an exception basis.

Require a Seller's "Risk Management Plan" on Complex Project Procurements

One of the conditions which makes it (perhaps) somewhat easier to manage risks associated with the purchased work, particularly the complex procurements done to the project's specification, is the fact that most sellers want new business. Most suppliers are eager to capture new work. Thus in the competitive environment to obtain a new order, sellers are often willing to come forth with their most innovative ideas in order to gain a competitive advantage over other suppliers.

Thus, it is not unusual for project buyers in their solicitation package, the formal Request for Proposal (RFP), to require that the prospective sellers respond with a proposal which includes a specific section typically called the *"Risk Management Plan."* This section would describe how the seller, should they be awarded the new order, will meet the risk challenges of providing the new product, component, subsystem, etc.

It is also not unusual for the buyer's RFP to indicate the percentage point values to be assigned to each section, for example, the *Risk Management Plan* might be worth say 25% of the proposal's overall evaluation. This approach certainly stimulates all prospective sellers to come forth with their most innovative ideas in their proposals competing for the new order.

While the precise outline for a *Risk Management Plan* will vary depending on the unique circumstances, a format for such plans might follow these lines:

In Summary

A half a century ago the United States and Russia were engaged in a belligerency commonly referred to as the Cold War. The hope of most people was that the relationship would never go hot!

At the time, in the 1950s, both the United States and Russia had a nuclear weapon capability. However, at the time neither nation had a new weapon delivery system called the Inter-Continental Ballistic Missile, or ICBM. This new weapon delivery system could send a nuclear weapon from one country to the other in just 30 minutes, from launch to impact. While most of the world believed that the United States would never use this weapon first, the other was not the case. The worst nightmare for many people was that Russia would develop their ICBM first, and then bring the entire free world into submission with the threat of launching ICBMs against them. It was a frightening prospect.

Thus, it was imperative that the United States beat Russia into achieving an operational ICBM capability. This was risk management at its finest. What did the United States Department of Defense (DOD) do? They chose to implement a "redundant" risk management strategy. In the mid 1950s the DOD initiated two completely redundant programs, both having the same mission, both to develop an ICBM capable of flying 5,000 miles or more to deliver a nuclear weapon. The first contract went to the Convair Company to develop the Atlas missile, and later a second contract went to the Martin Company to develop the Titan missile.

The United States eventually won the race. Both missile systems went into an operational status within months of each other, both ahead of the Russians. The free world was saved from enslavement.

However, that was not the end of the story. Later certain members of United States Congress openly criticized the DOD for wasting taxpayer's money. The issue: Why did the DOD have to develop two ICBM missile systems when only one was needed:

> *The dual approach program whereby the Titan was being developed concurrently was criticized as "over-insurance."* [7]

Two lessons emerge from this successful story of project risk management at its finest:

- One, it always costs some up-front money to mitigate project risks, although in the long run it likely may well save considerable money.

- Two, it is never possible to satisfy all members of the United States Congress at the same time. Never!

7. Edmund Beard, *Developing the ICBM-A study in bureaucratic politics*, (New York: Columbia University Press, 1976) page 142.

CHAPTER 6

Selecting the Appropriate Contract Type [1]

A wide selection of contract types is available to the Government and contractors in order to provide needed flexibility in acquiring the large variety and volume of supplies and services required by agencies. The contract types are grouped into two broad categories: fixed-price contracts and cost-reimbursement contracts. [2]

Selecting the contract type is generally a matter for negotiation and requires the exercise of sound judgment. Negotiating the contract type and negotiating prices are closely related and should be considered together. The objective is to negotiate a contract type and price (or estimated cost and fee) that will result in reasonable contractor risk and provide the contractor with the greatest incentive for efficient and economical performance. [3]

It is comforting to know that there are a wide selection of contract types available to help buyers better manage their project procurements. However, many of us would also find it interesting to note that although there are many contract types available to projects, most private companies and most Government agencies typically elect to use only one contract type: the firm-fixed-price (FFP) contract. If you could somehow sneak into and examine the procurement activities (sometimes called purchasing, material, materiel, and most recently supply-chain management) of most companies you would find that

---

1. Most of the precise definitions on contract types for this chapter are taken from the United States Government's Federal Acquisition Regulation (FAR), dated September 2001. While many commercial companies are not subject to the FAR regulations, most courts in the United States would likely accept the FAR definitions on contract types.
2. FAR, Subpart 16.101. Underlining done by the author to emphasize key points.
3. FAR, Subpart 16.103. Underlining done by the author to emphasize key points.

their procurement processes center around only one type of contract for use by project buyers: the firm-fixed-price (FFP) contract. An interesting contradiction of what's available to projects versus what is commonly practiced.

The reason for this apparent disparity is the feeling of security that comes to management with the use of FFP contacts. The FFP contract type is truly the safest contract form to use if, and this is a big if: (1) you know exactly what you want to buy, (2) you can describe it in precise detail, and (3) you are not apt to later change your requirements. However, if you are uncertain about the requirements for a given procurement, and or, you need flexibility due to project uncertainty, the FFP contract can be overly restrictive. Each redirection by the project presents an "opportunity" for the sellers to "get well" with change orders. We cannot hold sellers responsible for a buyer's choice of the wrong contract type.

The choice of contract type is a critical issue for both the buyer and seller. It is something which should build on the consideration of many factors. Some of the more important issues to consider would include the life cycle of the project, the known risks facing the project, technology challenges, and of course, the ability of the project to describe what it wants to buy, without later changing these requirements.

These are all critical issues for project procurements and are illustrated in Figure 6.1. The selection of the appropriate contract type is truly an art at best. The full spectrum of contract types runs from fixed-price, to cost reimbursable, with an intermediate hybrid contract type called the time and materials contracts. Each contract type has its advantages and its disadvantages as will be discussed below. Also, in many cases the project may elect to use multiple contract forms in a single relationship.

However, unless some justification can be demonstrated which will allow for use of another kind of contract, most companies will automatically "default" to the firm-fixed-price (FFP) model. In order to properly make the right decision, particularly on any complex procurements of new items being created according to the project's unique specification, we need to fully understand the range of contractual options which are available to projects.

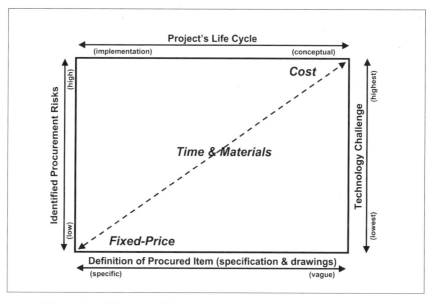

Figure 6.1 The Art of Selecting a Contract Type

The Two Major Contractual Options

There are two broad families of contracts available for projects to use, and each has its unique characteristics. We need to understand the general distinction between these two generic families because a dozen or so unique contract variations have sprung from use of these two major groups. The first family is the fixed price contract. It places the greatest risks of performance on the seller . . . if the buyer has structured it properly.

Fixed-Price Contracts

They are a family of contract types defined as follows:

Fixed-price contracts provide for a firm price or, in appropriate cases, an adjustable price. Fixed-price contracts providing for an adjustable price may include a ceiling price, a target price (including target cost), or both. Unless otherwise specified in the

> *contract, the ceiling price or target price is subject to adjustment only by operation of contract clauses providing for equitable adjustment or other revision of the contract under stated circumstances. The contracting officer shall use firm-fixed price or fixed-price with economic price adjustment contracts when acquiring commercial items.* [4]

Typically under fixed-price contracting the price will be set at the outset of the relationship. Most contracts in this category will be classified as firm-fixed-price, wherein an absolute value is placed within the contract. However, sometimes the fixed price will be adjustable, to provide incentives to the seller to complete the job by spending less money, portions of which the seller may get to keep according to a stated formula in the contract. Other fixed price arrangements set a fixed price, but the price may be subject to adjustments caused by changes in economic conditions beyond the control of either the buyer or seller. These are typically contracts for services or commodities scheduled for performance over long periods of time.

The key feature of the fixed price contractual arrangement is the obligation it places on the seller. It is absolute. Under the fixed price contract the seller "must produce," in other words, is "obligated" to finish the job under contract, regardless of the circumstances that may happen later. If the job involves more costs or risks or effort than was originally envisioned, so be it. No additional costs for the contracted work will be made available to a seller merely because the job turns out to be more difficult than was originally anticipated, by either party. If the seller does not finish the fixed price job, walks away from the obligation, the buyer can sue the seller for any damages incurred.

The use of fixed price contracts typically require less administrative oversight than cost type arrangements. However, if progress payments are included in the fixed-price relationship, typically monthly payments, oversight of seller performance by the project is essential to make sure that progress is in fact being made prior to making such payments.

---

4. FAR 16.201.

Because procurements made under fixed price arrangements place a higher risk on the seller, logic would suggest that they should receive higher profits. However, this is not always the case, particularly in instances where aggressive competitions are held, as with publicly bid construction jobs.

It must be emphasized that there can be risks and disadvantages to any project even with the use of fixed-price contracting. The risks are that the project may not know precisely what it wants the seller to do, or that the job may change after the contract is let. Changes in scope in fixed-price contracts are painful to the project. The term "getting well with changes" is familiar to anyone who has used firm-fixed-price contracting, only to later have to re-direct the supplier down another path. Changes in scope can always be accommodated, but at a price. Each new change presents an "opportunity" to a seller.

Cost-Reimbursement Contracts:

The second broad family of contract types is the cost reimbursable model:

> *Cost-reimbursement types of contracts provide for payment of allowable incurred costs, to the extent prescribed in the contract. These contracts establish an estimate of the total cost for the purpose of obligating funds and establishing a ceiling that the contractor may not exceed (except at its own risk) without the approval of the contracting officer.* [5]

By contrast, the key feature of the cost reimbursable type contract is the obligation of the seller. Under the cost reimbursable type contract the seller's obligation is merely to provide a "best efforts" commitment to complete all of the work as stipulated in the contract. If the seller incurs all of the costs as authorized in the contract, but does not finish the entire scope of work, the seller cannot be sued for the difference. Their legal commitment is to provide their best effort only to finish the job.

---

5. FAR 16.301-1.

However, the buyer must fund the entire job to its completion, to the limit of their contractual arrangement. Sellers are normally obligated to notify the buyer in advance if they anticipate exceeding the authorized funding levels, typically set at about the 70% to 80% point of contract value. Once notified, the buyer must decide whether or not to continue to fund the job, or to terminate the effort.

The major concern with the use of the cost reimbursable type contracts is the "opportunity" they can provide to any unscrupulous seller. Any supplier which has an under-utilized work force, or idle plant facilities, or surplus assets, or ambitious plans for growth, could, and sometimes have in the past, abused this type of arrangement by shifting their assets to the cost type contract in an attempt to keep their capital fully employed. Such practices border on the illegal, particularly with Government contracting, but such abuses with cost contracts have been known to happen in the past. It is a major concern of many companies, and thus the use of cost reimbursable contracting is typically severely restricted, even when a cost type arrangement may be in the best interests of a particular project.

The advantages to a project with the use of cost type contracts is the flexibility they can provide. It is always easier to accommodate changes in the direction of a supplier when operating under a cost type arrangement, than with a fixed-price contract.

Since the risks of seller performance on cost type contracts is lower, one would expect that suppliers should receive less fees for their work. Such is not always the case. Often, cost type contracts provide substantial profit opportunities to suppliers. One major disadvantage to the use of cost type contracts is the need for continuous oversight of seller performance by the project team.

The major distinctions between the use of fixed-price versus cost reimbursement type contracts are summarized in Figure 6.2.

Two Modifying Contractual Fee Provisions

There are two fee provisions which can be added to contracts which can be employed independently or together, which can provide

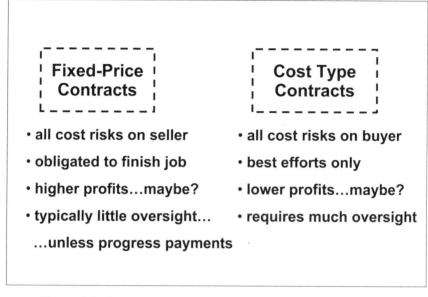

Figure 6.2 Contract Types: two generic families

strong inducements on the performing sellers. These provisions insert "incentive fees" and "award fees" into contractual relationships. The two fee types are distinct, but are often misunderstood by individuals involved in the contracting process. We need to clearly understand what constitutes an incentive versus an award fee provision.

Incentive Fee Contracts:

Incentive contracts . . . are appropriate when a firm-fixed-price contract is not appropriate and the required supplies or services can be acquired at lower costs and, in certain instances, with improved delivery or technical performance, by relating the amount of profit or fee payable under the contract to the contractor's performance . . . The two basic categories of incentive contracts are fixed-price incentive contracts and cost-reimbursement incentive contracts.

Cost Incentives. Most incentive contracts include only cost incentives, which take the form of a profit or fee adjustment

*formula and are intended to motivate the contractor to effective-
ly manage costs. No incentive contract may provide for other
incentives without also providing a cost incentive (or constraint).*

*Performance Incentives. Performance incentives may be con-
sidered in connection with specific product characteristics . . . or
other specific elements of the contractor's performance. These
incentives should be designed to relate profit or fee to results
achieved by the contractor, compared with specified targets.* [6]

The incentive fee type derivative may be used with either a cost
or fixed price type contract. This contractual variation is appropriate whenever there are uncertainties of performance associated with
a particular undertaking. Any costs associated with overruns or
under runs to the target costs are shared between the buyer and seller in accordance with a formula agreed to at the outset by both parties. These formulas will adjust the final seller fees upward or
downward to the maximum or minimum fee arrangement specified
in their contract. The cost sharing formula under incentive type
contracts may be set at any rate formula which adds to 100%, but
typically they will be set in the ranges of 90/10; 80/20; 70/30;
60/40, etc. The higher values shown on the left side will apply
against the target costs, and the lower values on the right apply to
adjustments in the seller's target fee.

An important distinction with incentive fee contracts is that there
be specific measurable metrics incorporated into the contract which
allows both the buyer and seller to objectively evaluate the seller's performance. Under the FAR rules one performance metric must always
include "cost" incentives, in order to also incorporate other types of
incentives such as schedule performance, quality, weight, reliability,
etc. In private contracting the two parties may go directly to these
other types of incentives without the use of cost incentives. In private
contracting the parties may incorporate any incentives into their contracts which can be objectively measured.

If there are professional differences of opinion between the buyer

---

6. FAR 16.401.

and the seller as to whether or not the contractual incentive fee provisions have been met, and if these differences cannot be negotiated between the parties, the seller can sue the project buyer seeking contractual relief. Incentive fee contracts thus should incorporate specific metrics which can be measured, and seller fees earned or lost based on achieving these defined objectives. As an example, a contract may incorporate a 10% bonus fee if the seller makes a delivery of a commodity "by the 15th of June."

Award Fee Contracts:

These contracts contain a provision which allows for payment of a specified fee to a seller based on the seller's achievement of broadly defined award fee performance criteria. Such award fee criteria will be unilaterally evaluated by the project team. These performance criteria can be defined for example as "meeting the overall schedule objectives", or "exceeding weight objectives", or "exceeding reliability goals", anything which can be specified in broad general performance terms. Note, the project buyer has the final say as to the amount of award fee given, thus this type of contractual arrangement provides the maximum influence of the project buyer over the seller's performance.

Award fee type contracts were initially thought of for use on cost reimbursable contracts, but of late they are also being employed on fixed price contracts. The award fee rewards the seller for outstanding performance and cooperation against broadly defined objectives set for the effort. Typically award fees are used as a supplement with other fee or profit arrangements.

As more buyers and sellers become comfortable with award fee contracting we are likely to see an expanded use in the future. The supplier's award fee is determined based on their satisfying the needs of the project, and are evaluated solely by the project's buyer. Under award fee contractual arrangements the seller typically waives their right of appeal of award fee determinations. Thus award fee determinations are generally not subject to any formal appeals process.

However, in order for the process to work, award fees provided must be considered fair and reasonable by both the buyer and seller.

Arbitrary or unreasonable fee awards can have a detrimental effect on any project. Sellers must be paid what they perceive is reasonable in order for award fees to have a positive influence on a project.

Perhaps the best illustration of an award fee is to compare it to the tip one leaves for service in a fine restaurant. If one likes the service provided by the waiter, one might leave a 15% to 25% fee. If the service is lousy, no tip is included with the check, or perhaps one thin dime to add an absolute insult.

The differences between incentive fees and award fees are important to understand, and are summarized in Figure 6.3.

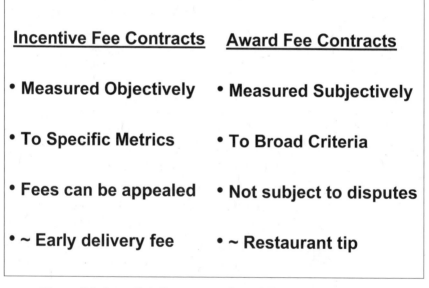

Incentive Fee Contracts   **Award Fee Contracts**

- **Measured Objectively**   - **Measured Subjectively**

- **To Specific Metrics**   - **To Broad Criteria**

- **Fees can be appealed**   - **Not subject to disputes**

- **~ Early delivery fee**   - **~ Restaurant tip**

Figure 6.3 Incentive Fee versus Award Fee Relationships

The "Fixed-Price" Contract Family

There are a multitude of specific contractual arrangements which have evolved from the two broad generic contract families: fixed-price and cost reimbursable. It is important that we understand the characteristics of the two varieties. Shown in Figure 6.4 are a listing of the

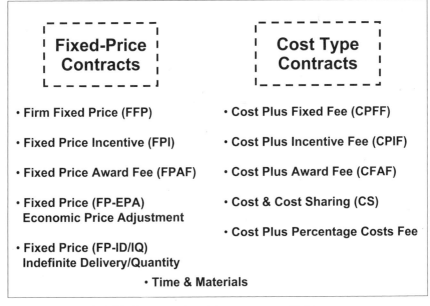

Figure 6.4 Various contract types are available

more significant contractual variations: five fixed-price, five cost type, and a popular hybrid type called the time and materials contract.

Described in this section will be the more common fixed-price type contracts in use, with a brief summary of each including the "pros" and "cons." The prospective will be that of the project buyer, as contrasted with the seller of goods. Later the cost reimbursable family will be covered.

One important point about the usage of contract types. Presented below are the various types, each described separately. This is done to better understand each contract type. However in actual business practice, it is not uncommon to have buyers incorporate two or even three types in a single contractual relationship, example: FFP/AF; FPI/AF; CPFF/IF; CPFF/AF, etc., to be described below.

Firm-Fixed-Price (FFP) Contracts:

A firm fixed-price contract provides for a price that is not subject to any adjustments on the basis of the contractor's cost experience in performing the contract. This contract type places upon the contractor maximum risk and full responsibility for all costs and resulting profit or loss. It provides maximum incentive for the contractor to control costs and perform effectively and imposes a minimum administrative burden upon the contracting parties. [7]

Without question, the Firm Fixed Price (FFP) contract is the most favored contract type by the United States government, and likely by most companies in private industry. The FFP is appropriate whenever definitive design and product performance specifications are available. This contract type places absolute cost risks and incentives on the seller to deliver the procured items in an efficient manner. The FFP contract type is not subject to subsequent price adjustments because of what a seller may experience during performance, and the supplier is under an absolute obligation to finish the job under contract. Damages can be sought if a seller fails to perform on a FFP contract.

But the FFP is not without certain limitations, and there are times when this contract type may be totally inappropriate. It is important that a buyer and seller know just when and when not to use the FFP contract.

In order for the FFP contract to be effectively employed, three conditions must exist at the time of the procurement: (1) the project's buyer must know exactly what it wants to procure; (2) the buyer must be able to specify the desired article in very precise terms, so as to agree on a price between the buyer and seller; and (3) the buyer must have reasonable confidence (probable assurances) that the item being procured will not subsequently change in specifications, or performance requirements, or terms, so as to require a redirection to the supplier. If these three requirements do not exist, it may well be advisable to consider some other form of contract type. Ambiguities in product specifications, and subsequent design changes, can sometimes make the FFP the wrong contract type for procurements, in deference to the government's and most company's preferred type.

---

7. FAR 16.202-1.

To properly use the FFP contract, the buyer must understand what is to be bought, and be able to define the desired article in clear and legally enforceable terms. A buyer requires a definitive procurement specification from engineering/manufacturing/technical in order to use the FFP contract. Both parties to the contract must have the same understanding as to what is being procured. Conversely, if the desired item to be bought cannot be specified except in very broad general terms, the use of the FFP contract type may well be unsuitable.

The other limitation with this most favored contract type is that the FFP leaves the buyer with little (perhaps no) flexibility to later change direction without paying a high cost for each change. Since the articles being procured must be specified in very precise terms, and all of the risks of cost growth are placed on the supplier, sellers cannot and typically will not accept redirection from a buyer without requesting additional costs to accept any changes. Any sellers which have struck lean (initial profits) deals will often try to "get well" through contract changes or redirection. Also, the FFP price values can change (as with other contract types) for defective pricing, for liquidated damages provisions, for defective workmanship or materials, for latent defects, and so forth.

One distinct advantage of the FFP contract is that they typically require the least administration and management involvement from the project team of any of the contractual options available. However, if progress payment provisions are included in the contract, even the FFP contract will require performance oversight from the project's buyer.

Fixed Price Incentive (FPI) Contracts:

A fixed-price incentive contract is a fixed-price contract that provides for adjusting profit and establishing the final contract price by application of a formula based on the relationship of total final negotiated cost to total target cost. The final price is subject to a price ceiling, negotiated at the outset. [8]

---

8.   FAR 16.403.

The Fixed Price Incentive (FPI) contract is one which is typically used when a project's procurement description is available, but there are some open issues to be settled. Often there may not be sufficient product specification data available to go directly with a Firm Fixed Price contract (FFP). The desired product can be defined, but not to the point where responsible sellers would be willing to commit to a FFP obligation. And at the other extreme, there is sufficient product data available so that the use of a cost reimbursement type contract would be inappropriate. The FPI contract gives both the buyer and seller some flexibility, while providing strong incentives to the seller to perform.

The FPI contract places positive incentives on the seller to completely satisfy a procurement, while incurring the lowest possible costs. Under the FPI contract the performing seller also participates in any cost savings, or even losses, according to a negotiated formula. The FPI contract is established with the understanding that the final contract profit and final price will be determined after performance, according to their agreed to formula. There will be a ceiling price specified in their contract, beyond which all costs are the responsibility of the seller. The FPI is a fixed-price relationship.

Typically the incentives in a FPI will be costs. But in addition to cost incentives, FPI contracts may also incorporate other performance incentives such as: timely deliveries according to a schedule, or even bettering the specified schedule dates, reliability, warranty, maintenance, weight objectives, etc. Anything that can quantified and objectively measured, can be incorporated into the FPI contract.

At the time of FPI contract award, the project buyer and seller must agree on certain provisions in their contract: (1) a target cost; (2) a target profit (without specifying either a profit ceiling or a floor); (3) a price ceiling (which is the maximum amount which can be paid to the seller, excluding any statement of work changes); and (4) a profit adjustment formula defining the cost sharing provisions.

The cost sharing formula under incentive contracts may be set at any rate formula which adds to 100%, but typically they will fall in the ranges of 90/10; 80/20; 70/30; 60/40 and so forth. The higher values on the left side apply against the target costs, and the lower values on the right apply to adjustments in the seller's target profit.

After the FPI contract has been completed, the buyer and seller will then negotiate the final agreed to costs, and resulting profits based on the performance adjustment formula. Final costs, plus final profits result in a final established price.

In order to best illustrate the use of the FPI contract, let us assume a given set of contract provisions, and then present three scenarios based on the performance of a seller. Assume the following FPI contract provisions: (1) a target cost of $100,000; (2) a target profit of 10% or $10,000 (without either a floor or ceiling for the target profits); (3) a price ceiling of $120,000, and (4) an adjustment share formula of 80/20. These three scenarios are summarized in Figure 6.5.

Scenario #1: the performing seller completes all of the work and incurs actual costs of $90,000, a $10,000 under run from target costs. Applying the 80/20 share ratio, the seller's share of the under run is 20% of $10,000, or a plus $2,000 in additional earned fee. The final value of this procurement is $90,000 in costs, plus a seller fee of $10,000 plus $2,000, or $12,000, for a final price of $102,000.

Baseline FPI Contract:
    Target Costs = $100,000; Target Profit @ 10% = $10,000;
    Contract Value = $110,000; Price Ceiling $120,000;
    Share Ratio 80/20

Scenario #1:
    Final Costs = $90,000; Actual Fee $10,000 + $2,000 = $12,000
    Final Price = $90,000 + $12,000 Fee = $102,000

Scenario #2:
    Final Costs = $110,000; Actual Fee $10,000 - $2,000 = $8,000
    Final Price = $110,000 + $8,000 Fee = $118,000

Scenario #3:
    Final Costs = $130,000; Actual Fee = zero, over Ceiling
    Final Price = $120,000 + No Fee = Price Ceiling

Figure 6.5 Fixed Price Incentive (FPI) Contracts

Scenario #2: the performing seller completes all of the work and incurs actual costs of $110,000, a $10,000 over run from target costs. Applying the 80/20 share ratio, the seller's share of the over run is 20% of $10,000, or a minus $2,000 in earned fee. The final value of this procurement is $110,000 in costs, plus a seller fee of $10,000 less $2,000, or $8,000, for a final price of $118,000.

Scenario # 3: the performing seller completes all of the work and incurs actual costs of $130,000, a $30,000 over run from target costs. Applying the 80/20 share ratio, the seller's share of the over run would be 20% of $30,000, or a minus $6,000 in earned fee. However, the final actual costs exceeded the contract ceiling price of $120,000. Thus the final price of this fixed price incentive procurement is $120,000 in price. The seller lost $10,000 on this job.

The Federal Acquisition Regulation (FAR) specifies that in order to use incentive type contracts, a seller must have an acceptable accounting system, and that adequate price or cost data must be available from the seller for review and settlement of a final price. Also, all FPI contracts must include a scheduled date for resolution or negotiation of all open target issues. These are all solid requirements which should be followed in any procurement with use on FPI contracts.

The FAR also defines two variations of the FPI contract: the FPI with firm targets, and the FPI with successive targets. For purposes of the preceding discussion, the FPI contract with firm targets has been discussed. The FPI with successive targets has a utility with completed development projects, which may be going into a limited production run, where the buyer is attempting to establish a reasonable repetitive unit cost for the production run. Therefore, we have restricted our discussion to FPI contracts with firm targets.

Anyone interested in repetitive production issues can review the subject in greater detail from the referenced FAR sections. [9]

Fixed-Price Contracts With Award Fees:

Award-fee provisions may be used in fixed-price contracts when

---

9. FAR 16.403-1 and 16.403-2.

the Government wishes to motivate a contractor and other incentives cannot be used because contractor performance cannot be measured objectively. Such contracts shall —

(1) Establish a fixed price (including normal profit) for the effort. This price will be paid for satisfactory contract performance. Award fee earned (if any) will be paid in addition to that fixed price; and

(2) Provide for periodic evaluation of the contractor's performance against an award-fee plan. [10]

When we think of contracts using "award fees" we typically think of cost reimbursable relationships. However, award fees can be used most effectively in any type of contract: fixed-price, cost reimbursable, or even a time and material type contract. An award fee provision in a contract is probably the strongest inducement provision that can be included between a buyer and a seller. An award fee is given based on the seller satisfying the buyer's broadly stated needs. They are based solely on the subjective determination by the buyer. All such buyer determinations are final, that is they cannot be appealed because the seller typically waives that right in their contract.

One point of clarification. You would likely never find a pure Fixed Price Award Fee contract used. Rather, the award fee provisions would be additive to another fixed price type contract: FFP/AF, or FPI/AF, or FP-EPA/AF. The award fee would be an additional inducement to stimulate extra performance from the seller.

An example of the use of an award fee with fixed price contracts might be where a seller would not make a commitment (firm fixed-price) to an early delivery date of a commodity, but would agree to an award fee provision should they be able to deliver early. If they missed the earlier delivery date, they merely loose extra fees. Any broad buyer objectives may be incorporated into an award fee provision.

A full discussion of the use of award fees will be also be covered below under cost type contracts using award fee provisions.

---

10. FAR 16.404.

Fixed-Price with Economic Price Adjustments (FP-EPA):

A fixed-price contract with economic price adjustment provides for upward and downward revision of the stated price upon the occurrence of specified contingencies. Economic price adjustments are of three general types: (a) Adjustments based on established prices. (b) Adjustments based on actual costs of labor or material. (c) Adjustments based on cost indexes of labor or material. [11]

The FP-EPA is another form of the firm fixed price contract. It allows for a fixed price contract to adjust the final negotiated price based on changes in economic conditions according to some agreed to formula or published index. The intent of this arrangement is to provide protection to both a buyer and a seller when they enter into a "long-term" contract to deliver a given product or perform services. Economic price adjustment arrangements are not intended to be a crutch on poor estimating practices, but to provide for economic conditions beyond the control of either party. Such agreements also tend to limit the total proposed costs of a product by eliminating the need for suppliers to include "pricing contingencies," which sometimes are included but do not happen over the term of contract performance. Typically no price ceiling or floor will be set for these kinds of contracts, but they could be if both parties so agreed.

This type of contract is appropriate only for planned long-term arrangements where there are possibilities for economic uncertainty during the performance period, where suppliers may be unwilling to enter into such long-term arrangements without the inclusion of price contingencies to protect them against unstable economic conditions. Sometimes these uncertainties never happen, in which case someone, often the seller, unjustly benefits from stable economic conditions.

The FP-EPA contract is intended to provide protection for both parties against long-term economic price changes, but it is not to be a substitute for bad estimating. It is <u>not</u> intended to cover contingencies for quantity or usage variances in either labor or material costs.

---

11. FAR 16.203-1.

As an example, assume that a seller proposes a new five-year job, and their estimate assumes 100,000 hours at $25.00 per hour, with their hourly rate based on a published labor index. If the job is completed with 125,000 hours, but there is no change in labor rates in the published labor index, no adjustment in contract price would be allowed. However if the original estimate of 100,000 hours were expended, but the published labor rate goes from $25.00 up to $30.00 per hour, an adjustment in contract price would be allowed covering the $5.00 per hour increase in economic rates.

Changes may take place upward or downward from the agreed to contract price. Three approaches are typically used in FP-EPA arrangements:

(1) Adjustments based on changes to "established prices" agreed upon in specific items or contract end-items. Certain basic commodities have established industry-wide prices which are published for everyone's use, which typically will include steel, aluminum, brass, copper, and certain other standard supply items. Currency rate changes between nations, for example the United States Dollar and the European Community EURO would fall into this category.

(2) Adjustments based on changes to labor or material costs using the "actual costs method." Changes from the values specified in their agreement may occur in certain cost items.

(3) Adjustments based on changes to labor or material costs using the "cost index method." Changes may occur from the values as specified in price indices referenced in the contract. Examples are: Bureau of Labor Statistics, Consumer Price Index, Standard Industrial Classification, Wholesale Price Index, etc.

A new aircraft development project spanning perhaps six years or more years, or an information technology outsourcing agreement covering perhaps five or six years, would both be good candidates for the FP-EPA contracts.

FP-EPA contracts require much administration and oversight and should only be used when necessary to protect both the buyer and seller in long-term relationships. These contracts may be used with either formally advertised or negotiated contracts.

Fixed-Price: Indefinite-Delivery, or, Indefinite-Quantity Contracts:

There is another category of fixed-price arrangements which are used frequently to procure items for projects in which the titles describe nicely their intended purpose. The first is a firm fixed-price contract with an indefinite delivery schedule. The buyer knows what they need, but at the time of contract execution cannot prescribe the precise dates the articles will be needed. That definition will come later. The second is also a firm fixed-price contract covering items, of an unspecified quantity, with the precise quantity to be later specified.

The set prices for either arrangement may vary based on the precise delivery dates or quantity later determined. Nevertheless, both contract types are considered firm fixed-price varieties.

The "Cost Reimbursable" Contract Family

There are four popular variations of cost reimbursable type contracts in use and each will be discussed below. In addition, there is the Cost Plus a Percentage of Costs Fee contract, which will be covered, but which should never be employed.

Cost-Plus-Fixed-Fee (CPFF):

A cost-plus-fixed-fee contract is a cost-reimbursement contract that provides for payment to the contractor of a negotiated fee that is fixed at inception of the contract. The fixed fee does not vary with actual cost, but may be adjusted as a result of changes in the work to be performed under the contract. This contract type permits contracting for efforts that might otherwise present too great a risk to contractors, but it provides the contractor only a minimum incentive to control costs. [12]

12. FAR 16.306.

When one thinks of a cost type contract, in all likelihood they are thinking of the CPFF or Cost Plus Fixed Fee contract. The CPFF contract is the "Granddaddy" of all cost reimbursement type contracts. While today the CPFF contracts may well be losing their popularity to the Cost Plus Incentive Fee (CPIF) or the Cost Plus Award Fee (CPAF) type contracts, these two normally build their contractual arrangements using the CPFF as the standard base. Therefore, it is important to understand the structure of the CPFF if for no better reason than to fully understand the newer and more popular cost contract types which have evolved.

The CPFF allows for the reimbursement of all reasonable, allowable, and allocable costs incurred by a seller up to the limits of the contract value. If a seller needs to incur costs above the contract value in order to finish a job, they must advise the buyer and get buyer approval to proceed. The seller is under a "best efforts" only legal obligation to perform on a project, provided that the buyer reimburses all legitimate costs incurred.

The fixed fee is set as a percentage of the agreed to costs in the contract, and does not change based on the seller's performance. The fee value remains constant and is only subject to change with an increase or decrease in the scope of contracted work. Should the seller under-run the costs, the seller's earned fee percentage will goes up. Conversely, should their costs exceed the contract value, their fee percentage will decrease. Cost overruns or under-runs do not change the original fixed fee.

For purposes of illustration, assume there is a new procurement consisting of $100,000 estimated costs, with a 10% fixed-fee of $10,000, for a contract value of $110,000. These two scenarios are summarized in Figure 6.6.

Scenario #1: the seller completes all of the authorized work while incurring only $80,000 in actual costs. The fixed-fee of $10,000 does not change, but now represents a seller profit of 12.5% on incurred costs. The total costs to the project will be $90,000.

Scenario #2: the seller completes all of the work, but incurs costs of $125,000. The fixed-fee amount stays constant at $10,000, but now represents a value of 8% of the costs incurred. The total costs to

---

Baseline CPFF Contract:
    Estimated costs = $100,000; Fixed Fee @ 10% = $10,000;
    Contract Value = $110,000

Scenario #1:
    Final costs = $80,000; Fixed Fee @ 10% = $10,000;
    Profit of $10,000 = 12.5%

Scenario #2:
    Final costs = $125,000; Fixed Fee @ 10% = $10,000;
    Profit of $10,000 = 8.0%

Figure 6.6 Cost Plus Fixed Fee (CPFF) Contracts

the project will be $135,000. The buyer had to agree on the funding increase to $135,000.

Sellers who want to maximize their profit percentages and create a reputation for efficient cost management will try hard to under-run their negotiated contract costs. However, there have been some unscrupulous suppliers who have been motivated to better utilize their firm's under-employed assets, perhaps even develop a new technical capability, and these suppliers have demonstrated little incentive to tightly control costs while performing on a CPFF contract. Thus, many people have an unfavorable impression of the CPFF contract for general use.

However, with all its shortfalls, there is a place for the CPFF type contract. CPFF contracts are appropriate anytime there are substantial cost uncertainties, where estimates of costs are difficult or impossible to accurately forecast. High technical uncertainty, challenging schedule goals, etc., can all justify this type of contractual arrangement. Another valid justification for the use of the CPFF can be the desire of the contracting parties to give themselves flexibility for incorporating contractual changes to cover re-directions for unknown events beyond their control.

Two types of CPFF contracts are in use: the "completion form" and the "term form." The "completion form" is the preferred type by the government, and is used whenever the scope of project work can be reasonably defined and an end-item deliverables can be identified. The end-items can take many forms, for example, a data report, a hardware item, software code, intellectual positions, etc. The seller's earned fee will be based on the satisfaction of the contract end-items.

The FAR defines the two basic forms — "completion" or "term" as follows:

(1) The completion form describes the scope of work by stating a definite goal or target and specifying an end product. This form of contract normally requires the contractor to complete and deliver the specified end product (e.g., a final report of research accomplishing the goal or target) within the estimated cost, if possible, as a condition for payment of the entire fixed fee. However, in the event the work cannot be completed within the estimated cost, the Government may require more effort without increase in fee, provided the Government increases the estimated cost.

(2) The term form describes the scope of work in general terms and obligates the contractor to devote a specified level of effort for a stated time period. Under this form, if the performance is considered satisfactory by the Government, the fixed fee is payable at the expiration of the agreed-upon period, upon contractor statement that the level of effort specified in the contract has been expended in performing the contract work. Renewal for further periods of performance is a new acquisition that involves new cost and fee arrangements.

(3) Because of the differences in obligation assumed by the contractor, the completion form is preferred over the term form whenever the work, or specific milestones for the work, can be defined well enough to permit development of estimates within which the contractor can be expected to complete the work.

(4) The term form shall not be used unless the contractor is

obligated by the contract to provide a specific level of effort within a definite time period. [13]

Under the "term form," the scope of contract work is general, and is only defined in terms of resources made available by a seller over a period of performance. Thus, the supplier is obligated to commit a level of resources over a specific time frame as a means of satisfying the contract. Seller fees are thus determined on the basis of the resources committed in the specified time frame. Should the term of performance need to be extended, the seller will then be entitled to additional fees covering the subsequent period. The use of term form CPFF contracts should be severely restricted.

The last undesirable aspect of the CPFF arrangement is the amount of effort required to administer these contracts on the part of the project's buyer. Because of the concern of overruns and potential of cost abuses with CPFF contracts, project management must closely monitor such procurements until completion. Thus, there is an inordinate amount of management oversight associated with the CPFF contract, as compared with other forms of contracts available.

Cost-Plus Incentive Fee (CPIF) Contracts:

The cost-plus-incentive-fee contract is a cost-reimbursement contract that provides for the initially negotiated fee to be adjusted later by a formula based on the relationship of total allowable costs to total target costs. This contract type specifies a target cost, a target fee, minimum and maximum fees, and a fee adjustment formula. After contract performance, the fee payable to the contractor is determined in accordance with the formula. The formula provides, within limits, for increases in fee above target fee when total allowable costs are less than target costs, and decreases in fee below target fee when total allowable costs exceed target costs. This increase or decrease is intended to provide an incentive for the contractor to manage the contract effectively. When total

---

13. FAR 16.306.

allowable cost is greater than or less than the range of costs with-
in which the fee-adjustment formula operates, the contractor is
paid total allowable costs, plus the minimum or maximum fee. [14]

The Cost Plus Incentive Fee (CPIF) contract type is similar in concept to the Fixed Price Incentive (FPI), but with one important difference: CPIF contracts contain no price ceiling beyond which the seller cannot recover costs. FPI contracts, by comparison, do have a ceiling. But what an important difference to the performing seller. CPIF contracts are appropriate whenever there exists considerable technical risks, and the buyer would like to encourage the seller to minimize costs.

Like the FPI contract, the CPIF contract type can be used by the buyer to incorporate additional performance incentives, in addition to cost incentives. Some examples of these performance incentives could be: deliveries of end-items ahead of schedule, product reliability, maintenance costs, weight of hardware, and so forth. Anything that can be measured can be used as a performance incentives. Should the seller not meet the technical performance thresholds, fee would be lost. To be an effective performance incentive, fees must have the potential of being increased or decreased to the seller.

CPIF contracts contain the following five elements: (1) a target cost; (2) a target fee; (3) a maximum allowable fee; (4) a minimum allowable fee; and (5) a fee adjustment formula based on seller performance between the maximum or minimum fee ranges. After the contract performance, the buyer and seller will negotiate the final contract fee between the allowable fee ranges, based on the actual performance of the supplier. A seller who under-runs target costs will receive a greater fee percentage, and conversely, an overrun from target costs will reduce the fees paid to the seller.

Just as it was with the FPI, under the CPIF the cost sharing formula may also be set with any rate formula which adds to 100%, but typically will fall in the ranges of 90/10; 80/20; 70/30; 60/40. The higher values on the left side apply against the target costs, and the

---

14. FAR 16.405-1.

lower values on the right apply to adjustments in the seller's target profit.

Many incentive type contracts (CPIF or FPI) will incorporate as an exhibit similar to that shown in Figure 6.7. The five elements of a CPIF contract are listed: target costs, target fee, maximum and minimum fee, and the share formula. Should the seller overrun costs, they would have their fee reduced by 20% of the overrun costs, down to the minimum fee of 6.0%. Conversely, should they under-run the target costs their fee would increase up to the maximum fee of 14.0%.

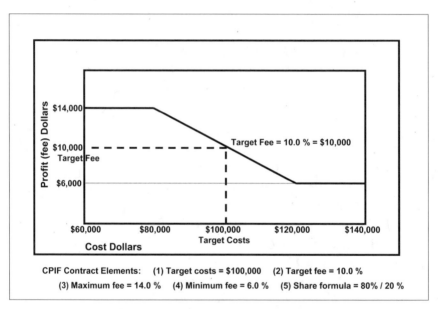

Figure 6.7 Cost Plus Incentive Fee (CPIF) Contracts

Cost Plus Award Fee (CPAF):

A cost-plus-award-fee contract is a cost-reimbursement contract that provides for a fee consisting of (1) a base amount fixed at inception of the contract and (2) an award amount that the contractor may earn in whole or in part during performance and that is sufficient to provide motivation for excellence in such areas as quality, timeliness, technical ingenuity, and cost-effective management.

The amount of the award fee to be paid is determined by the Government's judgmental evaluation of the contractor's performance in terms of the criteria stated in the contract. This determination and the methodology for determining the award fee are unilateral decisions made solely at the discretion of the Government.

The number of evaluation criteria and the requirements they represent will differ widely among contracts. The criteria and rating plan should motivate the contractor to improve performance in the areas rated, but not at the expense of at least minimum acceptable performance in all other areas.

Cost-plus-award-fee contracts shall provide for evaluation at stated intervals during performance, so that the contractor will periodically be informed of the quality of its performance and the areas in which improvement is expected. Partial payment of fee shall generally correspond to the evaluation periods. [15]

Another form of cost reimbursable type contract which has evolved from the CPFF is the Cost Plus Award Fee (CPAF) contract. This arrangement provides maximum incentives on a seller to perform to the fullest "satisfaction" of the project buyer. The buyer's determination of award fee amounts is unilateral, and the seller contractually waives their right to appeal such decisions. Thus the CPAF contract has a tremendous impact on the performance of the seller. Award fee contracts have such an impact on a seller's profit that some companies have actually refused to accept award fee contracts. However, award fee contracts appear to be gaining in popularity, at least with the buyers.

CPAF contracts with the Department of Defense, which pioneered in the use of these type contracts over two decades ago, typically contain six elements: (1) total estimated costs; (2) a "base fee," stated as a percentage of total estimated costs; (3) an "award fee," also stated as a percentage of total estimated costs; (4) the award fee's broadly defined "performance criteria"; (5) an award fee "evaluation

---

15. FAR 16.405-2.

board"; and (6) a "fee determining official," typically a senior executive, often the program manager or even the next most senior executive. Award fee contracts in the private sector may contain whatever the parties agree to, but typically follow the same general format.

The "base fee" in the CPAF is not subject to change based on seller's performance, and such fees are earned by performing to the statement of work. In concept base fees resemble a CPFF fee. Typically most base fees are limited to about three percentage points of estimated contract costs.

The "award fee" is conferred on top of the base fee. It is given out based on the periodic (yearly, semi-annually, quarterly), subjective and unilateral determination of a seller's performance by the buyer's evaluation board. It is paid to a seller according to a predetermined award fee schedule as defined in their contract. Because of the very high administrative effort required on both parties, award fee periods are best evaluated on an annual basis, certainly not more frequently than twice a year. Some companies have tried award fees on a quarterly or even monthly basis, but typically abandon this practice because of the high administrative effort. Award fee determinations take considerable time from both the buyer and seller personnel to determine a fair award fee amount.

The intent of the CPAF contract is to stimulate top performance from the seller by exerting maximum influence over a supplier — into future periods. Any fee amounts not earned in a given evaluation period may, or may not, be carried over into a later period, at the sole discretion of the buyer's fee determining official, or as specified in the contract. The buyer's award fee evaluation board is normally comprised of multi-functional management personnel. To work properly, this board must be represented by all functions involved in the project management process.

Because the award fee evaluation board's findings are subjective — but always final — and are not subject to a disputes procedure, persons who serve on an evaluation board must be perceived by the seller as being reasonable, impartial, and above reproach. Any hint of arbitrary or capricious findings from an evaluation board can destroy any benefits to be gained from the CPAF contract. If a seller actually performs well, but award fee is arbitrarily withheld from them, such actions can have a negative impact on their performance in the later periods.

Performance criteria used for award fee inducements will be defined in the contractual document itself, in broadly stated criteria, and may fall into such general categories as: technical achievements, management performance, allocation of adequate resources, product reproducibility, etc., whatever is important to the success of the project. Whatever is important to a given project may change from period to period, in which case the award fee criteria specified in the contract may need to be modified, but subject to re-negotiation by both parties.

The use of such broad criteria as "design to cost objectives" or "hardware weight savings" or "manufacturing process improvements" or "earned value management system implementation", all have make good candidates for award fee goals. Unlike incentive fee provisions, award fee criteria are not to be subject to a mathematical formula, nor are they quantifiable. Rather, the award fees are given out based on the "subjective" determination of the evaluation board, typically requiring concurrence by the superior fee determining executive who has the final say. The more senior fee determining official is often added to the process as assurance that award fee determinations will be fair and reasonable.

With government contracting, the use of a CPAF contract is subject to the same maximum combined contract fee ceilings as those of the CPFF and CPIF contracts. And the same FAR requirements dictating an acceptable accounting system, findings and determination, etc., also apply to the CPAF contracts. All award fee payments to a seller are classified for accounting purposes as contractor "costs incurred."

While the award fee type contract is normally used on cost reimbursable type contracts, it can also work well on any type of contract, even fixed-price contracts, time and material contracts, etc., with the agreement of both parties. In situations where the award fee is used in conjunction with other fee types, the practice is to refer to the contract type with a designation of "/AF" at the end, as for example a "CPFF/AF" or "CPIF/AF" or FPIF/AF" or "FFP/AF" type contract.

Cost Contracts:

> *A cost contract is a cost-reimbursement contract in which the con-tractor receives no fee. A cost contract may be appropriate for research and development work, particularly with nonprofit edu-cational institutions or other nonprofit organizations, and for facilities contracts.* [16]

Cost Sharing Contracts:

> *A cost-sharing contract is a cost-reimbursement contract in which the contractor receives no fee and is reimbursed only for an agreed-upon portion of its allowable costs. A cost-sharing contract may be used when the contractor agrees to absorb a portion of the costs, in the expectation of substantial compensating benefits.* [17]

The "cost" only contract and the "cost sharing" contracts are simi-lar in nature, and are essentially forms of joint enterprise arrangements, in which both the buyer and seller should benefit from the relationship. The seller agrees to receive no fee (no profit) for the effort, and some-times agrees further to absorb some percentage of their total costs incurred according to a formula specified in their agreement. These arrangements often work well on basic research and applied research types of contracts, particularly with colleges and universities.

Sellers will typically enter into such arrangements with the expec-tation that they will receive some future benefit from their invest-ments. Examples used to justify cost sharing arrangements by suppliers are: improved competitive position, access to technologies or to commercial markets not presently available to them, and so forth. Cost sharing agreements will vary from as low as 1% to 5% of the costs incurred for non-profit or educational organizations, to as much as 5% to 50% of the costs for commercial enterprises. Such cost shar-ing arrangements should benefit both the buyer and the seller.

---

16. FAR 16.302.
17. FAR 16.303.

Methods used for cost sharing will vary by industry, but generally fall into four types of arrangements. The sellers will agree to share costs: (1) as a fixed percentage of their total costs incurred; (2) as a fixed percentage of overhead costs; (3) as a fixed not-to-exceed value of overhead costs; and sometimes (4) by the exclusion of specific items of costs. The possible combinations of cost sharing can be endless.

While most of these arrangements are of the cost type in which the seller only agrees to perform a "best effort" to complete the job, in the 1980s the government got "innovative" and extended the cost sharing concept into firm fixed price work where sellers had to complete the job. Many private defense contractors competed for and won firm fixed-price cost sharing contracts, some large multi-billion dollar efforts, often for major new system developments. This experience was less than satisfactory for industry, and many contractors incurred substantial losses. Both the government and most private contractors have since backed away from any cost sharing arrangement under fixed price terms. Good.

Finally, there are some issues for buyers to consider and perhaps to avoid. Buyers should generally not employ a cost sharing contract based on the best deal, the greatest amount of cost sharing investments they can extract from a seller. Other non-dollar factors (seller qualifications) should dictate their final source selection. Also, contract awards should not be made with a statement of work in which logic suggests is greater than the funds allocated.

Lastly, cost sharing arrangements should not commit any buyer or company to subsequent contract awards based on the cost sharing investments of a seller. These are general rules which should be followed, but sometimes are not.

Cost Plus a Percentage of Costs Fee (CPPCF):

The CPPCF type contracts are not allowed under United States and most governmental contracting. Their origin traces back to World War I where expediency of performance was more important than negotiating a reasonable business deal. Also today, it is questionable whether any commercial business firm should ever use this type of arrangement. But they sometimes do.

Under the CPPCF contract, the seller's earned fee, or profit, increases as a stipulated percentage rate of funds actually expended. There is no incentive on a seller to keep costs down to a minimum, in fact, the incentive is to spend more money and thus get a greater fee. The CPPCF contract is a bad business arrangement for any project.

As a related issue, the United States Government is highly critical of the use of Letter Contracts to get sellers started, until the project at some point in the future can define a scope of work for the seller, and the parties can finally negotiate a firm contractual relationship. These are valid concerns. Why: because letter contracts are similar in nature to CPPCF contracts. Sellers start work under letter contracts, and get reimbursed as a percentage of all funds expended, until they can reach a firm relationship. A letter contract functions just like a CPPCF contract.

CPPCF contracts should never be used by anyone.

Other General Contract Types of Importance

There are other contractual variations which are worthy of mention in order to round out the discussion of contract types. Each will be discussed below.

Time and Materials (T & M) Contracts:

A time-and-materials contract provides for acquiring supplies or services on the basis (1) Direct labor hours at specified fixed hourly rates that includes wages, overhead, general and administrative expenses, and profit; and (2) Materials at cost, including if appropriate, material handling costs, as a part of material costs. [18]

In addition to this FAR definition of Time and Material contracts, the year 2000 update to the PMBOK Guide provided a definition of this popular contract type:

---

18. FAR 16.601.

Time and Material (T&M) contracts . . . are a hybrid type of contractual arrangement that contains aspects of both cost-reimbursable and fixed-price-type arrangements. T&M contracts resemble cost-type arrangements in that they are open ended, because the full value of the arrangement is not defined at the time of the award. Thus, T&M contracts can grow in contract value as if they were cost-reimbursable-type arrangements. Conversely, T&M arrangements can also resemble fixed-unit arrangements when, for example, the unit rates are preset by the buyer and seller, as when both parties agree on the rates for the category of "senior engineers." [19]

These types of contracts are considered appropriate in those circumstances when it is not possible at the time of award to estimate accurately the extent, or duration, or costs of a job with any degree of confidence. Labor costs typically carry all indirect expenses including profit, but material costs may carry material handing costs only, and are sometimes billed without profits. The T & M contracts are used primarily to procure emergency services, repairs, maintenance, overhauls, but are also used extensively to procure engineering and technical services as purchased labor, where the direct supervision of the purchased people is done by project staff.

Since a seller in effect receives a cost plus percentage of costs fee type arrangement on at least the labor portion, the buyer must monitor closely the performance of the supplier. The T & M type of contract can be easily abused since there is almost a contractual incentive to increase labor costs to the maximum, and thereby increase a contractor's profits. Abuses may also take place whenever a seller can substitute a lower-caliber of labor than was priced and envisioned in the negotiated hourly rate.

Because of the risks of cost growth, the T & M type contracts are normally discouraged without justification. Good business practices would suggest some form of restriction on their use; that they be used

---

19. *A Guide to the Project Management Body of Knowledge (PMBOK Guide)*, (Newtown Square, Pennsylvania: Project Management Institute, 2000) page 151.

only with approval of senior management, and include a limitation of costs or a ceiling on the amount authorized for the contract.

Labor-Hour Contracts:

A labor-hour contract is a variation of the time-and-materials contract, differing only in that materials are not supplied by the contractor. [20]

The "Labor-Hour" contract is a variation of the Time & Material (T&M) contract, but as the name implies, is restricted to labor services only, without materials supplied in the contractual arrangement.

Letter Contracts:

A letter contract is a written preliminary contractual instrument that authorizes the contractor to begin immediately manufacturing supplies or performing services. A letter contract may be used when the Government's interests demand that the contractor be given a binding commitment so that work can start immediately and nego-tiating a definitive contract is not possible in sufficient time to meet the requirement. However, a letter contract should be as complete and definite as feasible under the circumstances. When a letter con-tract award is based on price competition, the contracting officer shall include an overall price ceiling in the letter contract. [21]

A "letter contract" is a legally binding contract. We can call them temporary, but they are nevertheless legally enforceable contracts. Letter contracts, however, lack one key thing most contracts have: a "statement of work." Talk about high risks. There is probably no con-tractual arrangement which has the potential of higher risks than with use of a letter contract. Why then would we ever consider using a let-ter contract? Simple: because we can't get our act together in time to

---

20. FAR 16.602.
21. FAR 16.603-1.

support the project's schedule. Everything is ready . . . except for the technical statement of work.

Letter contracts are used in circumstances when a seller must be authorized to start work immediately in order to support the project's effort, and a negotiated definitive contract is not possible in the time available. In all cases, it is desirable to make the letter contract as complete as is practicable, within the time-frame needed to start the supplier. Among the minimum issues which should be covered by clauses in any letter contract are: how changes are to be handled, progress payments if provided, delivery or performance schedules, termination, and other clauses as appropriate for good business practice.

All letter contracts in government (FAR) work must be superseded by a definitive contract within 180 days of award, or when 40% of the authorized funds are expended, whichever happens first. They are governed by the FAR contract clause 52.216-25, which should be incorporated into the letter contract document. This FAR clause is specific as to its requirements, which requires among other things: the type of resulting contract anticipated by the parties, and a promise by the seller to submit a proposal of the same type; a schedule of dates for submission of a proposal, for start of negotiations, and for conclusion of negotiations. If the letter contract was based on a price competition, a not-to-exceed value of contract price must be specified.

As was mentioned earlier, letter contracts are essentially a Cost Plus a Percentage of Costs Fee type of contractual arrangement in that at the point of final negotiation the seller is paid a negotiated fee as a percentage of all costs actually spent. Sounds like a CPPCF type arrangement doesn't it. Letter contracts are a bad practice, and they should be watched closely by senior management.

Basic Ordering Agreements (BOA):

A basic ordering agreement is a written instrument of understanding, negotiated between an agency, contracting activity, or contracting office and a contractor, that contains (1) terms and clauses applying to future contracts (orders) between the parties during its term, (2) a description, as specific as practicable, of supplies or services to be provided, and (3) methods for pricing, issuing, and delivering future orders under the basic ordering agreement. A basic ordering agreement is not a contract. [22]

The "Basic Agreement" (FAR 16.702) and "Basic Ordering Agreement" are defined by the FAR as <u>not</u> being contracts. However, they certainly resemble a contract in all key respects. Rather, these are defined by the FAR as agreements that set forth the clauses which will be incorporated by reference in any subsequent resulting contract between the parties.

Private companies will sometimes have similar type agreements with selected approved sellers for use on their repetitive type purchases such as spares, catalog parts, and so forth. Often they will use different titles to describe the same generic concepts, such as a "master purchase order" agreements, "master terms and conditions" agreements, etc.

Determining the Appropriate Contract Type

Attempts have been made over the years both within the government and in private industry to take into consideration all of the relevant factors for a given new acquisition and then to make a selection of contract type based on some sort of weighted point value. Thus far, none of these initiatives have ever worked. Selection of a seller contract type for each procurement should be based on sound management choices, taking into consideration all aspects of the new procurement. Weighted scientific models do not work. There is no "silver bullet" in project procurement to determine an appropriate contract type.

The careful selection of contract types can be used to balance project risks. What any project will want to do is to achieve a proper balance — a parity — between the obligations the project has accepted, and what they subsequently will want to obligate from their sellers. This is called risk management. Often projects can balance their own risks with their key suppliers. See Figure 6.8.

---

22. FAR 16.703.

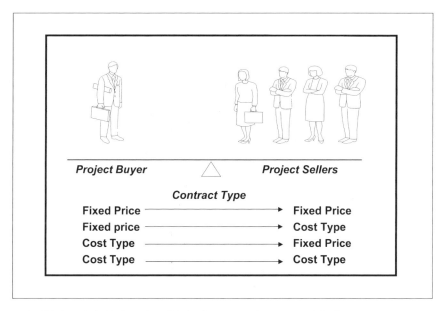

Figure 6.8 Balancing Risks between Buyer and Seller

By carefully choosing the right contract for each key procurement, projects can mitigate risks with their supplier base.

In Summary

There would appear to be a strong bias on the part of both the government and private industry to (blindly) gravitate toward fixed price contracts, particularly the firm-fixed price (FFP) contract. However, under many conditions, the FFP may well be the wrong contract type to employ.

Take for example one (anonymous) major developmental subcontract which was finalized with issuance of a FFP type contract. Then, over the course of the next twenty-four months, engineering issued over 1,000 design changes to the FFP procurement specification! In retrospect, some contract type other than a FFP likely would have worked better for both parties, particularly the buyer.

No one could have predicted the level of design changes that were

ahead of this procurement. However, the moral: if you cannot precisely specify what you want to procure, and or have reason to believe
that your procurement specification will change (perhaps 1,000
times), consider using some type of cost reimbursable contract. The
selection of a FFP contract type gave this project zero latitude to
accommodate the profusion of design changes, without paying excessive costs adjustments to the seller. Contract changes — the redirec-
tions of scope — can always be accommodated . . . but at a painful
price. Needless to say, this particular subcontract grew exponentially
in value from the original amount contained in the initial firm fixed-
price (FFP) value.

Some general guidelines for determining the selection of an appropriate contract type for each procurement are recommended:

1. Determinations of contract type are best done by a multi-
functional procurement committee representing a broad
cross-section of interests, for example procurement, engineering, manufacturing, contracts, finance, legal, quality, etc.
2. The best interests of both parties — the project and the seller
— should be balanced, and both parties should mutually benefit from the final choice as to the contract type.
3. Any contract type other than a FFP must be justified on its
own merits, and have a rationale to support the selection of a
type other than a FFP.
4. However, it should be understood that even a FFP type contract can be the wrong type, whenever there are unknowns in
the procurement statement of work and specification, and the
potential sellers in any competition are likely to incorporate
pricing "contingencies" into their contract proposals, in order
to cover the unknown risks.

With all factors carefully understood, a project can make an intelligent selection of the appropriate contract type for each new procurement. The selection of the proper contract type is one of the more
important decisions to be made in the project procurement process.

CHAPTER 7

The Procurement Management Plan

I keep six honest serving men (They taught me all I knew);
Their names are What and Why and When and How and Where and Who

Rudyard Kipling, *Just So Stories for Little Children*, 1902

Plans are worthless, but planning is everything.

President Dwight D. Eisenhower, November 17, 1957

Without an adequate plan . . . success will be a matter of luck.

Russell D. Archibald, 1992 [1]

The British poet and story teller Rudyard Kipling had it right when he said that having friends like What, and Why, and When, and How, and Where, and Who . . . are important. Perhaps he was thinking about project management when he wrote those words. And our former President Ike, while still a General in the Army, demonstrated to the world the importance of planning, creating detailed plans, and execution according to plans, when his Armies successfully invaded Europe in 1944. The D-day, 6th of June invasion represented planning at its very finest.

Lastly, Russ Archibald, a dear friend, and Project Management Institute (PMI) Fellow, made the case for the importance of plans in his best selling book on project management. You need to force yourself into planning, developing a plan, then executing the plan in order to successfully manage any project with a minimum of risks.

---

1. Russell D. Archibald, *Managing High-Technology Programs and Projects* (New York: John Wiley & Sons, 2nd Edition, 1992) page 180.

We are now at the end of the first of the six processes of Project Procurement entitled *"Procurement Planning—determining what to procure and when."*[2]. One of the key tangible outputs from this process is the *"Procurement Management Plan."* A procurement plan to support a major project can be a separate volume, with great supporting detail, and schedules, etc. Or a procurement plan can be as simple as a single page Bill of Materials, describing the items to be bought, the quantities required, and the need dates to support the project's master schedule.

An important point to stress: project procurements are too critical to the success of any project to be left to chance. Projects should follow Kipling's advise of a century ago in his story to little children. While all six serving men are important, the what, and when, and how much are particularly critical to successful project management. These three dimensions are often referred to as the triple constraint in project management: the scope, the schedule and the budget. [3]

All project procurements must pass through three distinct phases, roughly paralleling the six procurement processes described earlier in the PMBOK Guide. Even minor commodity buys experience three phases as are depicted in Figure 7.1. First the project must define what it wants to buy, as shown on the left. Next the project must select a seller for the product, or service. And lastly, after award of a contract, the chosen seller must execute the contract and deliver the goods.

This critical work is done best when executed according to a *Procurement Management Plan.*

The Definition of Scope: Deciding the "What" the Project Will Procure

The definition of the "what" will be procured by the project, and then preparing a plan of execution for these items can be one of the most important aspects of managing a project.

2. *A Guide to the Project Management Body of Knowledge (PMBOK Guide)*, (Newtown Square, Pennsylvania: Project Management Institute, 2000) page 147.

3. Milton D. Rosenau, Jr., *Successful Project Management* (Belmont, California: Lifetime Learning Publications, 1981), page 16.

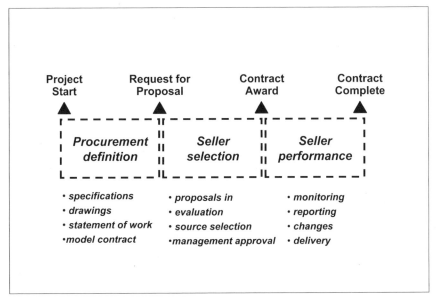

Figure 7.1 Project Procurements have three distinct phases

Once the project has been fully defined typically with use of a Work Breakdown Structure (WBS), a determination must then be made as to who will perform the work. The WBS display lends itself nicely to this process, and facilitates the important "make or buy" choices. The final output will be a listing of buys, representing those items which must be procured for the project. The "make or buy" process was discussed earlier and was displayed in Figure 3.1 and Figure 3.2.

After the make or buy analysis has been completed, the buy items should be assessed and placed into five generic categories, as was also shown earlier in Figure 2.1. Why do this? Simply because each of the five categories presents a different management challenge. The project must organize and manage differently each of the three categories of procurements, representing: (1) Major Complexity procurements, (buying something new to a project's specification); (2) Minor Complexity procurements (to the supplier's specification); and (3) Routine COTS procurements. Also, should special conditions come into play, like a (4) Corporate Teaming Agreement; or (5) an Inter-Divisional purchasing arrangement, the project must address them differently.

Likely the two categories of (1) Major Complexity Procurements, and (2) Minor Complexity Procurements will constitute perhaps 80% of the procurement costs, but perhaps only 20% of the purchased part numbers. Most important, these two initial categories alone will likely represent the greatest concentration of risks to the project. By contrast, the Category (3) procurements of the routine commercial off-the-shelf (COTS) items would likely constitute perhaps 80% of the purchased part items, but only 20% of the procurement costs. Vilfredo Pareto's law, sometimes called the 80-20 rule, works well in classifying project procurements.

Why is all this detailed preparation necessary: simply because the project will need to place specific responsibility assignments for each critical procurement . . . as early as possible. For example, the project will need to identify the responsible engineer, by name, so that the critical technical definition can start. This individual has the job to prepare the procurement specification and drawings necessary to buy major complex items. You do not procure a complex new item without having a precise technical definition, and that job will be assigned to the technical staff, not to the buying staff. There is perhaps no single issue more critical to successful project procurements than the early assignment of technical responsibilities.

Also critical, the project needs to identify the responsible buyer, procurement manager, or contracting officer, by name, to start preparation of the model contract containing all the appropriate terms and conditions and special provisions. The model contract will incorporate the technical specification to authorize the contract award. Some additional issues need to be determined: when does the project need the technical procurement package, the model contract, the Request for Proposal, etc? Who are the potential sellers of these products or services? What type of contractual arrangement would work best for the project and minimize its risks? These are all issues which must be addressed in the project procurement plan. A Project Procurement Matrix defining responsibility assignments should be developed, as was shown earlier in Figure 3.3.

Scope definition, outlining the "what" the project is going to buy, is essential to successful project management. Scope creep can only be prevented . . . with an adequately defined project scope.

Scheduling: Deciding "When" Each Procurement Must Happen

The next critical issue for any procurement plan is to decide "when" each procurement must happen in order to support the project's master schedule. One of the more common risks facing any project is that key procured items will not be delivered to the project in the time-frame needed to support the schedule. While no project master schedule will need to specify all of the procured items required by the project, certainly each of the major-critical buys must be displayed prominently as a separate line item.

Figure 7.2 depicts a Project Master Schedule listing three critical buys entitled Procurements "A" and "B" and "C." The required Delivery Dates (3) are listed for each procurement. Note: there are two milestones which must precede the required Delivery Dates (3). They are the seller's required performance lead-time for each procurement (2), and the Contract Award Dates (1).

Critical Issue: determining when each buy "must" be awarded to support the master schedule

The Project Master Schedule should display for each major critical buy item at a minimum the three key dates and the required time-spans, as is shown in Figure 7.2. This approach simply schedules backwards from the project's need date to isolate the contract award date for each buy. The identification of contract award dates is critical to start the management of project procurements. Each procurement must be authorized, and to do so you must be ready to place the award.

Scheduling backwards in Figure 7.2, milestone (3) for these procurements specifies the date the components are required by the project in order to support the master schedule. Such planned dates must be met in order to complete the overall project within the time-frame expected by management. Late deliveries by sellers can have an adverse impact on any project.

The second key item the master schedule must display is the seller's required time/duration (2) needed to perform their contractual

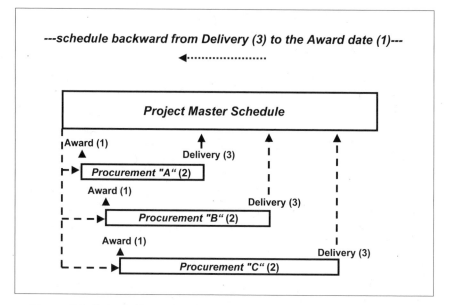

Figure 7.2 Scheduling: deciding when each buy "must be" Awarded

work. This is a critical time-span, but likely the most difficult for any project to estimate. Ideally, each seller would specify the required duration they need to support the proposed new contract. However, until the procured item has been defined and a solicitation made, seller inputs into the schedule are typically not available to a project. In the interim the project must rely on their experienced buyers and schedulers to estimate how much time will be needed for each critical procurement. The term "educated guess" best fits this approach. But the seller's performance time-frame will be needed in order to isolate the next key procurement date.

The last date required is most important to the procurement process. Milestone (1) is the date that each seller must receive a Contract Award. It is a date derived by working backwards, from the (3) Master Schedule Delivery date, less the (2) seller lead-time to produce the article, resulting in the identification of the (1) Contract Award date.

Each project procurement must be awarded in time to support the master schedule need date. Late contract awards will compress the seller's performance schedule, typically adding costs to the procurements, and put in jeopardy the orderly completion of the project.

Critical Issue: determining when each buy "can" be awarded . . .
    "getting our act together"

Sometimes we may encounter difficulty authorizing procurement awards in time to support the project need dates, as defined in the master schedule. Sometimes out of desperation we attempt to overcome these difficulties by resorting to "dumb" actions, like issuing letter contracts, or arbitrarily compressing the seller's lead-times, or worse yet, buying major critical items with a procurement specification which is incomplete or deficient. These actions have all been done before, typically with painful results to the projects.

Unscrupulous sellers love to encounter these conditions because they always result in change orders (growth) to their contracts. Contract values will grow in direct proportion to questionable procurement practices. See Figure 7.3 to follow this discussion.

In order to determine when can we place each order we must now

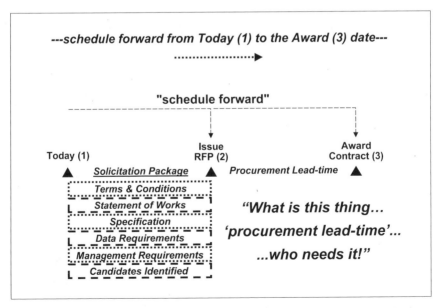

Figure 7.3 Scheduling: deciding when each buy "can be" Awarded

schedule forward as shown from milestone (1) today's date, and isolate each step needed leading up to making the contract award, number (3). There are a number of important concurrent tasks which must be performed prior to the placement of any new order. The second key required milestone is achieved when there is a formal (2) Request for Proposal (RFP) ready to release to prospective sellers. A typical RFP will contain multiple sections, for example, terms and conditions, statement of work, specifications, data and management requirements, payment provisions, etc.

However, the single most critical part in any RFP will be the technical specification of the new product. If the item to be procured is new, or it doesn't exist, it is imperative that we define precisely what we want done by the seller. Complex procurements require precise specifications.

It sometimes comes as a surprise to many that the critical work of preparing the "procurement specification" will be done, not by the company buyers, but by the technical staff. The end product of the technical staff will typically be drawings, specifications, and perhaps a process description. Any changes to the technical specification after a contract has been awarded, during the seller's performance period, constitutes the number one cause of cost growth: "scope creep."

In addition to the technical description, the business definition must also be prepared by the responsible buyer who will be assigned to support the project by the procurement organization. The designated buyer and the responsible engineer must work closely as a cohesive team to make all major-critical procurements work well.

The buyer will pull together the model contract with the RFP consisting of a number of sections. The responsible engineer will also have a key role in preparing the model contract, but subordinate to that of the buyer. Usually the model contract will come together nicely, it is a fairly routine document. But the RFP will often be delayed pending completion of the technical package, the drawings and specifications.

Once the RFP is ready, it will be released to selected sellers, who must be given a reasonable time to adequately respond. The sellers will respond to the RFP with their formal proposals, which must each be evaluated, and a final recommended choice be made for approval by management. From the point of issuance of the RFP until a final recommended choice is made is typically referred to as the "procurement lead-time." Procurement lead-times are a necessary and vital part of source selection. However, a funny thing sometimes happens in this process.

Engineers will sometimes (frequently?) be late on the completion of their critical technical specification. And remember, virtually nothing in procurement is more important to a successful buy than having a quality procurement specification. The engineers will at this point begin to feel the pressure of meeting a schedule release date, and then discover that they are being pressured to allow for procurement lead-time! The engineer's lament: "What is this thing called procurement lead-time, who needs it!"

Demands will often be made by the same delinquent engineers to shorten the allocated procurement lead-time, to give them more time to work on their procurement specification. And there is another emotional issue which needs to be considered: most engineers didn't go to school and take perhaps the most difficult curriculum to write a "dammed" procurement spec! That is why the critical job of writing the technical procurement definition often falls on the junior staff members. Resentment sets in. The delicate relationship between engineer and buyer often becomes strained.

An important point: procurement lead-times are an essential part of the procurement process. They should never be arbitrarily shortened to compensate for other factors, like the late release of technical specifications. See Figure 7.4. There are four critical parts of procurement lead-times. The first is to give a seller a reasonable time to respond to the RFP, resulting in a firm proposal. Next is to allow adequate time to evaluate each seller's proposal, and then to make a final source selection, subject to management approval. Lastly, we need to obtain management's approval for the final recommended source. How much time is needed for this procurement lead-time process? It all depends on the complexity of the procurement.

A seller's proposal for a simple (existing) shelf item can be done in minutes. Perhaps the best example of these types of buys are the per-

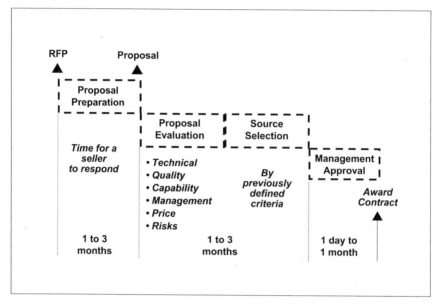

Figure 7.4 Procurement Lead-Time: essential to the process

sonal computers which can be defined on-line by the consumer, then priced in a matter of seconds. While the final computer product may be complex, it is simply a matter of packaging existing components.

However, a major complexity procurement of a Category (1) variety (discussed in Chapter 2) would likely take a seller anywhere from 1 to 3 months to respond. Not only must the respondent comply with each and every term and condition specified in the RFP, but in a competitive situation would have to decide how much risk they might consider underwriting in an effort to win the job.

Once the proposals are received, how much time will be needed to properly evaluate them, to make a source selection based on specific criteria, then prepare a recommendations for management's consideration. Once again, depending on the complexity of the item, anywhere from 1 to 3 months will typically be needed.

Lastly, once a final selection is made, executive management must approve the final choice. Obtaining management approval can take as little as one day (rarely), to a week or even a month, depending on how often senior management formally meets to approve such matters.

Sometimes management doesn't like the recommended seller, or has some concerns with the process, in which case they may reject the entire procurement, and the team must start all over. It all depends.

Procurement lead-times are a necessary part of the orderly procurement process. They must happen in a sequential manner without disruption. Any project procurement which is made by circumventing or arbitrarily shortening the procurement lead-time will likely later experience problems in managing seller performance.

Special Issue: Critical project procurements <u>do not</u> support the master schedule

There is an unfavorable condition sometimes encountered in the scheduling of a project which is referred to as having "negative float." This term means simply that there is not enough time to adequately do the job. It is not uncommon to encounter negative float when a project is first scheduled. Once exposed, it is then up to the project team to finds ways to eliminate the negative condition so that they are in concert with management's expectations of a completion date.

A negative float condition for a major critical procurement is portrayed in Figure 7.5. By scheduling forward to indicate the date when we "can" award a contract, and then by scheduling backwards to reflect when we "must" award a contract, a negative schedule condition can be determined. Issue: how can we get rid of this adverse condition without adding risks to the project?

In order to give a seller adequate time to do their work, and to make a delivery in time to support the master schedule, we sometimes find that we should have awarded the contract . . . last month! Or, conversely, by the time we get our act together and prepare a formal RFP, we will have to cut the seller's required lead-time in half in order to meet the schedule! Either solution would be unacceptable. However, in order to support the project master schedule we must find a way to eliminate any negative schedule condition.

One approach some projects have taken with selected critical sellers in order to shorten their procurement lead-times is to bring selected critical sellers directly into their team, immediately make

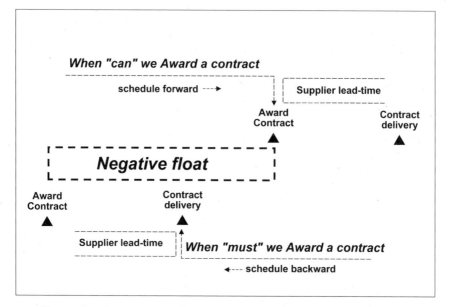

Figure 7.5 Procurements sometimes encounter negative float

them a part of the overall project team. True, this approach would essentially eliminate competition for the selected critical items. But quite frankly, some formal competitions are a farce. There are often "preferred" sellers, qualified suppliers with proven records of prior performance. Quite often, particularly in the commercial sector, contracts with selected preferred sellers are negotiated directly, with most satisfactory results.

See Figure 7.6. The more traditional competition approach is displayed across the top of the chart. On the bottom of the chart the project negotiates a contract directly with a qualified seller, thus eliminating the competition lead-time, and improving the overall project schedule.

By negotiating directly with a preferred and qualified source, the 2 to 6 months of procurement lead-times can be reduced down to just one or two weeks. Bringing preferred suppliers immediately on one's team, by skillful negotiation, can sometimes eliminate a negative schedule condition. Not everyone would agree with this approach. But it is an approach often done with projects in the commercial sector. Publicly funded projects might have difficulties

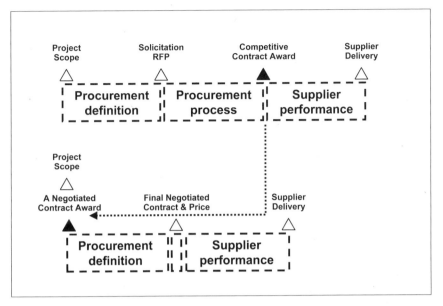

Figure 7.6 Teaming Agreements can sometimes shorten a schedule

with this approach, and it is always wise to get your customer involved before trying this approach.

All procurements, particularly major critical buys, must be awarded and performed in time to support the master schedule. The project procurement plan must address the timing of each buy.

Budgeting: Estimating "How Much" Each Procurement Will Cost

The final mandatory component of any viable procurement plan must round out what is commonly referred to as the triple constraint: the <u>costs</u> required to accomplish the defined <u>scope</u> of work within the allotted time-frame or <u>schedule</u>. At the start of each new project every task, every major component, every purchased item will get a budget. COTS items are typically budgeted in broad, bulk categories. Hopefully each authorized budget will be reasonable, achievable, and have some logical basis for the cost estimate.

Cost estimates for a new project become available based on vari-

---

- ***Analogy (rule of thumb) relationships***

  (top-down estimates based on similar work; expert judgment)

- ***Parametric modeling***

  (component weight: square feet; lines code; function points)

- ***Bottom-up estimates***

  (summary of detailed estimates for individual packages)

- ***Computerized estimating tools***

  (incorporating actual historical experience)

- ***Firm proposals from viable sellers***

Figure 7.7 How much will each Procurement cost

ous forecasting models. Displayed in Figure 7.7 are five of the more recognized methods to estimate required costs and subsequently set budgets for a new project.

Each of these methods needs to be understood.

Analogy (expert judgment . . . rule of thumb) relationships

These estimates are sometimes referred to as top-down estimating, or sometimes estimates by expert judgment. They are used initially whenever there is little detailed information on a new project, often in the early stages of the project. They are considered to be the least costly to prepare, but also the least accurate of other estimating methods.

The project estimator will focus on similar work which has been done before, and attempt to establish a relationship to the current new job. Sometimes when the new work is more complex, or less complex, or other factors such as unknowns come into play, the estimator will add or take away some percentage value from the projected new work.

A similar job which might have cost the organization $400,000 before, might now be estimated at perhaps $450,000 based on acknowledging simply the increased labor costs and inflationary factors. Or, perhaps it may now be estimated at $495,000, considering both inflation and an additional complexity factor of say 10%.

Parametric modeling

One of the more respected methods to estimate future costs of a new project is with parametric modeling. This method sets parameters based on historical performance, typically by industry, but some performance data will apply to multiple industries. In information technology projects such issues as costs for lines of computer software code, function points analysis, Constructive Cost Model (COCO-MO) and COCOMO II, are commonly used.

On construction projects square footage is often used as the basis for cost estimates before detail drawings become available. Construction square footage estimates can be further broken down into single or double residential home square footage, apartment footage, single story industrial footage, high-rise footage, and other types of buildings. Assuming comparable labor and materials costs, and site conditions, these preliminary estimates can be quite accurate.

The aircraft industry has used parametric modeling quite well. They have in the past been successful in forecasting future costs based on the expected weight of the aircraft types, separating aircraft into fighter, bomber, transport, unmanned, sea based, etc. Most recently they have had to incorporate other factors into their parametric models such as the use of exotic light weight materials, heat resistant materials, stealth materials, etc.

Since both the analogy and parametric forms of estimating are top-down forms of estimates, they are more difficult to subsequently budget in detail at project implementation.

Bottom-up estimates

This approach to forecasting future costs takes a new job and breaks it down into small pieces. A detailed estimate is then prepared for each piece or task or segment of work. The costs for the tasks are then summarized to obtain a total cost for the job. The various levels of the project Work Breakdown Structure (WBS) lends itself nicely to this type of estimating. A separate estimate would be prepared for each WBS element displayed.

One drawback to preparing bottoms-up cost estimates is that this method takes considerable time to prepare an estimate for a new job. Also, this type of estimate works best when some design information becomes available providing a basis for the detailed estimates.

Some people have complained that this estimating method takes an inordinate amount of time. That may be true. But they also provide a very detailed cost estimate, by task, and one that can be quickly converted into formal authorized budgets at the point of project implementation. Since neither the Analogy nor the Parametric cost estimates contain bottom-up detail, they are effectively gross top-down estimates, and much time will be eventually required developing detailed budgets at the point of project initiation.

Computerized estimating tools

Through the combination of keeping accurate historical records by industry, and project, and breaking actual performance results down into subordinate pieces, some companies have developed some rather sophisticated computer estimating techniques. Such techniques often rely on a combination of internal records and the use of electronic spreadsheets.

Also, some industries have carefully documented their performance actuals, which have allowed for commercial software pricing packages to become available. There are several such cost estimating models available, particularly for use in the aerospace and defense industry.

Firm proposals from viable sellers

The final method to determine a reasonable cost estimate for any procurement is by simply laying out the responses from trusted suppliers, preferably three or more in a competitive bid environment. Assuming that an adequate and complete RFP was issued, and there is no collusion on the part of the responding sellers, there can be no better source of estimated costs than from analysis of the firm responses received from suppliers who will actually perform the work.

Other Procurement Planning Issues of Importance

In addition to the triple constraint issues covering scope, schedule, and costs, there are a number of other important matters which must be included in any viable procurement plan. In order to be complete, the plan for the management of project procurements must include some additional subjects of importance.

Project Organization and Staffing Plans for Procurement Management

Most companies have in place the necessary processes and controls allowing them to order, track the delivery, inspect, and put in place the many commodities, purchased parts, and raw materials needed by the project. These items will be managed nicely under what is typically called a Material Resource Planning system (MRP), which is sometimes a subset of a more sophisticated process called Enterprise Resource Planning (ERP).

The MRP and ERP systems will work nicely with the 80 to 90 percent of the articles (parts) to be bought for the project. But how about the other 10 percent of the articles needed, which might represent perhaps 90 percent of the purchased costs, and perhaps 90 or more percent of the risks associated with such procurements. While the bulk of the purchased commodities can be tracked adequately with the MRP and ERP systems, the management of selected high value, highly complex, high-risk buys must be performed by people not computers. Automated systems, no matter how good, will not do the job. Whenever a project has procurements which require people skills, the project must organize itself accordingly.

Shown in Figure 7.8 is an imaginary project which has one Teaming Agreement buy, and one Major Complex buy. In these circumstances

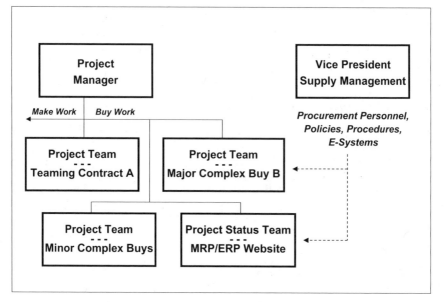

Figure 7.8 Organizing for Project Procurements

the project manager will likely want to form separate project teams to deal exclusively with these two highly complex buys. They constitute procuring something new to the project's unique specification. Typically such buys represent considerable risks, large dollar investments, and extend for the full life-cycle of the project.

Also, this same project might have a number of what may be considered minor complexity procurements which could represent high monetary values, but the articles would be classified as low risk because they are available from identified sellers, according to the seller's own product specification. Often a single project team can manage several large commodity purchases, as long as they represent articles which exist from dependable suppliers.

The majority of the purchased articles can be secured with use of the company MRP or ERP or e-systems, which will allow for the continuous tracking and status of all procured items, often available to the project team with a separate website.

The last critical player in the project's organization will be the senior executive who will go by the title of Vice President of Purchasing,

Procurement, or most recently Supply-Management. This individual will provide the project with experienced professional buyers, who will support the project's procurement needs, but always conducted strictly in accordance with the formal purchasing policies, procedures, and instructions.

The procurement plan should specify the organizational arrangement the project manager proposes to employ to buy the necessary work scope from external sources. Such plans must also include the staffing levels and timing of personnel requirements, particularly those professionals who must be assigned from other functional organizations, like Supply-Management, Inspection, Transportation, Warehousing, etc.

Small Business, Small Disadvantaged Business, Women Owned Small Business, etc.

All government funded projects, and this will include federal, state, and local government funding, will encounter project objectives in addition to simply performance against the contractual statement of work. These objectives will be the "social" community goals which are an established part of most government funded work. Such goals are typically stated as a percentage target of total project dollars which must be directed to assist certain business enterprises broadly classified as Small Business Concerns, with a number of various subcategories. Such objectives can be contractually described simply as goals to be achieved. Or they can be tied into precise incentive or award fees to be earned or lost, which would certainly get management's attention.

The FAR defines their requirement for small business set-asides as follows:

> *Any contactor receiving a contract . . . must agree in the contract that small business, veteran-owned small business, service-disabled veteran-owned small business, HUBZone small business, small disadvantaged business, and women-owned small business concerns will have the maximum practicable opportunity to participate in*

contract performance consistent with its efficient performance. [4]

Ten years ago this same FAR section read "shall agree" where it now reads "must agree." Thus any procurement plan prepared on a project funded with government monies must address the issue of placing some portion of new contract awards to one of the classes of small businesses, as specified in the prime contract.

How big a challenge can this be for any project? It can be routine or it can be massive. Let's review one specific contract which was awarded by the United States Navy in October, 2000. The project is called the Navy Marine Corps Intranet (NMCI) contract. In the year leading up to the award there was a fierce competition among all of the major information technology outsourcing firms. The project was expected to be in the $10 billion dollar range. But when the award was made to Electronic Data Systems (EDS), the total contract value was reduced down $6.9 billion. One significant provision of this new contract was the required small business set aside:

> *The NMCI contract requires that the prime contractor use small business for at least 35% of the work, and includes incentives for exceeding that figure.* [5]

Think about this contractual requirement, which would appear to have incentive fee attached to meeting these objectives. EDS must place 35%, or some $2.4 billion in contracts to small business concerns! If they exceed this amount, they could earn higher incentives. But if they failed to award $2.4 billion in contracts to small business concerns, the result could be costly. Obviously, a major issue for any procurement plan done by EDS for their NMCI project would have to address how they intend to meet the challenges of small business awards, which contractually "must" be met.

---

4. FAR 19.702. Note: the term "HUBZone" means "Historically Underutilized Business Zone", sometimes referred to as economically depressed areas.

5. Department of Navy, Information Management/Information Technology: http://www.don-imit.navy.mil.

Issue: how would any project address this challenge? Likely they would expand their project management office to add a new team of specialists whose sole job would be to locate and in some cases nurture small business concerns which would allow them to meet this objective. The project organization described above with Figure 7.8, would now look more like that shown in Figure 7.9. The Vice President of Supply Management would likely take the lead role in promoting and securing such new small businesses to meet the requirements in their contract.

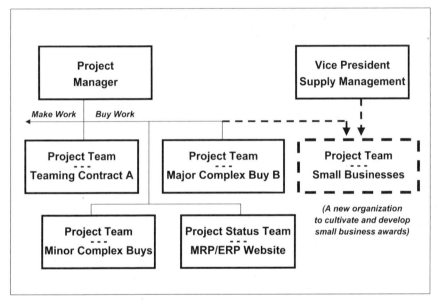

Figure 7.9 Organizing for Project "Small Business" Procurements

Competition Planning: Single and Sole Source Procurements

All procurement organizations like competition. With competition between qualified sellers, the best price and terms will be obtained. Sometimes, however, it can be in the best interests of a project to not hold a competition. These conditions can occur when there may be only one source available to produce a given product. These are called Sole Source procurements.

Other times there may be more than one source available to produce a given product, but for business reasons, which should be justified, the project has elected to solicit from only one source. These are referred to as Single Source procurements.

The waiving or reduction in competition, the use of single or sole sources for products will typically represent a departure from the approved procurement policies. Thus any planned use of these methods should be described for management's concurrence in the procurement plan.

Preliminary Contract Type Selection

If all of the planned project procurements are expected to be routine, with use of a firm fixed price (FFP) contract type, then this section of the plan would not be needed. If however, the project management team anticipates issuing contracts of a type other than FFP, they should identify (preliminarily) such plans so that senior management will be aware of these intentions and can register their concerns early, should they have them.

The routine contract type for all project procurements is the FFP. Any contract type of a cost, or incentive, or award-fee, or time and materials constitutes a departure from the routine. Senior management should be apprised early of such planned departures from the norm.

Who Will Manage Each Major-Critical and Teaming Arrangement Procurement

This may seem like a insignificant issue, but many a seller has played the "who's in charge" issue to their advantage throughout the life-cycle of a major critical procurement. If not specified and agreed to by everyone on the project team, there are at least three organizations who will make their case that: "I am in charge of this procurement." See Figure 7.10.

First, which individual has procurement authority. Who can execute contracts to sellers on behalf of the company. The answer will always be the buyer, or purchasing agent, or subcontracts manager, or

- ## The b**uyer or purchasing manager**
  (has the procurement authority)

- ## *The engineer or technical manager*
  (writes the procurement specification)

- ## The *Project Manager*
  (has the most at stake)

  ---pre-nuptial agreements are recommended---

Figure 7.10 Who will manage each Procurement

contracting officer. Many people who hold these titles believe strongly that since they alone can execute a contract on behalf of their organization, that they are best suited to manage the procurement. This typically is not the case.

The second person who can make an argument for being in change of a procurement is the chief technical person. After all, the technical person will be the one who will write the technical description of the item to be procured. Without question, the technical description is the single most important item in a major complex buy. Stated another way, the technical description is likely the single issue which if done poorly will case major cost growth in the contract value. However, not all technical people are cut out to be managers, and this sometimes causes a problem.

The last person who can make claim to being in charge of a critical procurement is the project manager. A project manager is like the coach of a sports team. When things go badly they are typically the first to go. Thus they have the most to lose.

This author is a strong advocate of the use of "project teams" sometimes called "integrated product teams" to manage major-complex buys. Project teams are generally organized consistent with the Work Breakdown Structure (WBS) centered around project deliverables. Multi-functional groups must work together in harmony as a team. Generally, with few exceptions, it will be the technical person who will be placed in charge of project teams. In the case of a major critical complex procurement, it would be a technical person who is put in charge of each team.

That technical person must be supported by a professional buyer, who would be subordinate deputy in hierarchy, but would be there to ensure that all procurement policies be strictly followed. An agreement as to who is in charge of procurements is often a difficult matter to resolve. The importance of management buy-in will be covered in the final section below.

The Purchasing System: Company Policies, Procedures, and Practices

All mature companies will operate under documented rules governing what employees must do particularly when they are performing any of the key corporate functions. One of the functions always deemed critical to any organization is the work of buying items on behalf of the organization. Every organization which has achieved any degree of maturity will have prescribed rules to follow in the purchase of items on behalf of the company. These rules will be prescribed in company policies, procedures, and sometimes detailed practices.

All procurements done for the project must be executed strictly in compliance with the corporate purchasing policies and procedures. In the event that a project deems it necessary to deviate from these established rules, such exceptions should be specifically cited in a section of the *Procurement Management Plan,* along with the justification for any departures. People are sometimes fired for violating company policy. This is precisely why only "buyers" or people with that general title have delegated procurement authority . . . so procurement policies will be followed.

A couple of examples of exceptions might help. The use of a cost reimbursable type contract might well represent an exception to a policy requiring only fixed price procurements. The waiver of competition, going directly to a preferred source, would likely be an exception to purchasing policy which requires competition on all procurements.

If any exceptions to established purchasing policies are anticipated by a project, they should be specifically cited along with the justification, so that management doesn't later get surprised.

Buyer/Seller/Customer Management Training (project team-building)

There is an interesting phenomena which sometimes affects new projects, even within mature companies, even with an experienced staff. The condition is that of responsibility mismatches: resulting in assignment "gaps" and performance "overlaps."

Critical project work is sometimes left unassigned. No one claims responsibility for certain work that must be done for the project. And sometimes the opposite condition will happen: more than one person or group believes that they should perform certain tasks. The result of this condition is performance inefficiencies, performance interference.

How big a problem can this be? It can sometimes can be catastrophic as when a certain space probe failed because part of the project was designing the system using United States measurements (Imperial measurements) while other team members were using the European metric system. The hardware components didn't fit resulting in a spectacular failure. There was obviously a "gap" in responsibility perhaps with a group performing the critical "systems engineering" function.

In certain industries it has become fashionable to organize using a concept called virtual teams. This approach is particularly popular with software projects where people around the world are assigned a piece of the software project to perform. These assignments are typically performed with great professionalism, and normally save considerable sums of money to the project. But virtual teams do have their own unique problems with "gaps" and "overlaps."

One very effective method to implement a new project with smooth efficiency is to conduct a pre-project team-building training session with inclusion of all members of the project who have a vested interest in its success. In addition to the project in-house staff, such sessions often include key sellers and sometimes the project's customer, sponsor, to the extent they are willing to participate.

Team building training sessions do cost money, early in a new project, particularly when some of the participants must travel half-way around the world to attend. But typically such training allows a project to get off to a smooth start, and perform well for the duration of the project.

Seller Risk Assessment, Analysis and Closure Planning

No procurement plan would be complete without an assessment of the risks associated with the purchased items. The buy items can cause risks to a project for a number of reasons. But any procured item for a new article, or commodities never been built before, has to be considered high-risk, until the product has been developed, tested, and delivered according to the project specification. This would include all Category (1) procurements, those items which are being created new for the project, in accordance with the project's unique specification.

Prior to the creation of a procurement plan, the project will have performed a risk assessment of all identified risks facing the project, those items which are made and those which are bought. This result will be a listing of all project risks, both make or buy work. This approach was displayed in Figure 5.4 earlier.

In addition, an assessment will have been made earlier to determine whether or not the project may be advised to employ a cost reimbursable or incentive or award fee type contract on selected procurements, or perhaps form a teaming partner, consistent with the language of their arrangement. In all cases, any cost or incentive type contract can result in higher risks to the project.

The procurement plan should specify the identified risks with all procurements, and indicate the approach the project intends to take to mitigate the known procurement risks.

Post Contract Award Management Approach

The time to start thinking about how you plan to manage critical procurements is early in the procurement processes, at the time you start the planning for them. Once a contract is let it is too late to then insert "after-thoughts" without paying an exorbitant price.

At a minimum you need to know at all times how your procurements are doing and whether or not they will arrive in time to support your master schedule. You will need schedule visibility on all buy items. Fixed price suppliers are often reluctant to provide schedule visibility "out of principle" after all it is a fixed-price work arrangement. However, sellers often abandon such feelings if you give them progress payments in return for their schedule visibility.

You will often want sellers of selected critical buys to participate in project status reviews, sometimes weekly, certainly not less frequently than monthly. If this support is needed it needs to be specified and requested early from all sellers.

Sometimes on major complexity buys the project will need to have their own resident representative at the seller's site to aid and assist the supplier. Most often this individual(s) will be a technical person, but sometimes these reps will also represent the business community.

The time to worry about management and management requirements is early in the procurement planning process.

Management Displays: a "War-Room" or Project Web Site

Most projects of any size and complexity have performance status summary reports available to the project manager . . . at all times. On smaller projects the project manager may simply keep a loose-leaf binder with critical project data like schedules, funding projections, action-items lists, etc.

On larger projects it is not uncommon to have a dedicated conference room with the same project status data available to the project team. Such rooms will often carry the title of "war rooms" or "status review rooms", etc., something which describes their intended purpose.

More recently with the advent of e-commerce, these status rooms are quickly being replaced by project websites which contain the same data, more up to date, easier to maintain, and with better security controls over the broad dissemination of such data. The procurement plan should give a sampling of the kind of data the project anticipates maintaining in their website. Critical project procurements would have a prominent place in the website.

Management's Buy-in to the "Procurement Management Plan"

Once the *Procurement Management Plan* is completed, and represents the best collective thinking of all organizations which have a vested interest in its success, there is one important step to take prior to execution: get management buy-in. There are two or perhaps three executives whose support is vital to the success of project procurements.

The first person who needs to support the plan will be the project manager. Everything which is done should be done in accordance with the direction of the project manager. Therefore, the project manager must approve any procurement plan.

Another individual who must concur in any procurement plan will be the most senior person who has been given procurement authority. These people will carry various titles, vice president or director of procurement, purchasing, supply-management, etc. They are sometimes superior in rank to many project managers, which sometimes can be an issue which needs to be addressed. This organizational disparity issue is often settled by their buy-in to the procurement plan.

A third person sometimes critical to getting buy-in would be the customer, which would be particularly important on government funded projects.

If there are professional differences of opinion as to what might be the best course of action dealing with project procurements, it is best to resolve them before the orders are specified, solicited, evaluated, and contract awards made to sellers.

CHAPTER 8

Plan Procurements (2 of 2)

(PMBOK ® - Third Edition 2004: 12.2 Plan Contracting)

The second process in project procurement management deals with the planning necessary to solicit proposals from qualified sellers. The old adage "be careful what you ask for . . . you may get it" immediately comes to mind. If there is a discrepancy between what we think we want and what we ask for in our solicitation, we cannot hold sellers responsible for giving us the wrong response. It is up to us to precisely define what we want sellers to do for us.

This process effectively begins the implementation of the *Procurement Management Plan*. One overriding consideration for all procurements is that they be executed consistent with the requirements prescribed in the project master schedule. One way or another, everything purchased must support the master schedule.

Solicitations will take different forms depending on what is to be procured. For example, the solicitation package for a commercial off-the-shelf (COTS) item will be vastly different from that required to develop a new commodity. For this reason the early analysis and classification of all procurements, as was covered in Chapter 2, is critical to effective procurement management.

Issues for Selecting Prospective Suppliers

There are a number of matters which must be considered when planning for the solicitation of bids from prospective sellers. Issue: do we have past experience dealing with similar purchases? Have we had experience, good or bad, with the sellers now being considered for solicitation. Some companies have rather sophisticated supplier rating systems which take a number of past factors into consideration: seller's record of on-time deliveries, the product quality, cost growth, claims, cooperation, and willingness to work out problems with the project team.

Issue: will we want to "pre-qualify" the potential suppliers prior to sending out a solicitation? This is often a wise practice on any procurement which requires producing something new, or is for technically challenging work. Pre-qualifications can consist of several factors, essentially requiring the seller to demonstrate, in person or on paper, that they can do the job being considered. You never want to solicit proposals from unqualified sellers, then have to eliminate them after you receive their final proposal. It is unfair to the seller to exercise them if they have no chance for the final award.

Issue: the dependability and stability of project funding. Is the project funded with private or government funding, it does make a difference? Private funding is typically more predictable. You can usually rely on it. Government funding, however, is subject to political pressures, where one legislative group must approve the new project, another legislative committee must appropriate the money, and finally the government executive must want the project. Government projects are subject to delays, false starts, reductions, slow-downs, stretch-outs, scope changes, etc. Why is this particularly critical for procurements? Because every change in project funding gives a fixed price seller an opportunity to submit a claim for equitable adjustment of contract price. Every change costs money.

Issue: will there be political pressures on the award of major procurements? Answer, likely. Should there be: no. But politicians will be politicians. And elected officials typically have little inhibition calling a company urging serious consideration to award a certain contract to a certain supplier, who happens to be in the politician's own district. This will happen. It presents no problem when the seller in question is on the preferred supplier list. But sometimes politicians will recommend a totally unqualified source, in their district, and this does present a problem for the project. Expect "help" from your local friendly politicians.

Issue: are there special considerations incorporated in the prime contract which must be addressed in selected procurements which will impact solicitation planning? Sometimes prime contracts will have special provisions which must be considered with selected procurements, often such procurements are listed within the prime contract. Sometimes these critical procurements require prior "approval" from the buying customer on selected major critical awards. If there are such restrictions contained in the prime contract, early involvement of the customer is important.

Another important issue which often arises on government funded projects is the requirement to place some percentage of procurement awards with special categories of businesses. Such required firms can take many forms calling themselves small businesses, socially disadvantaged businesses, women owned businesses, native American businesses, etc. If the prime contract has such provisions, and most government funded projects will have such provisions, they must be addressed in the planning for solicitations. This subject was discussed in the last chapter and can present an important challenge to any project.

The Buying Approach: Advertise, Solicit, Negotiate, Compete

Whenever a project has commodities to buy, and most do, the assigned buyer must decide on the best approach to secure the items for the project. Most mature companies will have an established purchasing organization that will assign buyers to the projects to obtain the needed articles. The best approach to be taken will likely be determined by the complexity of the items needed by the project.

The best place to start this process would be the "buy" listing which resulted from the make or buy analysis as a part of the scope definition process. If done systematically the buy listing will have identified all/most articles listed in descending order, with the most complex items at the top. For purposes of discussion, let us begin at the bottom of the list, with the more simple items.

In the last few years with the increased usage of the internet, the great majority of the project procurements now come directly from the internet, in which cases no formal solicitations or advertising will need to take place. The buyers simply place their orders, often done with use of corporate master purchase agreements, and the commodities arrive a few days later. Even fairly sophisticated items like computers and electronic components can be secured in this manner.

If a solicitation must take place, various companies use different methods and forms, often to achieve the same purpose. Some companies will issue an Invitation to Bid (ITB) or sometimes an Invitation for Bid (IFB) to obtain written requests for quotes, bids, best prices from suppliers. When only information on a product or on a given company is desired the buyer will often issue a Request for Information (RFI) form to the prospective companies. Some firms will use a Request for Quote (RFQ) to obtain data, information, and sometimes firm quotes leading to a subsequent buy.

Point: different companies will have different standard forms to achieve the same purpose. There is no absolute standard or meaning to any of the specific forms just mentioned. Forms will vary from company to company and it does not matter. The results are typically the same.

However, if the item needed by the project is a complex buy, something new which must be developed according to the project's unique specification, most companies do employ a similar process: the use of the Request for Proposal, the RFP. The RFP is a robust document which will contain many subsections such as a Statement of Work (SOW), Technical Specifications, sometimes drawings, management requirements, terms and conditions, special provisions, etc. The RFPs can be directed to multiple competing sources, or to a single source to provide a basis for subsequent negotiations. Usually a RFP will be directed to a corporate teaming member to provide a basis for final contract negotiations. The RFP document will be discussed in greater detail in a later section of this chapter.

With all complex buys, the assigned buyer will typically work closely with a technical and business representative who will provide expert advice to guide the complex procurement. Many firms elect to use outside consultants and or retired employees to provide such expert guidance.

Defining the "What" we plan to Buy

One of the most important and yet challenging issues in the management of project procurements is to define, in legally enforceable terms, what you expect sellers to do for you. Existing commodities, commercially available shelf item products are easy to define: "I'll take one of these, two of these, six of those . . . "

But when you ask a seller to create something new, (e.g., a new product or technology which has never been done before, a major complexity procurement) this is always a challenge to management. Perhaps it is best to break this critical requirement into two parts: the "business" definition and the "technical" definition.

An opinion of the author: the "business" definition should be easy, it should be routine, it should build on the past experiences of the professional purchasing (supply-management, procurement, etc.) staff. They have bought these things before and the projects must rely on these professionals to guide them.

However, it is the "technical" definition which presents the greatest risk to any project. Often, the critical technical definition will be done by novices, engineers or scientists who may have never been involved in buying a complex product before. And yet, it is the technical staff who will be defining the critical heart of any complex buy. If not done well, every change of technical requirements presents an opportunity to submit a claim from sellers. This condition is typically called "scope creep." Scope creep will be the number one cause of cost growth with project procurements.

The "Business" Definition

The definition of the business requirements will start with the preparation of what is sometimes called a model contract. While the precise format will vary from company to company, the makeup of a model contract will often contain the elements as displayed in Figure 8.1. The assigned purchasing or contracts professionals will typically take the lead role in defining and assembling the model contract, capturing the requirements of the project. While the work of preparing a

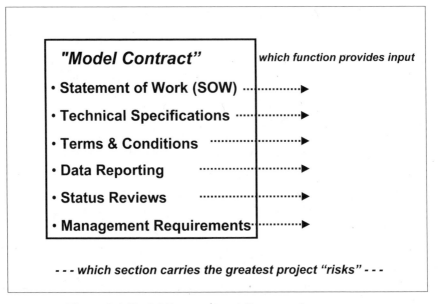

Figure 8.1 Model Procurement Document

model contract is important, it typically is a routine effort. Reason: the professional buyers and contract administrators have done it before, many times. They are good at it.

A couple of points concerning the model contract. Issue: which function provides the key inputs by section to the model contract. While the exact determination will vary by company, there are some traditional roles. The Statement of Work (SOW) is typically prepared by a business specialist from the procurement department. The technical specifications will always come in from the technical or scientific people. Terms & conditions will come from purchasing. Requirements for status reviews and management oversight needs will normally be set by the project manager. Data submittals from sellers will be defined by most functions supporting the project. Word of caution: challenge excessive demands for data submittals. Make sure they are truly needed by the requestor.

Another critical issue for the model contract: which section carries with it the greatest risks to the project? Answer: the technical definition contained in the procurement specifications. Most change orders, most cost growth, most schedule delays will typically result from changes to the technical scope of work. For this reason (and others) many companies have gone to a project teams approach, where the technical engineers are given overall responsibility for performance of their technical team. Empirically, project teams have demonstrated spectacular performance results.

Business Definition: the Seller's Statement of Work (SOW)

Many consider the SOW to be the single most critical document in the acquisition process. [1]

We should take note: the Statement of Work (SOW) would appear to be an important document in the procurement process. We had better have a solid understanding of this critical document. Perhaps a couple of other definitions might help.

Statement of Work (SOW)-A description of a product or service to be procured under a contract; a statement of requirements. [2]

The SOW in the request for proposals (RFP) is the only official description of the work requirement. Accordingly, it must provide the contractor with enough information to develop and price the proposal—without the need for further explanation. [3]

Question: if the Statement of Work (SOW) is so important, and it appears to be, why is it that most procurements do not contain what is called a SOW document? Answer: all procurements do in fact contain a SOW, they are just not called the SOW. But all procurements whether they go under the title of a purchase order, a contract,

1. *Project Management Basics Education: Project Procurement Management*, (Project Management Institute, Upper Darby, PA, 1996) page 10.
2. David I. Cleland and Harold Kerzner, *A Project Management Dictionary of Terms*, (New York: Van Nostrand Reinhold Company, 1985), page 237.
3. Peter S. Cole, *How to Write a Statement of Work*, (Management Concepts, Inc., Vienna, VA, 1999) page 5.

a subcontract, etc., will always contain the generic equivalent of a statement of requirements, i.e., a SOW.

The SOW is essentially a scope statement for the prospective sellers. It is typically written by a business person, often the buyer or contract administrator, rarely ever by a technical person. Often the individual preparing the SOW will be experienced in preparing such documents and will use such words as "must" in lieu of "may." Must requirements are easier to price than may, which gives the respondents a wide latitude in pricing the new job. Some professional SOW writers are quite versed and quite adept at describing not only what the sellers are expected to provide, and will also try to provide a listing of some of the work which is not to be included, to the extent that such exclusions can be defined.

A typical seller statement of work (SOW) might thus include the following items:

- The objectives of the procurement
- A listing of the procurement deliverables, hardware, software, and reporting
- Performance standards
- Commitment of specific personnel
- A schedule or period of performance
- Location(s) description of where work will be performed
- Documents incorporated into the SOW by reference, including terms and conditions
- The order of precedence of all specified documents
- Other items of importance to the project

The Statement of Work (SOW) is an important component of all procurements.

Question: Might the Seller's SOW someday be superceded by the "Project WBS Dictionary"?

There is a school of thought which is developing among some technical groups, primarily the systems engineers, which suggests that the seller's Statement of Work (SOW) has become a obsolete document on most projects. Their point is that if a project truly employs a Work Breakdown Structure (WBS) to define their work, then takes the next step to describe the defined project work in the form of a WBS Dictionary, there is no further need to prepare a separate document for sellers. This idea has some merit.

Rather than bring in a procurement person and have that individual write a separate document to describe what a seller is to do for the project, why not use the project's WBS Dictionary as the procurement Statement of Work. Not only would this approach eliminate the need to prepare a separate document, but the project would have both the project team and the seller working with the same understanding of the work to be done, the deliverables to be produced, etc.

Sometimes on projects there can be a disconnect between the expectations of the project team and the work being done by the suppliers because the sellers work to their contractual SOW, and the team may be working to another set of requirements, perhaps as specified in the project WBS Dictionary.

If this were to happen it would be critical that the assigned buyer be brought onto the project team early in the scope definition process, and the buyer would have to take an active role in the definition of each procurement, at the appropriate WBS element level. This approach would likely result in a higher quality, more complete WBS Dictionary for the project. Not a bad idea to consider in the future.

Business Definition: Terms & Conditions (T&Cs)

One of the most important members of any project team whenever there are critical procurements to be made will be the assigned buyer, the subcontracting manager, the contracting officer, etc., whatever titles they may be given. These individuals will be the professional procurement specialists who will be assigned to the project to provide assistance in all procurement matters. It is critical that such assignments be made early to support all major critical buys. Any delays in the assignment of buyers to a project will simply add risks to the process because their early counsel is critical for the success of such procurements.

One important contribution the professional buyer can make to a project is in the selection of terms and conditions (T&Cs) to be incorporated into critical procurements. On government funded projects there is less discretionary room because many of the T&Cs will be mandated by government regulation. However, even with government funded work there is some room for tailoring because only certain of the T&Cs are mandatory, while others are discretionary.

Terms and Conditions (T&Cs) can cover a wide range of issues as are illustrated in Figure 8.2. These are but a small sampling of the T&Cs but it does demonstrate their importance. T&Cs can cover such critical issues as how one makes changes to an existing procurement, if there are conflicts in contractual requirements what is the order of precedence, how does one terminate a relationship, when does title pass from the seller to the buyer, payments or no payments to the supplier, etc. It is critical that the appropriate T&Cs be incorporated into the legal relationship.

However, blindly incorporating superfluous T&Cs needlessly wastes money, requiring sellers to respond to legal requirements which

---

- **SOW & Changes to**   • **Governing Laws**

- **Specifications**   • **Title**

- **Order of precedence**   • **Termination**

- **Testing & Inspection**   • **Arbitration**

- **Delivery**   • **Back-charges**

- **Warranty**   • **Payments**

- - - projects must rely on buying professionals - - -

Figure 8.2 Contract/Subcontract Clauses...a small sampling

may not be necessary for success. Therefore, it is recommended that care be given to the inclusion of each T&C into procurements, and only those T&Cs that are needed for success be incorporated into buys. Discrimination in the application of T&Cs in procurements is always recommended.

Displayed in Figure 8.3 is a flow-down matrix of T&Cs, an approach which is sometimes used to assess whether or not the right mix of requirements is being employed. Note, mandatory T&C requirements are excluded from this process. Shown in the vertical column to the left will be the listing of all project procurements, listing the major complexity buys first, then the major but non-complex buys next, and so forth. Across the top row will be a listing of the specific T&Cs being considered for application to each procurement.

Once the matrix is complete the buyer would be expected coordinate it, to gain an endorsement of key players. At a minimum the key players would be the procurement organization, the project manager, the technical organization, and sometimes the buying customer, perhaps the government or another commercial company.

	Terms & Conditions flow-down clauses (excludes mandatory clauses)			
Item # 1	Yes	No	Yes	No
Item # 2	No	No	Yes	No
Item # 3	Yes	No	Yes	Yes
Item # 4	Yes	Yes	Yes	No
Item # 5	No	No	No	No

(List of identified Procurements)

Key Players in the process:
(1) Purchasing (2) Project Manager (3) Technical (4) Customer

Figure 8.3 Terms & Conditions Flow-down Matrix

You need the right mix of T&Cs on all procurements. But too much money is often wasted in procurements by imposing excessive, superfluous T&Cs on suppliers.

Business Definition: the Requirements for Management Oversight

The project manager and the project team should assess each major procurement and determine what will be needed to properly manage the selected critical buys. The routine purchased items will normally be tracked adequately by the automated E-Systems: MRP, MRP-II, ERP, etc. However all complex and major critical buys require special management oversight.

A number of factors will need to be considered by the project team including: an assessment of the known risks, a determination of how technically challenging the work may be, any past experiences with the proposed seller, etc. One thing which should be required from all suppliers on critical procurements is a copy of their internal working schedule to support each procurement.

Displayed in Figure 8.4 is a recommended sample format for a seller's monthly reporting schedule. Typically such schedules would represent a top summary, but supported by other schedules containing greater detail, perhaps other Gantt (bar) charts, or a critical path method (CPM) network. The particular display as shown in the figure provides a wealth of information on this assumed buy, (a $1 million construction project).

Five elements of data should be required from any schedule as are shown across the bottom of the chart: (1) a listing of all key tasks required to support the procurement; (2) a time phasing for each task; (3) a percentage or absolute dollar value for each task, which must sum to the total contract value; (4) a monthly percentage complete estimate for each specified task; and finally (5) the earned value for each task, which is simply item (3) times item (4) which equals item (5).

By tracking the performance of Column (5) against column (3), the project is essentially employing a simple form of "earned value" measurement. Earned value measurement will help to expose potential cost growth problems, early enough to be managed.

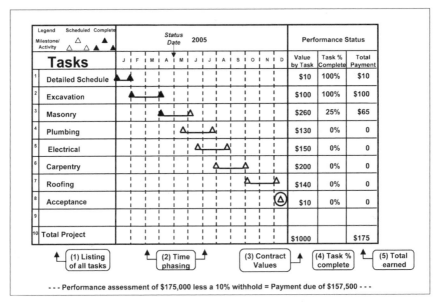

Figure 8.4 Always Require a Seller's Schedule...always

Always require a seller's schedule on all complex or major critical procurements . . . always! This is the case whether the procurements be of a cost type or fixed-price contract. On all cost type procurements a baseline schedule and monthly updates should be mandatory as a condition for all cost reimbursements. On fixed-price work a monthly schedule should also be required, exchanged in return for providing monthly progress payments.

The "Technical" Definition: Specifications & Drawings

The purpose of the technical specification is to define the features and functions that the purchased product will perform, the physical attributes, the limitations, design requirements, constraints, and the environment in which the product will be used. The purpose of the drawings is to provide the specific physical dimensions and materials for the procured item.

Without question, the technical definition in procurements constitutes the greatest risks for cost growth to any project which is buying a complex new product, something which does not exist. Remember, procurements create legal relationships between a buyer (representing the project) and a seller. It is critical that the buyer defines well what the seller is expected to do to satisfy the contract, and then not change the requirements once stated. Each change constitutes an opportunity for claims, or as it is commonly called "scope creep."

Specifications will exist within companies under various titles: Procurement Specifications; Product Specifications; Performance Specifications; Design Specifications; Detailed Specifications; Functional Specifications; Brand-name or Equal Specifications; Form fit or function Specifications; etc. Why all these titles and what do they really mean? You cannot tell from simply reading the titles. Generically specifications really fall into two broad categories as one authority states:

> *There are two types of technical specifications. The first type of specification provides virtually all of the technical information that a supplier needs to fabricate materials or equipment . . . The second type of specification provides performance criteria for the materials or equipment.* [4]

The first type is typically called a "Detail Design Specification", while the second type provides a "Performance Specification."

There is another important function which the specification should provide. It should define for both parties how one measures success, or completion of the procured effort:

> *Specification means a description of the technical requirements for a material, product, or service that includes the criteria for determining whether these requirements are met.* [5]

4. Charles L. Huston, *Management of Project Procurement*, (New York: McGraw-Hill, 1996) pages 138-139.
5. Thomas P. Cassidy, *Specifications and Standards Training Manual*, (Vienna, VA: National Contract Management Association, 1991) pages 10-11.

Likely there is nothing more important to successful project procurements than a complete and unchanging definition of the technical requirements. And keep in mind, this critical work is performed, not by the business or procurement community, but by the technical staff. Perhaps this is one of the many reasons why so many companies have gone to the use of project teams, or integrated product development teams, which are typically lead by technical personnel.

Procurement Competition

Competition in commercial business relations is good. We learned that notion a long time ago in our "Business 101" class. It is the American Way to foster free and full competition in business. Competition is, by definition:

> *Competition. Contest between two rivals. The effort of two or more parties, acting independently, to secure the business of a third party by the offer of the most favorable terms. It is the struggle between rivals for the same trade at the same time; the act of seeking or endeavoring to gain what another is endeavoring to gain at the same time. The term implies the idea of endeavoring by two or more to obtain the same object or result.* [6]

Like many things in life, we find that the concept of competition comes in various flavors and various shades.

At the one extreme, at the very highest level, is pure or "perfect" competition. This theoretical condition can exist only when there are multiple buyers and multiple sellers, each of approximately equal size and importance, the products produced by them are somewhat homogeneous, and firms can enter or leave the marketplace easily. Pure or perfect competition rarely exists in our world today.

At the other extreme from pure competition is competition at its

---

6. *Black's Law Dictionary*, 5th edition (St. Paul, Minnesota: West Publishing Company, 1979) page 257.

lowest form, the condition of "monopoly," which is essentially no competition at all. People must buy a given product because they have no other choice. The consumer, the ultimate user of the products ends up paying exorbitant prices for the items they use. The government often attempts to intercede in monopolies to protect the public.

While in theory there are numerous variations of competition possible, in the management of projects we can likely reduce them down to a minimal number. There are essentially three forms of competition we will encounter:

1. Full and open competition, anyone can bid on the job.

2. Limited competition among pre-qualified sellers, sometimes called two step procurements.

3. Competition among selected sources (Small Business-Disadvantaged Business Enterprise-Women Owned Business)

Full and open competition

Full and open procurement competition is likely the preferred approach by most governmental agencies and many procurement organizations. However, full and open procurement competition can often be a disaster and actually increase the risks on your project. The reason is simple: not every supplier is qualified to perform on your procurements. Some suppliers have earned a reputation of constantly bidding low, winning the new job, eliminating the competition, and then continuously demanding changes in order to financially recover from their low bids. Unfortunately this practice happens, but it does not result in good project performance.

Full and open competition can be employed on items which can be described adequately taking the form of sealed bids, as when an Invitation to Bid (IFB) form may be used. In these cases price is always the final determining factor. The IFP is most often used when the final desired product can be precisely described.

Other times when the deliverable end product must be tailored to meet the needs of the project, the buyer will employ a Request for Proposal (RFP), a robust document used to describe a complex new product which must be developed. Often, with RFP procurements the final price is only one of several factors to be considered in source selection.

Full and open procurement competition can sometimes work, but sometimes will lead to problems in the contractual relationship between the buyer and seller. One such case comes to mind but the names must be withheld. This major project was funded by the Federal Government. And because they were using Federal funds, the project manager felt that they had to allow all firms to bid. They held an open competition and allowed everyone to bid. Guess what happened: the low bidder was someone who had won two other jobs from this same agency, and both other projects were currently in a heated litigation! Likely they will end up with three litigations with a single unqualified seller!

Issue: How do you avoid encountering this same result? Answer: The project manager and project team must work closely with their legal counsel to find a legitimate way to disqualify the unqualified suppliers. It can be done, but it takes close cooperation between the project manager and legal counsel. Eliminate bad contractors before the solicitation is sent out.

Which essentially brings us to the next form of competition: the two-step competition.

Limited competition among pre-qualified sellers: two-step procurements

Likely the most desirable form of competition is achieved with what is sometimes called a two-step procurement process. Yes you conduct an aggressive competition among multiple sources, but all of the prospective sources will have one thing in common: each and every one of the sellers should have been pre-judged, determined by the buyer and the full project team to be qualified to do the job if so selected. The risks of a contract award going to an unqualified supplier have been reduced. Two-step procurements can work well with either sealed bidding (IFB) or request for proposal (RFP) type solicitations.

STEP ONE consists of soliciting information from prospective sellers sufficient to allow the project buyer and technical and business team to determine whether or not a prospective seller is qualified to perform the job, should they ultimately be the winner. The evaluation should be based on previously defined selection criteria which applies equally to all potential sources. Sometimes the project team may visit the prospective seller's plant, and or request formal presentations from all prospective suppliers.

Typically the buyer, or someone representing the procurement organization will lead this process, to make certain that all suppliers are treated equally. During step one some prospective sellers are accepted for the next phase, and some are dropped from the solicitation list. Many suppliers will object to being dropped from further competition, which is why the creation of reasonable and objective selection criteria is so important.

STEP TWO consists of a pricing contest among the final limited sources. If the process used sealed bidding (IFB) likely the final selection will be made solely on the lowest submitted price. If the process used a request for proposal (RFP) with several factors to be considered in addition to price, step two may result in the elimination of all but one or two final sources, who are then called in for final negotiations. Final negotiations will be conducted by the assigned project buyer, and all other project team members will play a subordinate role to the chief negotiator.

The two-step procurement competition is the preferred method of project acquisition by this author.

Competition among selected sources

As an example of this type competition, in the last chapter we discussed the $6.9 billion Navy Marine Corps Intranet (NMCI) contract which was awarded to the Electronic Data Systems (EDS) company. One of the key provisions of this huge contract was the requirement to award 35% of the contract value to companies classified as "small business" firms. EDS will obviously want to hold competitions for that portion of the contract they will procure, but many of their solicitations will be directed specifically at firms which meet the classification of "small business" companies.

Applying Competition . . . but with Intelligence

Let's not kid ourselves, competitions can sometimes be a farce. They are sometimes held merely to satisfy a particular law or regulation or company procedure. They are sometimes perfunctory at best. Yes, we should always strive for competition for the purpose of keeping our suppliers honest, but we should avoid blindly competing each and every purchase we make.

One of the most successful project management organizations in history has been the Lockheed Corporation's Skunk Works organization managed by the legendary Clarence "Kelly" Johnson and his deputy Ben Rich. This organization created their own project management rules and produced such incredible high-tech products as the U-2, SR-71, and the F-117 Stealth fighter.

How did this organization approach the subject of competition. Ben Rich in his autobiography summed it up nicely:

> *Another sound management practice that is gospel at the Skunk Works is to stick with reliable suppliers. Japanese auto manufacturers discovered long ago that periodically switching suppliers and selecting new ones on the basis of lowest bidders is a costly blunder. New suppliers frequently underbid just to gain a foothold in an industry, then meet their expenses by providing inferior parts and quality that can seriously impair overall performance standards . . . Japanese manufacturers usually form lasting relationships with proven suppliers . . . We believe that trouble-free relationships with old suppliers will ultimately keep the price of our products lower than if we were to periodically put their contracts up for the lowest bid.* [7]

---

7. Ben R, Rich and Leo Janos, *Skunk Works*, (Boston: Little, Brown and Company, 1994) page 333.

Yes we should always let our suppliers know that we will compete our procurements if we must to assure that we are getting a good deal. But constantly holding a competition on every buy simply to lower the prices may well be self-defeating. Price is but one issue in the delicate buyer-seller relationship. The trusts and experience we develop with our suppliers is also important.

The Request for Proposal (RFP)

The final document which will go to the prospective suppliers on major or minor complexity procurements is typically called the Request for Proposal (RFP). The RFP is a critical document which must be clear, complete, and allow for a competitive response from all sellers who are interested in competing for the award. While the precise format for the RFP will vary by company, it will normally contain at a minimum the following components:

- The cover letter, which will serve as the table of contents for the RFP, including a listing of all RFP attachments, the order of precedence for RFP documents, and the individual by name who will represent the project, typically the project's assigned buyer;

- The proposed Statement of Work (SOW);

- All Technical Specifications and supporting Drawings if necessary;

- Any Special Proposal Requirements like Bonding requirements, the names of key seller individuals and their bios, etc.;

- Contract Data Requirements Listing (CDRL) to be imposed in the resulting contract;

- Cost or Pricing format requirements, including a declaration of intended contract type;

- Proposal certifications, who will sign for seller, their organizational title;

- Requirements for special proposal sections, like quality, risk management, etc.;

- A statement as to whether alternate methods may be proposed by the seller;

- Proposal submittal requirements: time due, location, number copies, format, expiration date;

- A Model Contract which will be complete in all respects except for seller's name, date, price;

- Any other special requirements to be imposed on the seller.

In order to get intelligent responses from prospective sellers, the Request for Proposal (RFP) document must be understandable. Far too often the formal RFP document is simply a stack of papers, perhaps 5 inches high, representing the uncoordinated inputs from multiple functions. Often the official RFP cannot be understood by the prospective sellers, who must spend an inordinate amount of critical proposal time addressing: "what the hell do they mean by this statement!"

To assure a quality and understandable RFP, some companies will conduct what is often called a "bidability" review of the RFP document, before it is sent out to prospective sellers. The final draft RPF will be reviewed by seasoned staff who will take the RFP and determine whether or not they themselves could respond to it in its present form. This process has rejected many a RFP, and sent the solicitation team back to re-assemble a document which can be understood and responded to with viable proposal.

One last point on the RFP requirements: take care not to incorporate "dumb" and superfluous demands from sellers. For example requiring a project manager with a "PhD" may not be necessary to manage the proposed contract. A "Project Management Professional (PMP)" designation may be nice, and even preferred, but not absolutely necessary to manage the seller's work. Be careful what you describe as "musts" because each must will add costs to the seller's proposals to you.

Planning for the Evaluation of Seller Proposals

The time to think about who will evaluate the seller proposals when they are received, and what criteria will be used, is before the solicitation document (the request for proposal-RFP) is issued to prospective suppliers. Once the proposals are received everyone, virtually everyone, wants to be a part of the source selection process. It is prestigious to be on the proposal selection committee. And besides, they typically are served free cookies and coffee.

You do not need everyone to be a part of this process. But you should have a balanced multi-functional team representing different perspectives. At a minimum you would want on the evaluation committee: the buyer, someone representing the project manager, technical, quality, and perhaps other selected key functions.

Proposal evaluation committees are often sequestered much like a jury. And like a jury, they are told not to discuss the proposals until a final selection is made and announced by management. The role of the proposal evaluation committee is to "recommend" a final choice to management. Typically managements are sensitive about their role in the final selection process. The evaluation committee makes a recommendation, and management makes the final choice and approval.

A funny thing: most project master schedules typically allow one day to obtain management approval. Fact: management approvals rarely ever happen in one day. Approval comes when management next meets. Management sometimes meets weekly, or monthly, and approval will come at that time, not before. Make sure the schedule is realistic about how long it takes to gain management approval. Sometimes management doesn't like the recommended choice, and rejects the selection altogether, in which case the committee reconvenes to start the process over again.

One of the more compelling reasons to establish the evaluation criteria before the RFP is issued is because you may want to include the selection criteria and their weighted values in the solicitation document (RFP) itself. See Figure 8.5 which illustrates this approach. Many firms find that the inclusion of selection criteria in the RFP actually improves the quality of the responses. It helps the sellers when they know what their proposals will be judged by. However, you would never include the selection committee names in any RFP.

Sometimes, when the items to be procured are standard commodities, which are fully definable, the final selection process will be determined by price only. In such cases the proposals are merely opened, typically in public and often with the respondents present. The buyer will list the proposed values on a board, and the winner is immediately known by all.

Evaluation Committee:	• **Technical**
	• **Procurement**
	• **Quality**
	• **Project Manager**
Evaluation Criteria:	• **Technical.........35%**
	• **Management.....15%**
	• **Quality.............20%**
	• **Warranty..........10%**
	• **Price................20%**
	Total..............100%

- - - determined before the RFP is issued - - -

Figure 8.5 Evaluation of Seller Proposals

When the final source is to be made based on a number of weighted criteria, as is displayed in Figure 8.5, the selection committee will review the entire proposal except the cost volume. Proposed costs are a sensitive issue and typically restricted to only the buyer, and project manager, and senior management.

One final issue on evaluation: whether will you want to bring in an independent estimator to assess the RFP and provide an independent rough-order-of-magnitude cost value. On major proposals some companies have found it advisable to secure an independent estimates of proposals to provide assurances to management that the sellers proposed costs are reasonable. Independent cost estimates are a good procurement practice, unfortunately, rarely employed by most firms.

CHAPTER 9

Legal Aspects of Project Procurement Management

There is an important distinction which should be made between the work of a project which is assigned inside of one's own company for performance (the make work) versus sending work outside of one's company (the buy work). The difference between the two is the "legal" relationship the purchased work creates. With internal make work you can describe what you want done in broad general terms. The tolerance for error is quite generous, and self adjusting with internal budgets. After all, "we all work for the same company."

But with the purchased effort you had better know what you want, and be able to describe those requirements precisely to the seller, possibly to the seller's attorneys, and ultimately to the courts so that they can understand. In procurement relationships it sometimes turns out to be our attorneys versus their attorneys.

Project managers need not become attorneys, or even trained in the law. But they should have a broad general understanding of certain fundamental legal concepts, if for no other reason than to be able to discuss their requirements intelligently with legal counsel.

In this chapter we will cover some of the more important legal issues surrounding the procurement of project scope. However, keep in mind there is no substitute for securing competent legal counsel to advise and represent you.

An Overview of Contract Law

There is perhaps no legal subject more relevant to procurement management than that of contract law, simply because every procurement made represents a contract. Numerous definitions of a contract are available, but many provide little understanding of what is involved in forming a contract. The project management team should have an understanding of when they have met the tests of forming a contract, and when they have not.

One source defines a contract as:

An agreement between two or more persons which creates an obligation to do or not to do a particular thing. Its essentials are competent parties, subject matter, a legal consideration, mutuality of agreement, and mutuality of obligation. [1]

This is likely one of the better legal definitions of a contract. However, if it is further broken down into the basic elements of a contract it may be easier for some to assimilate.

A contract must meet the following ten tests:

1. A contract is an agreement between two or more parties;

2. The parties must have legal capacity to contract, mental capacity, and age capacity;

3. The parties must promise to do, or not to do, a particular thing;

4. There must be an offer communicated from one side;

5. There must be an unconditional acceptance of that offer by the other side.

6. Note: A modification of an offer, a partial acceptance only, will constitute a rejection of the original offer, and form a new offer. The process of forming a contract does not take place until there is an offer given and unconditional acceptance of that offer;

---

1. *Black's Law Dictionary*, (St. Paul, Minnesota: West Publishing Company).

7.   There must be mutual assent by all parties, the parties must agree on the same thing;

8.   The contract, in fact all contracts, must be supported by "consideration," providing something of value for the promise, but not necessarily something of equal value;

9.   The contract must be for a legal purpose, illegal purpose contracts are unenforceable;

10.   The agreement must be in a form as required by law. Some contracts must be in writing, typically all real estate transactions, time periods exceeding a certain duration, specific dollar amounts, etc.

Why is having a knowledge of basic contract law important? Because the project team may on occasion inadvertently enter into a contractual relationship . . . without knowing it. Or conversely, a project may think they have executed a contract, when in fact they have not met all the necessary requirements to form a contract, as perhaps when their agreement may lack consideration.

The Project Management Institute (PMI) defines a contract in a narrow way, representing simply a sale between a buyer and seller. It is a proper definition of a contract, but simply a narrow one. In the management of projects, contracts are often needed for purposes other than sales.

The PMI definition of a contract is:

A contract is a mutually binding agreement that obligates the seller to provide the specified product and obligates the buyer to pay for it. [2]

Many projects exist in an environment of teaming arrangements,

---

2.   *A Guide to the Project Management Body of Knowledge (PMBOK Guide)*, (Newtown Square, Pennsylvania: Project Management Institute, 2000) page 199.

joint ventures and partnerships where their legal obligation is to perform something, not simply to sell something. Thus in most instances
the project will use the broader definition of a contract.

An Overview of Agency Law

Agency law is important in the management of projects simply
because most (perhaps all) of the work performed on projects will be
done by someone other than the project manager. Agency law covers
the relationship between two persons whereby one person is authorized to act for and on behalf of the other person.

When the project manager authorizes an internal budget, or initi-
ates a purchase requisition leading to purchased scope, the law of
agency comes into play. The individual authorized to act for another
is called the agent, and the one for whom the agent acts is called the
principal. In the management of projects, the principal would typically be the project manager.

But agency law and the authority conveyed from principal to
agents come in shades, and this is where it can get interesting.

"Express" Authority given to an Agent

The highest form of authority is that which is conveyed "expressly." The principal specifically conveys to the agent authority to act for
them by either spoken or written authority.

The delegation of authority to buy things on behalf of a company
would be express authority. Most project managers lack such procurement authority. Rather, authority to buy on behalf of most companies
is limited to procurement professionals, typically called buyers, who
are assigned to support a given project.

In government transactions, only those individuals with the job
title of "contracting officer" may authorize new work or purchases for
the government, and these individuals have been given express authority to act.

"Implied" Authority given to an Agent

The relationship between two individuals can sometimes confer delegations to act as agent, but without expressly authorizing all such acts in writing or with words.

Whenever a company appoints someone to function as a project manager, and the executive in charge of the organization issues a written announcement to that effect, the announcement would be considered "express" authority. But beyond that express authority would be numerous "implied" authorities delegated to the project manager. For example, it would be assumed by all that the project manager can define the work to be done, issue schedules, issue budgets, call status meetings, etc. These latter duties would be implied authorities which go with the job of being project manager.

"Apparent" Authority given to an Agent

This last area of agency law, "apparent" authority, is one which can be ambiguous, delicate, and cause problems in the management of projects.

Sometimes individuals can assume authority to act as agent for a principal by virtue of circumstances. They can have "apparent" authority not as a result of any specific delegation, but by virtue of the principal's silence on the subject. If the circumstances are such that a reasonable person could conclude that one has authority, and no one says otherwise, apparent authority to act may come into play. Sometimes the organizational position one holds will give one apparent authority.

Assume that a given project is being managed by a person with the title of project manager, a mid-management company position. This project has a major complex procurement to develop something new for it. The company's Vice President of Engineering visits the supplier to get a status update and expresses concern about the direction the supplier has taken. The Engineering VP casually suggests a different technical approach. What we have here is likely a constructive claim for a re-direction by someone who has "apparent" authority to act for the project. Interestingly, the project manager and the buyer may be the last to know about this change of direction.

The Uniform Commercial Code (UCC)

Up to the creation of the Uniform Commercial Code (UCC) starting in 1951, each state had its own variation of the law as it pertained to commercial transactions. With Pennsylvania leading the way in 1953, all states plus the District of Columbia and the Virgin Islands have now adopted the UCC as their commercial law. Because the state of Louisiana is based on civil law, versus common law, this state has only partially adopted the UCC.

The UCC is still evolving, with periodic revisions and additions to the original eleven articles of the UCC. All commercial procurements are subject to the UCC with the exception of government contracts which are subject to the Federal Acquisition Regulation (FAR). While the code covers a variety of subjects, Article 2 on Sales is particularly applicable. It might be useful if we touch on some of the sections which mandate how we are to manage project procurements.

UCC Article 2-309 Notice of Termination

In all commercial transactions if one party wants to terminate their relationship proper notification to that effect must be communicated to the other party. Silence alone will not terminate an agreement. One exception might be where an agreed to event should it occur would terminate the agreement, which would take the place of notification. Giving notice is an important part of commercial law.

UCC Article 2-312 Warranty of Title

In a contract for the sale of goods, there is a warranty placed on the seller to the effect that the seller conveys a valid title which can be transferred to the buyer, and that the goods are free from liens or encumbrances.

UCC Article 2-313 Express Warranty

Express warranties on the seller are created when a seller makes a statement of fact or promise about the product being sold. A description of the goods sold, or a sample of the product would also constitute an express warranty.

UCC Article 2-314 Implied Warranty

The implied warranty merely asserts that goods sold will serve the purpose for which they are intended. Note: an express warranty is superior to an implied warranty.

UCC Article 2-513 Buyer's Right to Inspect Goods

The buyer of an item has the absolute right to inspect goods prior to paying the seller for the goods. But with these rights also come duties on the buyer.

The inspection of goods by the buyer must take place within a reasonable time after delivery, or an inspection will be assumed to have taken place. Inspection of goods must be consistent with what was originally purchased, i.e., new more stringent requirements cannot be added to the items being bought. And finally, if the goods on inspection are not acceptable to the buyer, a notification to that effect must be communicated to the seller.

UCC 2-718 Liquidation or Limitation of Damages

This article covers damages caused by a breach of contract by either side, and a settlement of the damages sustained based on an agreed to formula specified in the contract. The UCC states:

Damages for breach by either party may be liquidated in the agreement but only at an amount which is reasonable in the light of the anticipated or actual harm caused by the breach . . . A term fixing unreasonably large liquidated damages is void as a penalty.

In order to understand the meaning of this UCC language we need to have an understanding of two of the more common types of damages: Compensatory Damages and Punitive Damages.

Compensatory Damages (also called actual damages) are those awarded to someone to cover the actual loss sustained. These damages are intended to make the person whole again, but not to enrich. Example, if someone were hit by a car and sustained $10,000 in hospital bills, the courts might award the injured party $10,000 in compensatory damages.

If however, the driver had a past driving record of reckless behavior, perhaps driving while intoxicated or on drugs, the courts might also award the injured party additional damages called punitive (or exemplary), to punish the wrongdoer.

Point in procurement management: Any damages incorporated into a contract under the category of liquidated damages must be construed by the courts to be compensatory. If the courts find them excessive or punitive, they may well be denied altogether.

Federal Acquisition Regulations (FAR) System

All projects which are funded by the United States Government are subject to the rules and regulations of a formal procurement process called the Federal Acquisition Regulations (FAR). The FAR was created to codify uniform policies and procedures for the acquisition of supplies and services for the Federal Government.

In addition to the FAR, selected other branches of the Federal Government have their respective extensions to the FAR. For example, the Department of Defense has a FAR Supplement commonly called the Defense Federal Acquisition Regulation Supplement, or simply the DFARS. In instances of conflict, the FAR rules would prevail.

The FAR is a robust document containing thousands of pages of acquisition rules for federal agencies to follow. It is divided into eight major sections called "Subchapters" items A through H. In addition these eight subchapters are further broken into some fifty-three (53) "Parts."

To illustrate the relevance of the FAR to project procurements, selected Parts will be described as they relate to the materials covered in this book.

FAR Subchapter B-Competition and Acquisition Planning
Part 6-Competition Requirements

When the United States Congress enacted a new law in 1984 called the Competition in Contracting Act, (CICA), the FAR was modified to comply with the provisions of the CICA. This law called for full and open competition for all government acquisitions, to the maximum extent practical. It called for federal agencies to appoint a "competition advocate" to promote full and open competition.

FAR Subchapter C- Contracting Methods and Contract
Part 16-Types of Contracts

Chapter 6 of this book described the various types of contracts in use today. Much of this material was obtained from Part 16 of the FAR. Reason: there is likely no better description of contract types available anywhere than that contained in the FAR.

FAR Subchapter D-Socioeconomic Programs
Part 19-Small Business Programs

The huge EDS NMCI contract mentioned earlier in this book which contained a provision for 35% of the contract value to be awarded to firms which qualify as "small businesses" was specifically related to the requirements specified in FAR Part 19.

FAR Subchapter E-General Contracting Requirements
Part 32-Contract Financing

One of the most powerful tools available to a project manager in the administration of fixed price type procurements is the requirement to oversee the supplier's performance by requiring a monthly submittal of their internal working schedules. This issue will be covered later in the chapter covering Contract Administration. Particularly important to this discussion will be the subject of Performance Based Payments, authorized in FAR 32.10, enacted into the FAR in October 1995.

FAR Subchapter G-Contract Management
Part 49-Termination of Contracts

Companies always have the right to terminate a contract for a "default" in performance, a form of breach of contract. In addition the Federal Government incorporates a provision allowing it to terminate a contract for their own "convenience." This is a good provision to incorporate into any procurement, which gives the project manager latitude in the management of buy items.

Bonding the Sellers: "Guarantor" versus "Surety" Obligations

There is an important legal distinction between the terms "guarantor" and "surety" although the two are sometimes used as if they were interchangeable. These are not interchangeable terms. While both a guarantor and a surety may ultimately be responsible for the contractual performance of another person, called the principal, the guarantor has a "secondary" liability, whereas the surety has a "primary" liability along with the principal. This subtle difference has great significance particularly in the enforcement of a contractual obligation.

In the event of a default of the contract by a principal, the injured party under a guarantor relationship must make every attempt to first enforce performance on the principal, and only after that fails, may go after the guarantor for performance. By comparison, under a surety arrangement, the injured party can go directly after the surety for contract performance, since the surety is on an equal standing with the principal.

The distinction of having a secondary versus primary contract liability is extremely important in the speedy completion of a project. It takes time to sequence the efforts of principal then the guarantor in order to complete a project. For this reason, most governmental requirements for seller bonding require that the obligation be one of a surety, over the guarantor.

Types of Seller Bonds in use

In projects for construction work, particularly with government funding, federal, state, or local, it is commonplace for the buyer to require bonding from the performing seller, the constructor. You rarely see bonding used in purely private construction where the emphasis is more on seller reputation and long-term relationships rather than legal enforcement. And the use of seller bonding does add costs to any project, which many in the private sector question the value being added.

There are essentially three types of bonding in use: bid bonds, payment bonds, and performance or completion bonds.

Bid Bonds

The purpose of the bid bonds is to guarantee the validity of the lowest bid, so that the project buyer can rely on the lowest bid. In the event that the low bid is accepted, but the bidder refuses to accept the contract award, the bonding company is liable for any difference between the lowest bid amount and the next lowest bid amount.

Payment Bonds: labor, materials, subcontractors

These types of bonds protect the unpaid laborers, trades-people, suppliers, and subcontractors for the work they have performed on projects. It guarantees them payment, in the event that the seller fails to make payment.

Completion (Performance) Bonds

When one thinks of bonding agreements as used in construction projects, one typically thinks of guarantees of completion of the project. These obligations go by two titles, completion or performance bonds. They are defined as follows:

> *Completion Bond. A form of surety or guaranty agreement which contains the promise of a third party, usually a bonding company, to complete or pay for the cost of completion of a construction contract if the construction contractor defaults.* [3]

> *Performance Bond. Type of contract bond which protects against loss due to the inability or refusal of a contractor to perform his contract. Such are normally required on public construction projects.* [4]

The bonding company, an insurance company, bank, or other lending institution typically provide such seller bonding.

Question: why is it that seller/constructor bonding is used on government funded construction projects, but rarely ever used in privately financed projects? Could it be the cost of the bonding? Quite possibly. More likely, it is the fact that the owners in the private sector do not see the benefit to be gained from requiring bonds from the seller/constructors. In the event that a constructor fails to complete a job, the surety is then obligated to find another constructor who will complete the project. Unfortunately, sometimes the replacement contractor is worse at performing than the one who walked away from the original job. Supplier claims and disputes are common in this environment.

A crusty old constructor manager in the commercial sector once remarked to the author: *"There is no substitute for a well qualified, reputable, and responsible seller, and all the bonds in the world will not make a difference."*

---

3. *Black's Law Dictionary*, (St. Paul, Minnesota: West Publishing Company).
4. *Black's Law Dictionary*, (St. Paul, Minnesota: West Publishing Company).

Special Contractual Terms

There are a number of critical issues which come into play between buyer and seller, of which the project manager and team are usually never aware. They are provisions quietly inserted into procurements by the buying professionals assigned to support the project. Nevertheless, these terms and conditions, (T & Cs), are an important part of project procurements.

We need to review a small sampling of the more important T & Cs as used in procurements.

Special Term: "Time is of the Essence"

Most project performance is time sensitive. The project must be completed by a certain date. When any project has procured components or services which are critical for its completion, and the project is dependent on the performance of a seller to complete the project, many firms rely on a "time is of the essence" clause to be inserted into the contract to emphasize that time is critical.

When the term "time is of the essence" is inserted into a contract, performance by all parties as scheduled is strictly required. If the seller is to do something by a certain date, or if both buyer and seller have specific dates to meet, and they fail to meet them, their failure to perform precisely on time constitutes <u>a breach of contract</u>.

In order for time to be critical in a contract, the contract must incorporate the phrase "time is of the essence" in this contract. If this phrase is not incorporated, time is felt to be important, but not fatal to performance on the contract.

Suggestion: take care in inserting this provision in any contract. Make sure that the scheduled dates are truly critical before using it. Ask yourself: do I really want to terminate a contract if the seller is one day late in meeting a scheduled delivery? Think about it: most scheduled dates are approximate, and have some plus or minus tolerances. This is a heavy contract provision to insert into most contracts. Use it with care.

Special Term: "Liquidated Damages"

A liquidated damages provision can also provide incentives on a seller to deliver their components on time. This provision may be inserted into a contract which specifies damages on the seller at certain specified values for each day they fail to deliver on time, say, $100.00 per day for every day they are late.

Remember the rule as stated in UCC article 2-718: with liquidated damages the damages can only be compensatory, not punitive. They must have some basis to be enforced by the courts. Often such damages are based on the reasonable estimated costs of the delay. Example: if a failure of a seller to provide a construction crane on a specified date causes monetary damages with a work crew, the values can be estimated and incorporated into the contract. A sheet of paper showing the estimated calculations for losses, initialed by buyer and seller, would be good proof that the damages are compensatory.

Special Term: "Force Majeure"

The term "force majeure" means literally a greater force. This term is frequently inserted in contracts to prevent incurring damages caused by circumstances beyond the control of a buyer or a seller. The condition should apply to both parties. It does not excuse performance outright, but rather gives an excusable time delay in performance.

The precise language as to what acts may provide an excusable time delay will vary from company to company, and is typically negotiable between the parties. Typically events which are covered would be "Acts of God", war, riots, natural disasters, and other events beyond the control of the obligated party.

Sometimes such terms allow delays for the failure of performance by a next lower tier supplier. However, since the management of the next lower tier supplier is within the reach of the seller, delays caused by suppliers sometimes causes problems with interpretation.

Special Term: Who has authority to act on the contract

Typically when the procurement contract contains a statement of work the SOW will define who is authorized to represent the buyer. Often such language will indicate that the buyer (by name) will handle all contractual matters, and the project manager (by name) is authorized to handle all technical matters. If the procurement is silent in the matter, a term may be inserted specifying who is responsible for what on the contract.

Special Term: Termination of Contract for Convenience

Under common law one party to a contract may terminate the contract upon default of performance by the other party. However, in commercial relationships today this may not be sufficient to protect the buyer.

It is becoming somewhat commonplace to also allow a buyer to terminate their relationship based on the "convenience of the buyer." This is a special provision negotiable by both parties. In the event the buyer elects to terminate a relationship early for its own convenience, the seller would be entitled to compensatory damages sufficient to recover all their costs, to make them whole again.

Special Term: Warranty

Under UCC articles 2-312, 2-313, 2-314 the subject of seller warranties is covered. Many buyers have found it advisable to specifically call out the type of warranty required by the seller.

One item which is critical to be specified in this term is the time period covered by a seller's warranty. Many a loss has been incurred by a buyer when seller components fail, but fail only after the warranty coverage has expired. Include an adequate time period for warranty coverage, sufficient to minimize risks.

Special Term: Right to Inspect Goods

The right of the buyer to inspect the purchased goods prior to making payment is provided under UCC article 2-513 described earlier. One important item to be specified is where the inspection will take place, at the buyer's or seller's location. Assume that the buyer and seller are located hundreds of miles apart, where will the inspection physically take place?

Sometimes these provisions will call for a preliminary inspection to take place at the seller's site, then a final inspection and acceptance at the buyer's site.

This is an important provision to include in the contract.

Special Term: Back-charges

What happens if the seller's goods are found on arrival and inspection to be defective? Does the buyer have to then re-pack the goods, ship them back to the seller for their repair, to be shipped back to the buyer. We are talking about significant time delays.

Sometimes the buyer will reserve the right to make the necessary repairs to the defective parts and charge the repair costs back to the seller. In order to allow for the buyer to make necessary repairs and the changes to be allocated back to the seller, firms must insert this provision giving them authority to do so.

Special Term: Bonding and Insurance

If the buyer requires the seller to provide bonds, such as performance bonds, and possibly other insurance provisions protecting the seller against third party lawsuits, a special term to that effect must be included in the contract.

Special Term: Progress Payments

Unless otherwise stated, payments to a seller are obligated only after the goods or services have been delivered, and verification made as to their adequacy, inspection. If payments are to be made periodically prior to final delivery, such provisions must be authorized in the agreement.

Payments made on a seller's progress, verified progress, are a good idea. The best way to verify progress is to require an updated schedule from the supplier, to support their request for payment.

Whether the progress payments will cover all costs, or all costs less a withhold (retention) of some value must also be covered in this provision. Withholds of payments typically run in the range of 5% to 10% to 20% of the amount of costs incurred by the seller.

Special Term: "Alternate Dispute Resolution (ADR)"

It is becoming commonplace, and a good practice, to insert into contracts a provision which will allow or sometimes mandate the process of Alternate Dispute Resolution (ADR) to settle disagreements without the pain and expense of litigation. The two most common forms of ADR are Mediation and Arbitration.

Mediation

Mediation is a kind of facilitated negotiation, but with use of an inter-mediator to bring both sides together to a settlement. The role of the mediator is to find a middle-ground which both sides will accept as reasonable.

Arbitration

Arbitration is the more formal of the two common ADR processes, and is in effect a simplified form of a mini-trial. A professional arbitrator (or panel of arbitrators) is hired, who will preside as a type of judge and jury However, the process is not subject to the more confining formal rules of common law evidence, the parties do not go through pre-trial discovery, and the final rulings are not necessarily made public. Findings in arbitration rulings can be by the terms of the agreement either binding, or consensual on the parties.

Arbitration agreements are gaining in popularity. To date, thirty-five states have adopted the Uniform Arbitration Act (UAA) into law. Arbitration has for years been a popular alternative to litigation in the construction, labor, and securities industries.

While arbitration is typically less costly than litigation, it is nevertheless a costly process where both sides must prepare to adequately present data favorable to their position.

■   ■   ■

These are but a small sampling of the special contractual terms which may be included in a contract, to protect the interests of both buyer and seller.

To repeat what was said earlier, this chapter provides simply a broad overview of some of the legal issues dealing with procurement management and is intended to enlighten the project team, but not to be a substitute for employing competent legal counsel. Topics which might be encountered by the team were only touched on lightly. Get competent legal support.

CHAPTER 10

Conduct Procurements (1 of 2)

(PMBOK ® - Third Edition 2004: 12.3 Request Seller Proposals)

The third of the six procurement processes specified by The Project Management Institute (PMI) *A Guide to the Project Management Body ok Knowledge (PMBOK Guide)* 2000 Edition is called solicitation. Its primary purpose is to obtain viable responses from prospective sellers, sufficient to satisfy the project's listing of buy work, the components, subsystems, services, support, purchased labor, whatever, which will be supplied from other companies.

This process starts with a definition of what is to be purchased, taking the form of an invitation or request which is sent by the assigned project's buyer to prospective sellers. The assigned project buyer will take an active role in this process in order to give all qualified sellers an opportunity to respond to the solicitations.

This chapter will discuss that segment of project procurements which occurs after the invitations or requests have been sent to sellers, but prior to the receipt of their responses. It is called the solicitation process. Its primary objective is to get viable responses from qualified sellers so as to satisfy the requirements of purchased work for the project. Another secondary objective of this process is to make sure that all sellers are treated fairly so that no one gains an unfair advantage over others. The solicitation process has been defined as follows

Solicitation is a generic term that includes invitation for bids, requests for proposals, requests for quotations, and any other method of soliciting prices from vendors and subcontractors. Procedures differ for these different methods. [1]

---

1. Elinor Sue Coates, CPCM, *The Subcontract Management Manual*, (San Francisco: Coates & Company, 1992) pages 59-60.

Increasingly, internet solicitations are on the rise, and formal advertising is likely on the decline. But the major complex procurements are still subject to formal Requests for Proposals (RFP) sent to prospective sellers recommended by experts on the subject: technical, supply management, project managers, and sometimes executive management will have suggestions.

Qualified Seller Lists (supplier database)

Most mature companies which have had purchasing (supply-chain) operations for any length of time have found it advisable to create a data base of approved suppliers for quick reference and use byheir buyers. Some of these databases are quite sophisticated and contain a rating system reflecting the past performance of their suppliers. Such things as on-time deliveries, quality of parts, cooperation, flexibility, responsiveness, etc., have been quantified and incorporated into these files.

One of the problems with supplier data bases is that they sometimes have become too large to be useful. Buyers need a few qualified sources, not hundreds of sources. The maintenance and updates of these supplier databases can be expensive. Sometimes a few "recommended" sources from the technical people who are writing the procurement specifications will be sufficient to provide for a reasonable competition. Also, many procurement organizations are organized along commodity lines, allowing buyers to become specialists with certain types of buys.

One problem procurement organizations have experienced in attempting to reduce the size of these databases is that word gets out that supplier "X" has been dropped from the approved supplier listing. Not only do these suppliers object themselves, but often they get their local elected representatives to object on their behalf. It's not easy to explain to an elected representative why one of their constituent companies was dropped from the approved list, particularly when your company may work on other government funded contracts.

Bidder Conferences (pre-bid conferences)

In many industries companies have found it a useful practice to hold what is called a bidder's conference on major procurements to allow for questions to be asked from prospective respondents. These conferences are to reinforce the requirements specified in the Request for Proposal (RFP). If the RFP were always a perfect document, containing everything needed to respond to the request, then bidder's conferences world never be needed. Since most RFPs are compiled in a rather hasty and haphazard manner, these meetings are often a good idea.

One of the ground rules on a bidder's conference is that every prospective bidder be kept on equal footing. It is a controlled meeting, typically with the project buyer acting as chairperson, supported by the project manager and the chief technical person. Questions from potential respondents are solicited in advance of the meeting so intelligent answers can be presented to all present. Sometimes additional questions may be allowed from the potential sellers in attendance, but sometimes not.

The practice of holding a pre-bid conference is a good one on major procurements. Sometimes the questions from prospective sellers are so good, that in some cases the buyer may in fact choose to modify the official RFP to incorporate additional or clarifying materials.

Sole Sourcing versus Single Sourcing

Sometimes it is not possible to solicit proposals from more than one source. Reason: there is only one source for a given product. This is called a "sole source" procurement. It is defined as:

Sole-source negotiation occurs when there is only one seller that can provide the needed product or service. Thus, a sole-source seller has a monopoly in its market and tremendous leverage with most buyers. [2]

---

2. Gregory A. Garrett, *World-Class Contracting*, (Arlington, Virginia: ESI International, 1997) page 57.

Other times there may be multiple suppliers who can provide a given product or service, but for reasons which should always be documented, a business decision is made to only go to one supplier to provide the product. This practice is called "single sourcing" and is defined as:

Single sourcing is the deliberate choice for one supplier. [3]

You find single sourcing quite frequently in commercial business-es where the reputation of the supplier and the long-term relationship which may exist between buyer and seller is paramount in the selection decision. With government funded projects the rationale for deliber-ately going to a single source must be documented properly in the procurement file.

Competition: Reasons to Not Hold, to Waive a Competition

Competition is good. We should compete all procurements to the greatest extent possible. Not necessarily. There can be situations where it is ill advised to hold a procurement competition.

Even when full and open competition was mandated by Congress after they passed the Competition In Contracting Act (CICA) of 1984, the act itself recognized seven legitimate reasons to waive the require-ment for competition and go directly to negotiated buys. They are:

1. *There is only one source available and no other product or service will fulfill the requirement.*

2. *Unusual and compelling urgency requires the number of sources to be limited; however, as many sources as possible must be solicited.*

3. *A particular award must be made to maintain a critical facility*

---

3. Arjan J. van Weele, *Purchasing and Supply Chain Management*, (United Kingdom: Thompson Learning, 2002) page 161.

or source for industrial mobilization or national emergency.

4. *A particular source is required by treaty or agreement with a foreign government.*

5. *A particular source or method is required by statute.*

6. *National security requires that sources be limited in cases where disclosure of needs would compromise security.*

7. *Head of the agency certifies to Congress that noncompetitive procedures are determined to be necessary in the public interest.* [4]

The role of the assigned buyer will be to make sure that any requests to waive competition are legitimate, and that they are adequately documented for the procurement file. In most cases, the waiving of competition will likely constitute a deviation from the established purchasing policies which usually will require full competition.

This is an area where there will often be professional differences of approach between the technical people (the engineers and scientists) and the procurement people (buyers). The technical community will want/demand that orders be placed immediately, "the heck with these silly rules." The professional buyers are assigned to projects to support them, but they must insist that the official procurement rules are followed. This is precisely why most project managers do not have "procurement authority."

Responding to Seller's Questions During Solicitation

Great care must be taken in responding to questions from prospective sellers wanting a clarification of language, or perhaps more technical

---

4. Louis A. Kratz and Jacques S. Gansler, "Effective Competition During Weapon System Acquisition", *Contract Management Magazine*, (National Contract Management Association, McLean, VA: 1985, 1-1).

detail. The reason: sellers who ask for and get more information are placed at a competitive advantage over those who have not raised the question and received either an official or informal response.

Some companies allow for questions from prospective sellers to be addressed to anyone in the buyer's company. However, most do not. In fact, it is a practice which should be carefully controlled. Try to manage these seller questions if possible. Typically it is not the project's buyer or project manager who will get such questions, but rather the technical person who wrote procurement specification. Make every attempt to control questions and funnel them through the project's buyer.

A fair way to handle such questions is to require that they be sent to the buyer, who will obtain an "official" response, and then send both the question and response to <u>all</u> prospective sellers who have expressed an interest in the procurement. Everyone must remain on equal footing in the solicitation process.

■   ■   ■

The solicitation process will end with the receipt of proposals from prospective sellers. If the final selection is to be made solely on price, the bids are opened, typically with the public present, and the winner announced. If the award is to be made based on several factors which must be evaluated by a select committee, then we enter the next procurement process: source selection.

CHAPTER 11

Conduct Procurements (2 of 2)

This critical process in procurement management covers that effort which takes the responses from sellers, proposals, makes an evaluation, and then determines which ones should be awarded the contract. Management then decides whether or not they agree with the recommendations.

Ethics in Procurement

People who work on projects are overwhelmingly honest. But some are not. And it is those few that make it necessary for companies to put strict purchasing procedures in place that reduce the chances of misbehaving. Project procurements present a unique opportunity for people to improperly enrich themselves at the expense of their companies if they are so inclined. Kick-backs, personal gifts, graft, are all possible with procurements, which do not exist with internal project budgeting.

Project managers rarely have delegated procurement authority, and this is deliberate. Rather projects are assigned someone who has such authority typically called a buyer or purchasing agent. Within the government, project managers also do not have authority to contract, rather that distinction is given to one with the job title of "contracting officer."

Typically anyone who has such delegated procurement authority must go through an annual certification stating that they do not have a financial interest in, or relatives who work for suppliers, or must specify such examples with each yearly certification. False statements on certification forms could be cause for a dismissal of one's procurement job. But interestingly other members of the project team do not have to make such certifications, and yet they also have considerable opportunities to improperly influence a final source selection, if they are so inclined.

In addition to outright bribes, larceny can happen in a number of more subtle ways. If a seller pays to have someone's house painted, pays for a vacation, hires someone's relative, gives tickets to concerts, etc., all these actions can have a tendency to influence the outcome of a source selection. The paramount rule in source selection: all sellers must be kept on equal footing during this process.

With project procurements it isn't always clear black or white issues that gets us in trouble. There are shades of gray which also need to be avoided. "Perception" of what one does is sometimes as important as the specific deeds themselves. For example, if you are the chief technical person, or project manager, or buyer, you need to take great care in not doing things with or for prospective sellers which could give the wrong impression. Having daily lunches with a prospective seller, attending ball games, social events, all can give the impression of being unduly influenced by a supplier, even if business deals are never discussed.

A case in point. In the fall of 2002, the United States Department of Labor sued the AFL-CIO executive council member and plumbers' union President Martin Maddaloni for misusing union pension funds to buy the Weston Diplomat Hotel & Spa in Hollywood, Florida. The Government's contention: there was no feasibility study, no budget, and no architectural plans to support the purchase of the hotel. But there was another issue which didn't look good to the public:

"Maddaloni has had to pay back the cost of a trip he and his wife took to Italy—paid for in part by a contractor with close union ties—to pick out marble for the hotel." [1]

---

1. *Business Week*, "Nice Place for a Speech Anyway," March 10, 2003, page 12.

Now it may well be that the union president and his wife were uniquely qualified to select marble for the hotel. That is not the issue. The overriding issue is that what they did looked improper, and thus their expense paid trip to Italy should have been avoided. In retrospect, they should have paid their own way to Italy, since there was a potential conflict of issue present.

Bottom line: buy your own lunches, pay for your own football tickets, save up for your own trip to Italy, etc. It is just not worth the risk of sending out the wrong impression.

Price Analysis, Cost Analysis, and Independent Cost Estimates

Many companies before they make an important new contract award find it advisable to perform some type of analysis of the costs of the procurement by a special group of individuals experienced in such work. These people are a part of what is commonly called a price and cost analysis group. Their job is to determine whether or not the seller's proposed costs are reasonable.

Price-Cost Analysis. The objective of analyzing prices and costs is to determine whether the price paid is a reasonable one in terms of the market, the industry, and the end use of the material bought. In addition, price analysis is a means of isolating and possibly eliminating items of unnecessary cost. [2]

Two types of such analysis can take place depending on whether the solicitation is for a cost type (including time and materials arrangements) or a fixed price type contract. On a major award of particular importance, management may also request an independent estimate of the proposed costs by a professional estimator, either on the company staff or from an outside consultant who specializes in preparing such estimates. The construction industry often employs outside consultants to prepare an independent estimate on major new jobs.

---

2. George W. Aljian, Paul V. Ferrell, *Aljian's Purchasing Handbook*, Fourth Edition, (New York: McGraw-Hill Book Company, 1982) page 11-16.

Price Analysis

This type of analysis, because detailed cost breakdowns are not available on fixed price work, will layout each of the seller's proposals and compare each response at the bottom-line price. However, sometimes the solicitation instructions can be structured so as to get some more detailed insight into what is being proposed, even on fixed price work.

For example, assume that the solicitation is for a new product which must be designed, built, tested, etc. Each of these individual work segments can be broken into separate contract line items in the solicitation. Line item #1-Design, line item #2-Manufacture, line item #3-Testing, etc. In the solicitation package the Request for Proposal (RFP) could ask for a price breakout of each line item being proposed, which will sum up to a total price. Price values would include the seller's proposed profit.

By requesting a separate breakdown price for each contract line item, some minimal but effective price analysis can be performed. Also, sometimes the project may solicit effort from sellers which may have questionable value to the project, but could add significant costs to a procurement. By requesting a separate breakout of such costs, for example, special testing, warranty coverage, special handling, the project team can make an intelligent assessment as to whether or not these items add sufficient value to the seller's price, or whether they can be deleted to save money.

This type of gross price analysis does give management some comfort in knowing that prospective sellers actually know what is involved in the work being proposed.

Cost Analysis

A cost analysis consists of a detailed look and comparison at each of the items of costs being proposed by the sellers. This type of analysis is used to assess the proposed costs on both cost reimbursable, and time and material type contracts. Detailed cost breakouts are rarely ever appropriate or available on fixed price or lump sum work.

This type of cost analysis goes into great detail. Proposed labor rates are analyzed by job classification. Indirect rates are assessed, usually by labor pools, for example, engineering, manufacturing, material, etc. The General & Administrative costs are reflected as a percentage of total costs through overheads. All other direct costs such as travel, materials, subcontracts, computers, etc., are all detailed in the respondent's cost proposal.

The cost analyst will provide a summary of cost elements laid out from each of the respondents typically isolating areas of concern or issues needing further clarification. These summaries will be used in negotiation with the top two or three respondents to settle on a final selected best choice. Often the cost analyst will become a critical person in such cost negotiations.

Cost analysis will try to verify the accuracy of the cost data, whether or not it is complete, current, and reasonable. Such issues as the assumed attrition, scrappage rates, learning improvements, will all be assessed by the cost analyst. If cost items which are typically charged into the seller's overhead pools are being charged directly to the project, like special insurance, special travel, computers, mobilization costs, they must be analyzed by the analyst and are issues for negotiation.

Independent Cost Estimates

Senior management will sometimes demand further assurances that the seller's proposed cost values are reasonable. In order to get such reassurances on major awards it is common to have an independent cost estimate prepared by persons experienced in cost estimating similar work.

Such cost estimates can be done by an examination of the RFP, and then a detailed bottoms-up cost estimate prepared for the proposed new job. These estimates should be done without knowledge of what was actually being proposed by the sellers. It needs to be an independent look.

However, such estimates can often be valid even when done with less than a detailed, bottoms-up look. The purpose is not to arrive at a precise value, but rather to provide a gross estimate to compare against what is being proposed by the sellers.

In construction work estimators typically will use the costs per square feet, by type of structure, as a way of arriving at an independent value. Manufacturing work will often use historical experiences with similar work to arrive at a figure. In software projects function point estimates are often sufficient to verify a reasonable cost value.

The independent cost estimates are to provide a comfort zone for management. Absolute precision is not needed. For example, if a company were about to negotiate a new contract and all the seller cost estimates were in the neighborhood of $100 million, but the independent cost estimate was at $60 million, management might well have legitimate concerns. But if the seller proposals were about $100 million, and the independent estimate were perhaps $80 million, they may authorize the procurement, recognizing that independent cost estimates are typically done with less precision.

Special Issue: Late Seller Proposals

Some procurement organizations take a very hard line with respect to holding fast to a proposal due date and the precise time deadline for submittal of proposals:

Late proposals are no longer accepted under any circumstances. There is no opportunity to blame it on the U.S. Postal Service or government mishandling. If a proposal is late it is not accepted. [3]

Well! It is easy to handle this issue when your least favorite source, yes we do have favorites, is late on meeting the deadline for proposal submission. You simply reject their offering and go on to the better sources. But what happens when the single most qualified source or sources are late? Do you toss out their proposals? Maybe yes, maybe

3. Mary Ann P. Wangemann, *2001 Subcontract Management Manual*, (San Diego: Harcourt Professional Publishing: 2000) page 518.

not. With government funded projects the rules are more rigid. But in a commercial enterprise, we typically can be more flexible.

Keep in mind: our primary mission is to successfully implement and complete a project. Everything else should be secondary. In a commercial enterprise under some circumstances it may be advisable to resolve the issue of late submittals by giving all respondents an equal extension of time, so as to allow critical but late suppliers to get their proposal in on time.

Special Issue: Unsolicited Proposals

Some of the best technical ideas/approaches come from unsolicited seller proposals. How do the sellers know what you need when you haven't specified your needs in a solicitation document? Simply put, word gets out that company X is working on a given new system, and many of the ideas, new concepts which have been generated by other companies, looking for the right opportunity, will make their way into your company. Often the marketing executives of companies will meet and ideas be discussed informally. Subsequently a formal presentation of the new concept will be delivered. Synergy sets in between buyer and seller organizations.

What should a company do when it gets an unsolicited proposal from another company? Should it hold a competition for the new system using the ideas gained from the other source? Not if you want additional good ideas from this same company.

A better approach would be to have both companies sit down and define their requirements, produce a baseline agreement, then let the professional negotiators of both companies subsequently sit down and work out a negotiated procurement. Unsolicited proposals can be a great source of new technical ideas. Do not spoil these sources by competing someone's ideas to save a few dollars initially, but do great harm in the long-term relationship of both companies. In procurement, building long-term business relationships is often more important than short term profit goals.

Special Issue: Alternate (non-responsive) Approach Proposals

An alternate proposal is technically a "non-responsive" proposal. The seller has looked at your request, may have responded to it, but also thinks they may have a better idea. Oftentimes, the alternate approach may in fact be a better solution than what you specified in your Request for Proposal (RFP). It may be technically better, or often times it may be more cost effective.

Alternate proposals can be a great source of new idea. However, not all solicitations allow for alternate approaches. Sometimes alternate approaches are specifically prohibited in the RFP.

Just like unsolicited proposals, alternate proposals can lead to another solicitation to hold a competition, but such practices actually discourage the flow of innovative ideas from sellers. It is likely a better approach to sit down with the seller and go directly to a negotiated contract incorporating their alternate approach.

Issues for Negotiation

Most large companies have professional negotiators on their staff. Typically they are housed in organizations called contracts, proposals, supply management, sometimes legal. These individuals all share a common trait: they can talk for hours . . . and commit themselves to doing nothing!

Certain of the ancient cultures in the world are particularly good at negotiating arrangements. People from Asia and the middle east are normally adept negotiators. People from the western cultures are not good negotiators. Reason: we are too direct. We want to get to the point, reach an agreement, and go on to something else. Impatience can lead to poor negotiation settlements.

One of the first issues for any negotiating team is to decide who is in charge. Every negotiating team needs to have a single leader. Once selected, everyone on the team will be subordinate to the team leader. If a team member has a question to ask, they should run it by the team leader, in private, prior to asking it in front of the other team. Questions should be asked and answered through the team leader. The team leader will speak for the team.

It is always a good strategy to ascertain the authority of the other team. Some negotiating teams lack the delegated authority to consummate an agreement, rather they are sent out to fact find only. You do not want to make concessions to a team that lacks authority to strike an agreement.

It is typically a good approach to have a multifunctional team assembled on both sides. That way a negotiation will not be stopped because no one can answer a simple technical question. Another matter of importance is to have both sides agree on the agenda, the timing and departure of both sides, and agree to document the negotiated results with signatures . . . before departing.

One of the quickest ways to undermine a negotiating team strategy is to allow your team to get out-of-control. Some people like to show others how smart they are, how large a role they may have played in preparation of the RFP. Others may simply like to "grandstand." Any of these actions can undermine the objectives of the negotiation. This point is particularly troublesome for vice presidents who may be present and feel compelled to say something important even if their remarks may weaken the negotiation.

The overall negotiating strategy for the team is an important issue to settle before starting. Such strategies may incorporate a "win-win" approach, to allow both sides to benefit from the agreement. The other extreme of this approach is one in which we "take no prisoners", we want to extract every concession from the other side. Fortunately, most companies recognize that both the buyer and seller are likely to be doing business for a long-term, thus both sides should benefit from the final arrangement. Long-term company to company relationships should prevail over short-term negotiating objectives.

Many issues should be settled before the two sides depart for home. Among the more obvious would be an agreement on the final statement of work, terms and conditions, the schedule of performance, perhaps specific milestones to meet, management oversight and reporting, interim or progress payments, and of course the final costs or price. There should be a prior understanding that the major points of the final settlement will be reduced to writing and initialed by the key participants prior to departure.

Best and Final Offer (BAFO)

Sometimes at the conclusion of negotiations, the buyer will then ask all remaining and responsive sellers to submit what is called their best and final offer (BAFO) of a price for the effort. Typically the BAFO is centered on price only, but other factors could come into play such as schedule, warranty, options, anything that was discussed in the negotiations.

Forming a Procurement Team to Manage Complex Buys

If you are buying nuts, bolts, and paints, or even expensive commodities, but commodities built to the seller's product specifications, you probably would not need to form a special team to manage these buys. They are fairly straightforward and the only issue is that the parts arrive when needed by the project, and that they work. Most companies have in place some type of procurement process in the form of an MRP, MRP II, or ERP system which handles the procurement of such items to support the project schedule. Typically these automated purchasing systems work quite well.

However, if the project is buying a major complex new item, something which has never been done before, or is procuring something in accordance with a corporate teaming arrangement, it is strongly recommended that the project consider forming a multi-functional team to manage such procurements. Why: because no one individual processes all the skills needed to adequately manage all of the issues which are certain to arise. The management of major complex procurements and teaming agreements requires the collective skills of multiple functions working together as a team.

To be sure, one individual needs to be placed in charge of each procurement team. But the team itself will be assembled from multiple functions, crossing organizational lines, intruding on fiefdom territories. Great interpersonal skills will be needed by anyone called the team leader.

The traditional roles of the project manager, the functional manager versus project teams

There are some traditional roles typically expected from anyone who has been given the title of project manager, versus others who are called functional line managers. The project manager is normally expected to: 1) define and authorize the work to be done on the project (provide a project statement of work); 2) define the timeframe for all authorized work (issue a schedule); and 3) provide the necessary funds to do the work (release a budget).

By contrast, the role of the functional manager is to review, take exception, and finally accept the project manager's definition of what is to be done, and then: 1) provide the needed staff to support the project; and 2) oversee and supervise the work being done. These are distinct and clearly defined organizational roles. In practice, the functional line managers will normally also play a critical role in helping the project manager to prepare the project's SOW, schedule and budget.

However, when projects form project teams to better manage their major subprojects like major complex buys, or teaming arrangements, the designated team leader's duties will somewhat encroach on the traditional roles done by the functional line managers. Team leaders typically make technical decisions and direct/oversee the staff. To repeat what was said above: great interpersonal skills are needed by anyone called the team leader. And yet, project teams have demonstrated great competence in the management of major critical procurements and/or teaming arrangements.

Issue: Just where does each project fit into the company organization

One of the first issues which needs to be considered in forming a procurement team is to determine where each project fits into the overall company hierarchy. If you are attempting to buy a new major complexity product for a project which is buried deep within the organization, so deep as to make it virtually impossible to notice, there may be a little problem forming a multi-functional procurement team to manage the buy. Issue: just where does my project fit in the organization?

Displayed in Figure 11.1 is a continuum of possible organizational placements for projects. Five possibilities are listed, although there could be more. To the left of the continuum would represent organizational arrangements in which the functional line managers would have the greatest influence over the management of projects. To the right of the continuum represents arrangements in which the organization has moved away from functional dominance of projects into some form of management by projects, often taking the form of matrix management.

The organizational arrangements depicted as items (A) and (B) are similar to each other in that the responsibility for the management of projects is assigned to a functional line manager. Likely, most of the projects in the world are represented by this approach. Such projects are initiated and managed within a single functional line organization.

Under arrangement (A) a Project Expeditor will coordinate the

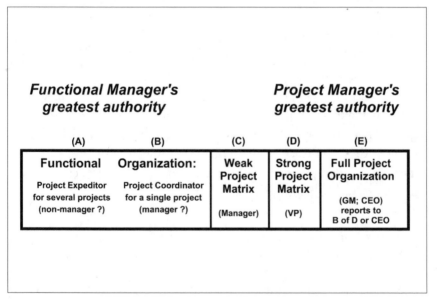

Figure 11.1 A continuum of Project Organizational Arrangements

activities of the project, reporting status and problems to the line manager for resolution. Often the Project Expeditor is responsible for multiple projects at the same time, and often this person may not have a job classification of manager within the organization. This arrangement represents the extreme of weak project organizations, but perhaps constitutes the majority of project placements.

Under arrangement (B) the work of the project is assigned to someone with perhaps a title of Project Coordinator. This person might be responsible for a single project, or limited projects, and will sometimes have a title of manager within the organization, but sometimes not. This arrangement would provide more authority to the project, but problem resolution still will go to the line manager. Problems still arise when a project is dependent on the functional performance from individuals in another line organization.

Projects which exist under arrangements (C) and (D) are similar. Both employ what is termed a matrix organizational approach, defined as follows:

> *The matrix organizational form is an attempt to combine the advantages of the pure functional structure and the product organizational structure. This form is ideally suited for companies . . . that are "project driven." . . . The project manager has total responsibility for project success.* [4]

The primary difference between the (C) approach, a weak project matrix, and (D) a strong project matrix is often simply the organizational classification of the project manager. If the project manager carries a job classification which is subordinate to the head of the functional organizations where the work is being performed, it would be considered a weak organizational arrangement. Example, a project manager with a job classification of a "manager" delegating tasks to a line organization headed by a person with a title of "vice president" would be considered a weak project matrix. The term "weak" suggests

---

4. Harold Kerzner, *Project Management-A systems Approach to Planning, Scheduling, and Controlling,* (New York: Van Nostrand Reinhold, 1995) page 118.

nothing more than the disparity of authority between a manager requesting the work versus a vice president performing the work.

By contrast, if the project manager were to be a vice president, or reported directly to a vice president, the project would be considered a strong project matrix. The organizational authority would have shifted from the functional line organization performing the work over to the project.

Under the full project organization, as depicted in (E), the firm will have gone over to a complete project arrangement, where everyone working on the project reports solid-line to the project manager. Rarely in practice to we find this type of a full project organization. Notable exceptions would be environmental projects, and certain major construction projects, newly formed and implemented at some remote new site, isolated from the corporate office.

What does all this mean to a project attempting to form a procurement team to better manage a major-complexity buy. Simply, that forming a team when one's project falls into either the categories of (A) or (B), which most projects likely do, will present a major challenge in the formation of a procurement team. In these situations, the project managers likely lack sufficient organizational clout to properly form a multi-functional team, which must cross organizational boundaries so as to better manage these complex buys. In particular these projects will be at a disadvantage with the assigned buyers, who may have their own personal agendas which could be at odds with project goals.

If a project has major-complexity buys, or procurements conducted under strategic teaming arrangements, a company would be well advised to place them organizationally into the categories of (C), or (D) as displayed in Figure 11.1. Projects placed into the organizational categories of (A) or (B) put the projects in a distinct disadvantage in the management of new major complex procurements and/or teaming arrangements. And yet most projects exist as categories (A) or (B).

Authorities, Duties and Responsibilities of Procurement Management Teams

In order to manage effectively the major complex procurements some projects encounter, including all corporate teaming arrangements, it is recommended that a multi-functional team arrangement be formed for each procurement which can cut across organizational lines. A single individual should lead each team, and be given both responsibility and commensurate authority for performance of the teams. Each designated team leader should report directly to the project manager.

What would be the mission of the teams? They would typically be expected to perform the following duties:

1. *To organize and plan for the procurement (planning for procurement).*

2. *To define the legal contractual document (planning for solicitation).*

3. *To formally implement the contractual arrangement (solicitation and source selection).*

4. *To monitor and manage and conclude the performance of the procurements (contract administration and contract close out).* [5]

Sounds a lot like the procurement teams should follow the six formal procurement processes as described in Chapter 12 of the Project Management Institute's *A Guide to the Project Management Body of Knowledge.* [6]

Source Selection and Management's Approval

The final selection of a new procurement should be based on previously established criteria, and performed by a previously specified evaluation team. These are issues which should be settled before the

---

5. Paraphrased from Quentin W. Fleming and Quentin J. Fleming, *Subcontract Project Management-Subcontract Planning and Organization* (Chicago, IL, Probus Publishing Company, 1993) pages 59-60.

6. Project Management Institute, Newtown Square, Pennsylvania, 2000.

RFP is released to prospective sellers. See Figure 8.5, covering evaluation of seller proposals.

Sometimes on major complex proposals the buyer may allow for or even request formal presentations by prospective sellers. At other times this practice will not be allowed, and each selection is based completely on the seller's written response.

A source selection committee must understand its role. The committee's role is to evaluate the formal seller responses, rank the acceptable responses, eliminate the unqualified responses, and make a final selection for management's consideration and approval. Management makes the final choice, not the evaluation committee.

Special issue: how long will it take to gain management's approval? Most master schedules typically show one day for management's approval on major awards. Rarely does approval ever come in a single day. Rather, approval will come the next time management meets to consider such issues. Sometimes management meets each week, sometimes each month, but rarely does management meet daily. Sometimes management does not like the evaluation committee's choice, and sends the procurement back to the committee for further evaluation.

Sometimes a source selection committee will select two or three top acceptable candidates, for management's final selection.

Contract Award and Go-ahead

Final management approval and even contract award does not always allow a seller to begin work. Sometimes contract go-ahead is delayed until a "kick-off meeting" is held. This practice allows the buyer to emphasize last minute key points to the seller. Often such meetings will emphasize critical matters in the new procurement like safety issues, regulatory matters, quality, prior approvals, etc., anything of particular importance to success of the new procurement.

CHAPTER 12

Administrator Procurements

(PMBOK ® - Third Edition 2004: 12.5 Contract Administration)

Some people are of the belief that procurement management begins with the award of a contract. Nothing could be further from the truth. Project procurement management begins at the point when the new project is initiated and detailed decisions are starting to be made as to what portion of the project will be performed with one's own staff, and what portion will be sent to another company for performance. At the time the make or buy decisions are made to purchase work or project critical components from another company, project procurement management must begin.

The most critical part of project procurement management is the planning that should take place before any contract is solicited, evaluated, and awarded. If not planned well, procurement management can be a bumpy road. If planned well, procurement management can add immensely to the successful implementation of any project.

In this process of procurement management, sometimes also called contract administration, there are essentially two key missions for the project team: the continuous monitoring of seller performance, and the management of all changes to the seller's authorized baseline.

Use a simple form of Earned Value to manage Major Complexity Procurements [1]

It is likely that most corporate financial executives today measure the cost performance of their projects using only two cost dimensions: the planned costs and the actual costs. Thus, if one spends all the

---

1. Major complexity procurements were defined earlier in Chapter 2, see Figure 2.1.

allotted money one is considered to be right on target. If you spend less than the allocation, it is considered an "under-run" of costs. If you spend more than the allocated costs this is an overrun of costs. What could be more ludicrous. This comparison is not cost performance, but rather expenditure performance. It measures nothing more than whether or not we spent the budget.

What is missing in the picture is the "value of the work performed" for the monies spent. Example: If your project budget was $100 million, and you spent $90 million, but had only accomplished $80 million of work, respectfully, this should be called what it is: an overrun of costs. The missing third dimension of most corporate project assessments is a measure of the value of the work accomplished. We call this earned value management, or EVM for short.

Over a century ago, the industrial engineers lead by the father of scientific management Frederick W. Taylor were correct in their understanding of what represented "true" cost performance in the factories. To these scientific engineers, cost performance represented the difference between the accomplished work, represented by earned standards, versus the actual costs spent to do the work. Cost performance was not the difference between the planned work and actual costs. Today many corporate executives still do not grasp this fundamentally simple concept and are content to focus on the planned expenditures versus the actual expenditures and refer to this as their cost performance. We should never confuse annual accounting with physical project performance. Accounting may re-baseline their cash accounts to zero at each year-end close. Projects which span two or more performance periods should never, repeat never, zero out their actual performance balances. To allow this practice is to destroy one's ability to predict the final project costs based on actual accomplishments.

The early industrial engineers created what they called their "planned standards" representing two elements: (1) the authorized physical work and (2) the authorized budget for the authorized work. However, planned standards represented only their baseline plan, not the accomplished work. It was only when such work was completed that they could determine their true cost performance.

Thus Taylor, et al, a century ago, focused on the "earned standards" which represented two elements: (1) the physical authorized work which had been accomplished, plus (2) the original authorized budget for this work. They then compared the earned standards against the actual hours expended to determine their true "cost performance." It worked a century ago in the factories. It works today in the management of projects, and sub-projects, i.e., procurements.

The Fundamentals of Earned Value Management (EVM)

The United States Department of Defense (DOD) was the first entity in modern times to adopt this early industrial engineering factory concept for use in the management of projects. In 1962, the DOD had underway a major capital project called the Minuteman Missile employing thousands of people and costing millions of taxpayer dollars. This major project spanned several fiscal years. The United States Air Force people who managed this project recognized their duty to the taxpayers to perform well, so they attempted to adopt this simple industrial engineering concept to a one time only project. To their pleasant surprise, earned value management worked for them.

They broke the project into discrete pieces, separate tasks, and to each task they added an authorized budget. When each task was completed they credited completion of the authorized physical task, plus they "earned" their authorized task budget. They compared this completed work, which they called the "earned value" against the costs actually spent to accomplish this work. The result was an accurate reflection of the true cost performance.

Since 1962 the Department of Defense Pentagon has kept track of the performance of hundreds of projects reflecting actual performance, the good, the bad, and even the downright ugly. In total they have now analyzed over 800 separate projects. The results have been spectacular in allowing them to predict the final project cost requirements.

The single most important tracking metric in EVM is what is called the "CPI" or the Cost Performance Index. This index expresses the relationship between the earned value (the physical work accomplished plus its authorized budget) versus the actual costs spent to accomplish the earned value. The cumulative CPI has been proven to be a stable predictor of performance at completion even as early as the 15 to 20 percent point of any project. Thus the CPI metric can be used to accurately forecast the true cost position of any project, even those spanning multiple years in performance. For example, if the cumulative CPI registers at a .80, it means that for every dollar that was spent, only 80 cents of value was earned. This can also be referred to as an overrun.

But most important is the fact that the cumulative CPI can be used, starting at the 20% completion point, to forecast the final project cost results with amazing accuracy. For example, if a five year $100 million dollar project has recorded a cumulative CPI of .80 at the 20% completion point, you can forecast the final results within a finite range. Simply take $100 million, and divide it by the cumulative CPI of .80. You can immediately forecast the final project costs at about $125 million, or a forecasted cost overrun of approximately $25 million. How good is this forecast? Empirical studies by the DOD support the position that it will be accurate within plus or minus 10% from the $125 million final costs:

> *DOD experience in more than 400 programs since 1977 indicates that without exception the cumulative CPI does not significantly improve during the period between 15% and 85% of contract performance; in fact, it tends to decline.* [2]

More recent extensions to this same DOD study brought the totals up to over 800 projects without altering their empirical findings. However, many projects managers today outright reject the DOD project experience saying that it has no relevance to their commercial type projects.

The author is of the belief that a project is a project, and that the fundamental characteristics of projects transcend all industries. And

2. Chester Paul Beach, Jr., *Administrative Inquiry Memorandum on the A-12 Cancellation*, (United States Department of Navy, November 28, 1990) page 5.

also keep in mind that many of the DOD projects included in their study are rather sophisticated and complex endeavors: like stealth aircraft, smart bombs, global positioning targeting, state-of-the-art software, etc. These can hardly be called simple projects.

One independent scholarly study done by the United States Air Force reinforced the belief that the cumulative CPI can be used to predict final project costs with amazing accuracy:

> *. . . the cumulative CPI did not change by more than 10 percent from the value at the 20 percent contract completion point.* [3]

Question: Can we now use the EVM technique to help manage the complex procurements which are often critical to the success of any project in any industry? Answer Yes, but we need to start by making the EVM process as simple as possible, and then separate the major complexity procurements into two fundamental procurement categories: the "cost reimbursable" contracts and the "fixed price" relationships. Each contract type must be managed differently.

Managing "Cost Type" Procurement Contracts Using Simple Earned Value

In order to employ earned value in the management of cost type procurements (or any project, or team, or sub-project, etc.) one must put in place a baseline capable of measuring performance. This does not just happen, it must be deliberately planned and developed. But it is not difficult. Earned value management is nothing more than a resource-loaded project schedule, with tangible metrics defined to convert the "planned values" into "earned values" as the work is accomplished. However, it does take some effort, and certainly discipline to keep the defined baseline plan in place.

---

3. Major David S. Christensen, and Captain Scott R. Heise, USAF, "Cost Performance Index Stability", *National Contract Management Association Journal*, Volume 25, #1, 1993, page 7.

Earlier in Chapter 8 we discussed the planning which should take place leading up to a release of a project solicitation document, called the Request for Proposal (RFP). In Figure 8.4 was displayed a suggested format for a Seller's Schedule. This type of schedule, which is used often in the construction industry, is typically referred to as a "schedule of values." It is a special schedule in that it requires four defined components, as have been repeated again in Figure 12.1. These components are: (1) a listing of all tasks (the scope) required to complete the procurement; (2) the time-phasing for each authorized task; and finally the (3) the value or budget assigned to each planned task (which must add up to 100% of the contract value). What we have here in this simple "schedule of values" format is an earned value baseline, which we refer to as representing the "planned value."

By tracking the progress of each authorized task, and reflecting (4) a percentage completion estimate for all the authorized work, we are able to accurately measure the "earned value" performance, monthly, or even weekly, etc. A seller's schedule, as displayed in Figure 12.1,

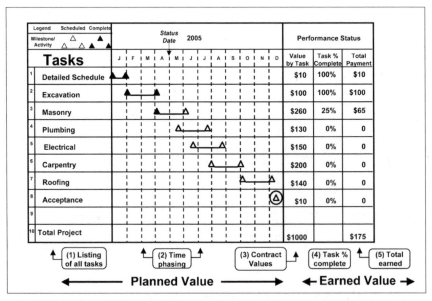

Figure 12.1 Utilize a Seller's Schedule...to employ a simple form of EVM

should always be required from suppliers performing on a cost type procurement . . . always.

In Figure 12.1 we have all we need to employ a simple form of EVM. Column's (1), plus (2), plus (3) provide the baseline, or the "planned value." Monthly updates to column (4) provide the "earned value" measurement of physical performance. If you then compare the seller's actual costs from their invoices, you have the ability to focus on the three dimensions of earned value management: the "Planned Value"; the "Earned Value", and the "Actual Costs." Any seller working on a cost reimbursable type procurement who is spending more money than they are physically earning should be monitored closely. When finished, they are likely to exceed the authorized contract value, and the earlier you know this condition exists the better the chance to work the issue.

Using a simple form of earned value management provides the following benefits to any project in the management of their cost reimbursable type procurements:

1. It allows the project to focus its attention on the physical earned value achieved to accurately measure the percentage completion of each procurement (Earned Value divided by the total Budget at Completion equals the percentage completion);

2. It allows the project to use seller's potential fee (Fixed or Award) as a motivator, authorizing their fee bookings only as the physical work is accomplished (not simply funds expended);

3. It allows the project to determine and continuously track the single most important and stable EVM metric called the Cost Performance Index-CPI (Earned Value divided by Actual Costs), which has been proven to stabilize from the 15 to 20% completion point on any project;

4. With a focus on the cumulative CPI the project's buyer can quickly and independently forecast the final required costs for the procurement by taking the total Budget at Completion and dividing it by the cumulative CPI, which will provide an

accurate forecast of the total required costs to complete the procurement.

EVM is not rocket science, rather it is a major adjunct to fundamental project management. And if the project cannot or will not fund the procurement to full completion, then some hard decisions must be made with respect to the buy. Bad news does not get better with the passage of time.

Managing "Fixed Price" Procurement Contracts Using Simple Earned Value

Fixed price project procurements can also employ a simple form of earned value management, not only to measure the performance of any procurement, but also to pay the seller only what they have earned . . . nothing more. Generally, cost actuals are not available on fixed-price procurements. But you do not need actual cost information. On fixed price procurements the project should focus on the physical work completed, and the budgeted value of the completed work.

As with cost type procurements, you need to establish an earned value baseline against which you can measure the seller's physical performance. Such baselines can be obtained by requiring from all sellers a "schedule of values" in the format displayed in Figure 12.1. On construction projects they typically require (as the first project milestone) a resource-loaded critical path method (CPM) network schedule, which serves the same purpose as a schedule of values.

Once the seller has provided their schedule of values you need to enlist the services of the seasoned project schedulers to evaluate the time phasing of the seller's proposed tasks. Some sellers have been known to phase planned work in their favor, by over-valuing the early tasks, and under-valuing the later tasks. Get an independent assessment from your schedulers.

What you essentially do with fixed-price procurements is to trade monthly progress payments to the sellers in return for their schedule status visibility. Issue: what happens if a seller declines your offer of progress payments in return for their providing schedule status? Answer: be cautious of any seller who declines progress payments. They are often making huge profits on the procurement, and do not want to provide information of any sort. You may want to reopen negotiations.

By paying a seller only what they have earned, you reduce the risks of sellers not completing a job. As with the independent assessment of the initial baseline, you also need to make sure that the monthly performance estimates of progress are not over-stated, resulting in an over payment to the sellers. Typically such assessments will be done by the technical managers overseeing supplier performance, or by the project schedulers.

FAR 32.5, Progress Payments Based on Costs, and 32.10, Performance-Based Payments.

Under contracts funded by the United States Government, progress payments have been provided to sellers based not on physical "progress" but on their "costs-incurred." Talk about an "oxymoron." Payments based on costs being incurred run the high risks of over-paying suppliers for their work accomplished, and many a project has incurred losses by overpaying their sellers.

There are some safeguards provided in the Federal Acquisition Regulation (FAR), subpart 32.5. Typically, only 80% of the actual costs incurred are paid to the sellers, which excludes all seller fees. These progress payments are but temporary loans, to be repaid when suppliers make actual deliveries of their products. But there can be a disparity between the physical work done and the costs incurred, particularly when the sellers encounter an overrun situation, as they sometimes do. Sellers are required by the FAR to acknowledge an overrun, in which case their progress payments are reduced in value by the overrun percentage. Talk about another contradiction.

Good news. In October 1995, the FAR was expanded with subpart 32.10 to add Performance Based Payments. While the FAR 32.10 never mentions earned value management by name, in fact,

Performance Based Payments is EVM at its very finest.

Under FAR 32.10, the project (or procurement) is divided into discrete deliverables (milestones), and a value is set for each milestone, the sum of which must add up to 100% of the authorized contract value. Each milestone includes all costs and seller's profit, in order to sum up to the contract value. As milestones are completed, the sellers receive the value of each completed milestone. Sounds like a simple form of EVM.

Project Status Displays: walls or website

In World War 2, British Prime Minister Winston Churchill would hold his cabinet meetings deep in an underground location which he called his "War Room." On the walls of this room were displays of all of the things they felt were necessary to reflect the status of the war effort.

Many projects today also follow Sir Winston's example and have

---

- **Diagram of the project (site, system, layout)**
- **Near-term objectives list**
- **Work Breakdown Structure (WBS)**
- **Major critical supplier charts**
- **Top Ten Concerns...the "worry list"**
- **Project Master Schedule (other schedules)**
- **Project "action item" list**
- **Personnel loading/phasing charts**
- **Cost/schedule performance (earned value)**

Figure 12.2 A project "War Room" or "website" display

their own "war rooms" to reflect the pulse of their efforts. While the precise data to be displayed will vary from project to project, a representative sampling of critical information might be as shown in Figure 12.2. Typically the Work Breakdown Structure (WBS) diagram will be displayed, together with the project schedule, cost plans, risks confronting the project, and usually a listing of action items.

As a starting point the project will typically want to depict their baseline plans , and compare actual results against the baseline. They will want to highlight departures from the baseline so as to determine the required course of action.

Today however, most projects may not need a piece of dedicated real estate to display their status. All they need is a project website to hold everything they need to monitor project status. With a project website they can reach all parts of their project: remote sites, major suppliers, work being done on the other side of the globe, virtual teams. The project website has essentially replaced the old war rooms. Sir Winston, if he were still with us, would be delighted with project websites, and likely drive us all crazy with his rapid-fire and continuous questions.

Project Status Reviews

Most major projects periodically hold status review meetings to determine how well, or poorly, the project is doing against their baseline plans. Such meetings are often held weekly, monthly, or even daily whenever they find themselves in trouble. Such meetings are normally chaired by the project manager, or the chief technical person on the project. Project managers have been known to remove all chairs from the meeting room, to make such meetings stand-up, as a sign that the project is in trouble. Chairs come back into the room when the project gets back on track.

Performance against their detailed plans and schedules are typically reviewed, along with the action-items which may have come from the prior meeting. Heaven help the person who surfaces a new problem which is older than the date of the last status review meeting. All problems are to be exposed for discussion whenever such meetings are held. It is a cardinal breach of personal conduct to withhold bad news in such meetings. The intent of these meetings is to expose problems so they can be worked. While such meetings are typically informal, action-items are usually recorded to remind people that they have been assigned specific tasks to complete.

Point: whenever there are major critical procurements on any project, these respective sellers must take part in such project status reviews. It would be foolish to think that the respective buyer or purchasing agent could represent the seller in such meetings. Information and accurate status must come first hand, directly from the sellers providing the critical procurements.

Privity of Contract Issues: dealing with 2nd and 3rd Level Suppliers

One of the important elements of contract law is that which deals with what is called privity of contract. It is defined as:

Privity of contract. That connection or relationship which exists between two or more contracting persons. [4]

Privity of contract means simply that there is a direct contractual relationship between two or more persons (companies) to a contract. There is no privity for persons outside of the direct contractual relationship.

This is an important matter to consider because many a "constructive claim" has arisen when an owner or a customer or the person ultimately paying the bills fails to understand that they cannot bark out orders to a second or a third tier sellers without running the high risks of originating claims from those lower tier suppliers. It is a wonderful position to be a lower tier supplier on a project where the ultimate customer likes to demonstrate that they are in charge. Claims, claims, claims.

4.   *Black's Law Dictionary*, (St. Paul, Minnesota: West Publishing Company).

The concept of Privity of Contract is illustrated in Figure 12.3. In this figure there are three companies listed: Companies X, Y, and Z. Company X has a contract with Company Y. There is privity between X and Y. In turn, Company Y has a separate contract with Company Z. There is a separate privity between Company Y and Z. These two separate contracts may have originated from a single project, and funded by the same ultimate source. However, there is no contractual privity between Company X and Company Z.

Thus, if Company X gives orders directly to Company Z, Company Z has the opportunity to pick and choose what it wants to do, and submit a claim for its services to Company Y. Since Company X may not know precisely the details contained in the contract between Company Y and Z, often such directions from Company X can be in conflict with the contract from Company Y to Z.

Solution: if Company X does not like what Company Z is doing, it must express its concerns directly to Company Y, who in turn must deal with Company Z. To do otherwise provides opportunities for Company Z to submit constructive claims to Company Y for the interferences caused by Company X.

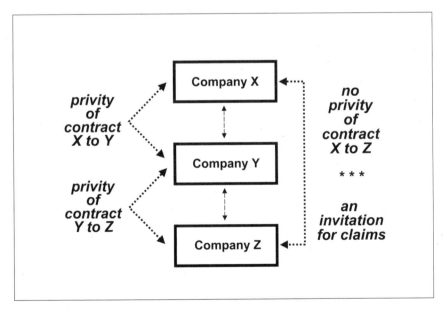

Figure 12.3 Privity of Contract Issues

Many projects today are managed with use of what is called "over-arching" integrated project teams (IPTs). Going back to Figure 12.3, the ultimate paying customer would be represented as Company X, which may represent a Department of Defense (DOD) or Department of Energy (DOE) component. These agencies may be relying on a single prime contractor to manage the project on their behalf, as represented by Company Y. Company Y may have in turn issued multiple next lower-tier subcontracts as could be represented by Companies Z1, Z2, Z3, etc.

The DOD or DOE agencies must exercise restraints on their conduct when giving directions to Companies Z1, Z2, Z3, or they invite constructive claims from these firms. For this reason many firms or agencies in the position of Company X will refuse to meet directly with lower-tier suppliers without having Company Y present in such meetings.

Managing Changes to Project Procurements

Changes in project scope are inevitable. Likely, no project could ever expect to completely eliminate all changes . . . the project would never get done. At some point all projects must assume they have set a reasonable position for themselves and then get on with the implementation or execution of that position. Important point: once the project has set its position, configuration control must then be established and each and every change from that point on must be managed. This is true for internal work. It is even more important where the project has created a series of legal relationships, called procurements, and each seller would love to accept changes in scope . . . for a new higher price.

The project manager (or the project manager's representative) must approve all changes. Only the project manager will have a broad perspective and can properly evaluate the technical, costs and time impact of implementing each change. Technical considerations are very important, but they must be balanced with the costs and time and other business issues.

All projects once they have set their baseline, must manage changes. As one information technology project manager put it:

As the project progresses through the implementation phase, the project manager must identify, evaluate, communicate, control, and coordinate all project changes. [5]

The costs of incorporating scope changes . . . will accelerate

Changes in scope, particularly with procurements, need to be addressed early, and approved or rejected at the earliest possible point. Changes get progressively more expensive the later they are implemented. Latent, lingering changes must be addressed, and either approved or rejected by the project manager. Subtle technical "niceties" are difficult to control, particularly if the organization has created a weak-project matrix and the project manager lacks the clout to say no to the functions.

In Figure 12.4 is portrayed the life cycle of a representative project. Four phases are shown although the exact number and terms will vary from industry to industry. Once the project has created its baseline, all subsequent changes to that baseline must be tightly managed, or the costs of incorporating changes will become prohibitive.

Project Procurements require a formal change control procedure

Likely, most mature project organizations will put in place some type of a formal process to manage changes. Such documented procedures often describe the process which must be followed to evaluate and incorporate all changes, including procurement changes.

A change control system is a formal, documented process that describes when and how official project documents may be changed. It also describes the people authorized to make changes, the paperwork required, and any automated or manual tracking

---

5. Dan Ono, "Project Evaluation at Lucent Technologies." From David I. Cleland, *Field Guide to Project Management*, (New York: Van Nostrand Reinhold, 1998) page 374.

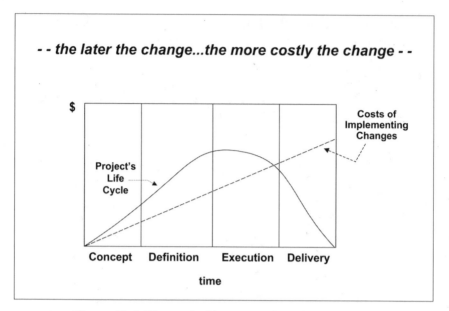

Figure 12.4 The cost of incorporating changes

systems the project will use. A change control system often includes a change control board (CCB), configuration management, and a process for communicating changes. [6]

Changes in scope will happen. But they must be aggressively managed.

Danger Ahead: Constructive Changes

There is a branch of law which has been evolving out of both construction projects and government contracting. The issue is what is commonly referred to as "constructive changes." Remember, project procurements create a legal relationship. It is the responsibility of the project's buyer to define the procured work. If the definition is not

6. Kathy Schwalbe, *Information Technology Project Management*, (Boston: Course Technology Thompson Learning, 2002) page 74.

adequate, or changes for whatever reason, or we interfere with a seller's performance, the performing seller may be entitled to extra compensation for their services.

A constructive change to a procurement can be an oral or written act, or an omission to act, by someone on the project who has actual or apparent authority to act, which is of such a nature that it can be construed to have the same effect as a written change order. For the most part constructive changes are presently limited to government and construction contracting, but the doctrine is likely to be expanded into the commercial sector in the near future. Constructive changes has been defined as:

> *The most straightforward type of constructive change occurs when the Government takes some action during contract administration which increases the cost of the work . . . If the contractor's view that the extra work was not required by the contract . . . the action will be held to be a constructive change (or breach of contract) and the contractor will be entitled to compensation for the extra costs that have been incurred.* [7]

What does this mean in the management of project procurements, particularly the second or third tier supplier? Be very careful which directions you give to suppliers . . . they may send you a bill. Some of the actions which can result in constructive changes are:

- accelerating or delaying the period of the supplier performance
- giving a seller a specification which contains defects
- changing the specification or statement of work or terms & conditions
- interfering with the performance of the supplier
- rejecting a seller's deliverables even though they meet the procurement specification

---

7. Donald P. Arnavas and Judge William J. Ruberry, *Government Contract Guidebook*, (Washington, DC: Federal Publications, Inc., 1987) page 10-15.

- adding additional and/or excessive testing
- stopping and starting the work of the supplier

Managing Time (only) and
Time & Materials (T&M) Procurements

All Time only, and Time & Materials (T&M) procurements for a project should be routine. You are simply buying two generic commodities: people by the hour, with or without supporting materials. Typically, but not always, T&M procurements will result in these commodities arriving at your door and the project team will supervise their consumption by the project. Under this approach, T&M buys would be considered a Category 3) All Other Routine-COTS Procurement, as was portrayed earlier in Figure 2.1. Buying the equivalent services of "ten senior designers" from January through June would be an example of this type of procurement. The daily work of the senior engineers would be supervised by the project. The seller's statement of work (SOW) is very simple.

But this is not the end of the story. In some organizations management will sometimes elect by policy to never allow Cost Type Procurements, but will allow T&M buys. In these environments any clever buyer can employ a T&M procurement with a unique statement of work (SOW) for the seller to perform against, in which case the buy essentially becomes a Category 1) Major Complexity Procurement, as was portrayed in Figure 2.1. The seller essentially works to their own SOW, within the bounds of the approved hours and materials limitations. These Category 1) procurements must be watched closely to minimize cost growth risks. Buying "construction management services" from January to June would be an example of this type of procurement. The daily work of the construction manager is typically not supervised by the project. However, it must be overseen by the project.

Watch T&M procurements closely to make sure you do not have a cost type arrangement in place in which costs can grow depending on the performance of the seller. The deciding issue:

who is supervising the seller's work, the buyer or the seller. If it is the seller that is responsible for the SOW, then you really have in place a cost type arrangement. Watch these buys closely for cost growth.

It is always a good practice to place boundaries around T&M procurements. You do this to minimize the risks of inadvertent cost growth. The rates the buyer will pay for labor should typically be preset at a wrapped-rate value, which will include the agreed to hourly rate by labor category, plus indirect burdens on the direct labor, and including seller's profit. Make sure you get what you bargained for, and that you do not pay senior engineers rates and get junior engineers.

Any accompanying materials can be priced at material costs only, but often include a small material handling burden, often without profit. Sometimes however, material costs will include a seller's profit. The practice varies.

Likely the most important T&M limitation should be in specifying the total authorized costs to be allowed by the seller, with a limitation of costs specified by month, by total contract, through the end of a specific time period. To not specify NTE values on T&M procurements is to create a pure cost reimbursable type contract. In practice, many T&M procurements certainly resemble cost type contracts, but are called T&M buys so as not to employ cost type contracts. It's a game.

CHAPTER 13

Close Procurements

(PMBOK ® - Third Edition 2004: 12.6 Contract Closure)

A great American by the name of Yogi Berra once said: *"It ain't over till it's over."* How true. This profound statement applies to both baseball, and to project procurements.

Just because the Seller has made all deliveries doesn't necessarily mean that a procurement is completed. There are often residual issues which must be addressed. Among them the orderly close out of each procurement, the storage of all files, and in particular the settlement of all outstanding changes and residual claims the Sellers may have against the Buyer. Claims do not settle themselves, and the passage of time works primarily in the Seller's favor, not the Buyer. The project team may want to go on to exciting new assignments. But the Sellers will want to get paid for everything they did during performance.

Termination of the Contractual (Procurement) Relationships

The best way for any procurement to end is to have the Seller completely satisfy the statement of work, make all deliveries as specified, and comply with all provisions of the contract. Without question, this is the preferred choice. But sometimes it doesn't happen that way.

There are circumstances in which the Buyer and sometimes the Seller may want to end their relationship before completion of the procurement. What are the legal ramifications of such actions. At this point the project will need to receive competent legal advice, coming either from their corporate legal counsel, or more likely from the professional purchasing organization assigned to support them.

There are essentially three situations in which the contractual relationships between the Buyer and Seller can be terminated early.

Scenario # 1: Termination for Cause or Default (actions by the Seller)

The most common cause of early termination will likely be through the actions of the Seller, which will fall short of fulfilling the critical requirements of their procurement contract. The Seller will breach their contract, which is defined as:

Failure, without legal excuse, to perform any promise which forms the whole or part of a contract. [1]

In short, the Seller fails to perform the critical obligations required by their contract, and these actions provide sufficient justification for the Buyer to terminate their contract.

We often hear the term "material" breach used, which means a big or an important breach of contract. The significance of the term material is that the action gives the injured party a legitimate excuse to not complete their end of the bargain. Note, minor, trivial, or annoying actions on the part of the Seller will not give the Buyer a cause to cancel a contract. A breach of contract must be based on a significant event, going to the core of their relationship.

However, in the world of commerce, often the breach of contract may not have taken place, rather the breach will be anticipated, or highly probable based on conditions surrounding the Seller. Two additional definitions of breach of contract come into play, anticipatory and constructive:

Anticipatory breach of contract. Such occurs when the promisor without justification and before he has committed a breach makes

---

1.   *Black's Law Dictionary*, (St. Paul, Minnesota: West Publishing Company).

a positive statement to promisee indicating he will not or cannot perform his contractual duties. [2]

Constructive breach. Such breach takes place when the party bound to perform disables himself from performance by some act, or declares, before the time comes, that he will not perform. [3]

Thus, if a Seller indicates to the Buyer that they have no intention or no capability of completing a particular procurement, such Seller actions would likely constitute an anticipatory breach of contract. If a construction project manager de-mobilizes the work force, sends everyone home, returns all equipment, in all likelihood a constructive breach will have occurred. These actions would give the Buyer the justification to hold the Seller in breach of their contract.

The effect of a Seller breach of contract can be costly to the Seller depending on the egregious nature of their actions. In such cases the Seller may not be able to recover all of their costs incurred. They are likely to be entitled to no profit for their work performed. Of greater consequence, the Seller will likely be liable for compensatory damages the Buyer may have to incur as they place the same procurement with another supplier in order to complete the project. In this case the Seller may be liable to the Buyer for the costs of taking the same work to another firm for performance.

A special issue will sometimes come into play dealing with the rights of the lower tier suppliers, whose contractual performance may have been proper. Question: Is the Buyer obligated to pay the costs for performance of lower-tier suppliers? Generally, if the contractual performance of lower-tier suppliers has been proper, the Buyer will have to settle all claims equitably with these suppliers, fully compensating them for all reasonable costs incurred, and also providing them with a reasonable profit for their efforts. Such settlements would add to the claim against the original Seller.

---

2. *Black's Law Dictionary*, (St. Paul, Minnesota: West Publishing Company).
3. *Black's Law Dictionary*, (St. Paul, Minnesota: West Publishing Company).

Scenario # 2: Termination for the Convenience (of the Buyer)

The concept of terminating a contract for the convenience of the Buyer comes directly from the United States Federal Procurement Law. Under the Federal Acquisition Regulation (FAR) the Government reserves the right to terminate any contract for their own convenience. Most other governmental agencies have since incorporated this same concept into their procurement systems so you find the right to terminate contracts for convenience of the Buyer with most government bodies, state, county, and local.

Private industry has also followed this model and it is likely that most procurement systems in industry also have similar clauses ready to be inserted into their purchase orders.

If the Buyer executes a termination for its convenience the Seller must be notified, and once notified must take positive steps to minimize the incurrence of further liabilities. The Buyer must then negotiate with the Seller to make them financially whole, to cover all their reasonable expenses, and pay them a reasonable profit for their effort up to the termination.

The courts have held that terminations for the convenience of a Buyer must be done in good faith. There must be a legitimate basis for the termination for convenience. Simply to secure a lower price from a new Seller would likely not be considered a good faith termination by the Buyer.

Court cases have gone back and forth on the issue of whether a particular contract termination is for default or convenience. What the Buyer and Seller are arguing over is the recovery of all Seller costs incurred, plus a profit for their services.

The most notable termination for default or convenience is the Navy's A-12 stealth bomber. In 1991 then Secretary of Defense Dick Cheney cancelled this major contract for "default" of the two contractors. The contractors then went into the courts claiming that it was actually a cancellation for the "convenience" of the Navy. Thus they wanted to keep their expenses of $1.3 billion, plus make a fair profit. Twelve years later the issue still has not been finally settled, and the claim has now grown to $2.6 billion with interest.

They are now starting to talk about big money. [4]

Scenario # 3: Absolute right to terminate the agreement (by either the Buyer or the Seller)

In unusual circumstances, the parties to a contractual relationship will sometimes (rarely) insert a contract provision allowing either of the parties to cancel their contract, by simply giving notice to the other party. This provision sort of negates the very purpose of a contract.

Such provisions are used infrequently, sometimes in employment contracts or contracts for professional services. Often the only stipulation is that termination will take place after a specified number of days have passed after notification to terminate.

This contract provision will rarely be used in the management of projects.

Notice of a Contract Termination

One important issue in contract law deals with "notice" by the parties involved. Notice is particularly important when dealing with the issue of terminating a contractual relationship. If one intends to conclude a contractual relationship with another, that fact must be communicated to all other parties to their relationship. Silence alone will not suffice. The Uniform Commercial Code is quite explicit on this point:

> *Termination of a contract by one party except on the happening of an agreed to event requires that reasonable notification be received by the other party and an agreement dispensing with notification is invalid if its operation would be unconscionable.* [5]

---

4. James P. Stevenson, *The $5 Billion Misunderstanding: The Collapse of the Navy's A-12 Stealth Bomber Program*, (Annapolis, Maryland: Naval Institute Press, 2001).
5. *Uniform Commercial Code,* article 2-309, (3).

Issue: Who will close-out the project, settle all claims, and complete each procurement

Funny things sometimes happen when working on projects. Not infrequently, projects are started and well underway before the project manager is finally designated and arrives on the scene. It is not supposed to happen that way according to the textbooks, but it often does. Project managers are sometimes late arrivals on the job.

And sometimes to compound this condition, often the very same project manager who came on the job late, is later re-assigned to another new and exciting project . . . before the current project is completed. In such cases the deputy project manager or most senior technical person will take over the project and make sure all items are completed properly. But sometimes the replacement project manager lacks the organizational punch to make things happen, and project loose-ends are never settled.

Perhaps the most serious issue at project close-out are supplier claims for equitable contract adjustment. Unattended supplier claims do not settle themselves simply by ignoring them. Claims only get worse as project people retire and go on to new assignments, sometimes with new companies. The transient nature of project management assignments can sometimes lead to serious financial consequences for any organization, when the project has not been closed out properly and all claims settled.

A good procurement system, which is in place with most mature organizations, should prevent the "un-settlement" of supplier claims. But even with mature organizations, which have approved purchasing systems and procurement procedures in place, claims can sometimes be a serious problem for an organization, because project managers by their creative nature like to build new things, not close-out all the required paper work. Claims settlement is better than income tax preparation . . . but not by much.

The Settlement of Seller Claims

Changes to projects and any resulting procurements are to be expected. Changes will happen. But changes must be managed. If uncontrolled, changes can adversely impact the satisfactory performance of any project. Project procurements can best be thought of as sub-projects of the higher project. But project procurements, perhaps because they exist as legal relationships, present unique challenges to any project in the final settlement of claims from the Sellers.

Seller claims for an equitable adjustment in their contract price can be settled in a number of ways, as are displayed in Figure 13.1. Without question, the single most desirable way to settle any claim is for the Buyer and the Seller to sit down and negotiate a fair and equitable agreement as shown at the top of the chart. By contrast, the least desirable approach is for the two parties to stand firm in their position, to initiate a lawsuit, and then settle their dispute(s) in a court of law. Nobody wins . . . but the lawyers.

However, between the two extremes as shown in Figure 13.1 is an

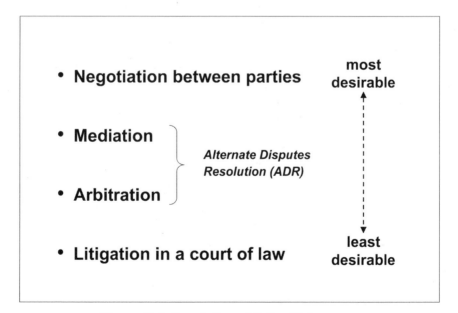

Figure 13.1 Resolution of Seller Claims

established claim settlement process called Alternate Disputes Resolution, or ADR for short. ADR as a claim settlement process which likely originated in the construction industry, and has been around for over a quarter of a century. It is now an established and respected settlement process which has been universally accepted in all industries. The ADR process can be used to settle professional differences of opinion in any contract, subcontract, procurement, and frequently in corporate teaming arrangements.

While there are various gradients in the ADR process which are still evolving, the two most common forms of ADR are Mediation and Arbitration. We should understand the differences between these two processes.

Settlement by Mediation

Mediation in a nutshell is a facilitated negotiation and settlement between the parties. The Buyer and Seller cannot reach a negotiated settlement by themselves, often as a result of emotions, they are "pissed-off" at each other, so they bring in an impartial third party, a mediator, to help reach an agreement. It often works.

The role of the mediator is to bring both sides together. Both sides are given the opportunity to present their position. A mediator will then attempt to gain concessions from both sides, until an agreement can be reached. Mediation is a flexible, informal process. Costs are minimal, often simply the hourly rate of a qualified professional mediator. The final results and settlement values are controlled by the Buyer and Seller, and are known only to them. Either side can accept or reject the position, it is entirely up to them. The mediator will often prepare a settlement memorandum for both parties to execute. It is a relatively fast process.

The settlement of Seller claims by mediation is highly desirable, and closely resembles the results of a negotiated settlement by both parties.

Settlement by Arbitration

The next more formal ADR settlement process is called arbitration.

Arbitration is perhaps more beneficial than formal litigation, but nevertheless more closely resembles a formal trial in a court of law. The disputing parties by their agreement bring in a professional arbitrator, or referee, or quasi-judge to settle their disputed issues.

By their Arbitration Clause inserted in the contract, the findings of the arbitrator can be "voluntarily accepted" which means they can also be rejected, or the findings can be "binding" on the parties, which means they cannot be rejected. However, most courts on appeal have generally supported the findings of the professional arbitrators.

While arbitration does resemble a court of law, and both sides are typically represented by their respective lawyers, the governing rules are more relaxed than with formal litigation. Both sides have greater opportunities to introduce evidence that would not normally be allowed in a court of law. Participants will give their testimony under oath, and there generally is pre-trial discovery to isolate the key issues.

Arbitration is usually less costly than litigation, but considerably more costly than mediation. If arbitration is to be used, an Arbitration clause should be inserted in the contract specifying the intent of all parties.

Project Close-out Checklist

The close-out of projects should be performed in an orderly and systematic way in order to best protect the interests of the project owner, the people who are paying the bills. An experienced project manager, one who has been there before, provided us with a checklist of issues which should be covered when closing out any project. He suggests that the following documentation should be preserved on any project:

A. *Project Office (PO) and Project Team Organization*
B. *Instructions and Procedures*
C. *Financial*
D. *Project Definition*
E. *Plans, Budgets, and Schedules*
F. *Work Authorization and Control*

G. *Project Evaluation and Control*
H. *Management and Customer Reporting*
I.   *Marketing and Contract Administration*
J.   *Extensions—New Business*
K. *Project Records Control*
L.   *Purchasing and Subcontracting Liaison and Policies*
M. *Engineering Documentation*
N. *Site Operations* [6]

Memo to the file: Lessons-learned

The last issue to be discussed in the systematic closeout of any project is something we know we should do, but rarely ever take the time.
That is the final position of the project manager, and the project team,
describing for the benefit of "future generations" just what went well,
and what could have been handled perhaps better on the project being
completed.

A critical part of such lessons-learned would be the procurements.
What could we have done better, and should we do differently on the
next similar project. How should we deal with a particular supplier,
and perhaps, should we use this seller again on the next project.

---

6. Russell D. Archibald, *Managing High-Technology Programs and Projects*, (New York: John
    Wiley & Sons, Inc., 1992), page 365.

CHAPTER 14

In Summary: Managing Project Procurements

We have come to the end of our discussion of project procurement management. Everything we buy to support our projects is important. All purchased items must work, and they must be available in time to support the requirements of the project.

But perhaps the unique aspect of the procured work, as compared with the internal effort, is that everything we buy is done under a legal relationship. Thus we must perform the procurement functions properly, or we will pay a dear price for this effort, perhaps even in a court of law.

Earlier, in Chapter 2, it was suggested that we place all procured work into three generic categories so as to better manage each type of procurement. These categories were:

1. Major (high risk) complexity procurements. The purchase of something new, something which does not presently exist, tailored to the project's unique specification. These would always be considered critical sub-projects.

2. Minor (low risk) complexity procurements. These items will often represent large monetary values, but the commodities exist, and will conform to the seller's existing product specification.

3. Routine buys of COTS (Commercial Off-The Shelf) commodities or purchased services. These items will constitute the largest category of buy items, but are low value and low risks.

Also, we sometimes buy these same items by implementing corporate teaming arrangements, and sometimes from other operating units of our own company, each of which presents project management with a unique set of challenges. Project procurements under corporate teaming agreements are just like any other procurement, except that the project gets a lot of help from above. Work sent to other operating divisions of our company are just like any other procurement, except you often get no respect!

However, without question, in the opinion of the author, the category (1) major complexity procured items constitute the most challenging aspect of project procurement management. These high-risk items must be managed well, in order to successfully complete our projects.

Ten steps to implement successful Project Procurement Management

Whenever we encounter procurements on any project, and certainly major complexity procurements, it is recommended that we take the following ten steps to successfully conclude this work:

1. At the time the initial project scope of work is being defined, a "make or buy" analysis must take place, isolating what tasks/effort will be performed in-house, and what tasks will be procured from other companies. Thus, at the conclusion of project scope definition, we should know precisely which items we are going to procure from another company.

2. The items which will be procured from another company should be analyzed, and placed into "three generic categories" as was described earlier: (1) Major-complexity procurements, items which do not exist; (2) the Minor-complexity procurements, which exist according to the seller's product specification; and (3) All other routine Commercial-Off-The-Shelf (COTS) buys, which will represent the largest category of purchased items, but are low risk.

3. Each (1) Major Complexity procurement must have a "designated team leader" identified and given both responsibility and commensurate authority to manage each defined procurement, as a sub-project, reporting directly to the project manager. In most cases these individuals should be the technical person responsible for preparing the product specification.

4. A "multi-functional team" should be designated to assist the identified leader in the management of the (1) Major Complexity procurement. An important deputy to the designated team leader will be the assigned buyer, the contracts person, that individual who has delegated procurement authority and who will enforce company procurement policies.

5. Each (1) Major Complexity procurement will have an "independent cost estimate" prepared of the estimated required costs, which will be used to compare to the solicited proposals when they are received.

6. All project procurements must be "scheduled" so as to support the project master schedule.

7. Each (1) Major complexity procurement must have a "risk analysis" performed so as to identify the associated risks. All high risk procurements should also have a risk mitigation plan prepared to bring the identified risks down to acceptable levels.

8. Each (1) major complex procurement should be assessed to determine the appropriate "contract type" to be employed, on a case by case basis.

9. The "management oversight requirements" including formal reporting, and project status reviews must be determined and specified in the Request for Proposal and resulting contract.

10. In all cases, a formal "Procurement Management Plan" should be developed and published and implemented to support the procurements on the project.

By following these ten basic steps, there should be a seamless relationship between all identified project tasks, those that are sent in-house for performance, and those which are procured from another company. But project procurements are different, and require unique treatment.

Appendix A to Chapter 4

Model Teaming Agreement

by Alan J. Gould, Esq. [1]

1. Used with permission of Mr. Alan Gould. This model appeared in Ms. Elinor Sue Coates, *The Subcontract Management Manual*, San Francisco: Coates & Company 1992) page 290.

MODEL TEAMING AGREEMENT

(Program Title)
XYZ Inc.-ABC Corporation

This agreement, made as of _____, 199__, between XYZ Inc., (hereafter called XYZ) and ABC Corporation (hereafter called ABC) covering the cooperation of the parties in conjunction with the submission of a proposal by XYZ to (Customer) in response to "(Program Title)" by said RFP. The parties anticipate that the contract to be awarded by (Customer) for the _____ Program will be of the (type contract) type, and relative to such Proposal and contract agree to the following:

1. *Each party will exert reasonable effort to prepare a Proposal which will result in the selection of XYZ as Prime Contractor by (XYZ Customer) and the acceptance of ABC as a Subcontractor therefore; and, each party agrees to continue to exert all reasonable effort toward this objective throughout any negotiations concerning a proposed contract or contracts which may follow the submission of such Proposal.*

2. *XYZ will have the responsibility for the preparation, evaluation and submission of the combined management, technical, price, and cost Proposal to (XYZ Customer). The Proposal will be submitted in the form selected by XYZ with ABC providing full assistance and advise. Each party will supply the necessary engineering management, technical, and other services as well as cost information, exhibits, designs and plans related to the work which it proposes to perform. All contracts with (XYZ Customer) pertaining to the preparation of a Proposal will be made through XYZ.*

3. *Neither party will charge the other for expenses and costs incurred by it during all phases of the preparation of the Proposal and any negotiation which may follow; and, neither party will be entitled to reimbursement or payment of compensation of any kind from the other in connection with the Proposal and negotiation efforts except as hereafter provided.*

4. *If XYZ is selected by (XYZ Customer) as the Prime Contractor for this*

Program, XYZ intends to subcontract to ABC Corporation upon a (type contract) basis and upon a price basis to be agreed upon for the work and services generally set forth in Exhibit "A" hereof with such changes as may result from mutual agreement. Any such subcontract or subcontracts, or changes or supplements thereto, shall be subject to the prior approval of the customer and shall be in accordance with the laws, regulations and terms of the XYZ prime contract. XYZ will use all reasonable efforts to secure such approval. ABC will, in the event of the award to XYZ of any Prime Contract, accept a subcontract to perform work and render services generally in accordance with Exhibit "A" "Subcontract Statement of Work" and on mutually acceptable terms and conditions.

5. *XYZ will keep ABC fully informed concerning preparations for, timing and status of the prime contract negotiations. ABC will support and participate in the prime contract negotiation meetings as requested by XYZ.*

6. *The parties shall devote their best efforts with respect to the subject Proposal and later phases of the _____ Program in the manner set forth herein; provided, however, except as otherwise provided in numbered paragraph 7, sub-paragraph H, this requirement shall terminate upon the earliest of the following:*

   A. *(XYZ Customer) declares its intentions not to contract with XYZ for any phase of the Program by notice of award to other contractors to the exclusion of XYZ; or,*

   B. *That either party of the Agreement is determined by (XYZ Customer) to be unacceptable to (XYZ Customer) in the role and functions set forth in this agreement and the Proposal, provided however, that if (XYZ Customer) requests a change in the role and/or functions of ABC and XYZ, this Agreement shall not be deemed terminated unless ABC and XYZ fail to agree to such changes within the time period permitted by (XYZ Customer); or,*

   C. *Cancellation of RFP by Customer; or,*

   D. *Execution by both parties of subcontract from XYZ to ABC; or,*

E.   *Expiration of two (2) years from date hereof.*

7.   *During the term of the Agreement, ABC and XYZ, to the extent of their right to do so, shall exchange such technical information and data as are reasonably required for each to perform its obligations hereunder. ABC and XYZ each agree to keep in confidence and prevent the disclosure to any person or persons outside their organizations or any unauthorized person or persons within such organization, all technical information which is designated in writing or by appropriate stamp or legend by the proper party to be of a proprietary nature, is received from the other under this Agreement, and which pertains to proprietary information, data or confidential information regarding its technological financial data, inventions, and research and development; provided however, that neither party shall be liable for disclosure of any such data if the same:*

A.   *Was in the public domain at the time it was disclosed; or,*

B.   *Was known to the party receiving it at the time of disclosure; or,*

C.   *Is disclosed inadvertently despite the exercise of the same degree of care as each party takes to preserve and safeguard its own proprietary information; or,*

D.   *Is disclosed to the customer or an authorized representative thereof in the performance of the obligations of either party under this Agreement or any resulting prime contract or sub-contract between the parties, provided that such information disclosed to the customer in a proposal shall be used only for evaluation of such proposal; or,*

E.   *Is disclosed with the written approval of the other party; or,*

F.   *Was independently developed by the receiving party; or,*

G.   *Becomes known to the receiving party from a source other than the disclosing party without breach of this Agreement by the receiving party; or,*

H. Is disclosed after three (3) years from the date of this Agreement, which three-year period shall survive the termination of this Agreement.

8. *During the course of the work called for by this Agreement, inventions conceived solely by ABC shall belong exclusively to ABC, and inventions conceived solely by XYZ shall belong exclusively to XYZ. Inventions conceived jointly by the parties shall be subject to the further agreement of the parties. This understanding is subject to modification as required by appropriate Government regulations or the terms of the prime contract. There shall be no license implied to either party under any patent except with respect to inventions conceived jointly by the parties as set forth in this paragraph.*

9. *This agreement is not intended to constitute, create, give effect to or otherwise recognize a joint venture, partnership or formal business entity of any kind, and the rights and obligations of the parties shall be limited to those expressly set forth herein. Nothing herein shall be construed as providing for the sharing of profits or losses arising from the efforts of either or both of the parties, except as may be provided for in any subcontract agreed to between the parties.*

10. *Any news release, public announcement, advertisement, or publicity proposed to be released by either party concerning the Program or its efforts in connection with the Proposal or any resulting contract will be subject to the written approval of XYZ prior to release. Full consideration and representation as to the roles and contributions of both parties shall be given in any such release, announcement, advertisement or publicity.*

11. *No party shall assign nor in any manner transfer its interests or any part thereof in this agreement, except to successors or wholly owned subsidiaries.*

12. *The employees of either XYZ or ABC shall obey all pertinent rules and regulations while on the premises of the other, including those relating to the safeguarding of classified information. The parties shall indemnify and save harmless one another from and against all claims for (a) bodily injuries, including death; or (b) damage to property caused by a negligent act or omission of the parties or their employees in connection with this agreement.*

13. *All notices, technical and other information transmitted pursuant to this agreement shall be forwarded by letter addressed as follows:*

<u>XYZ:, Inc.</u>   <u>ABC: Corporation</u>

It is agreed that the address identified herein may be changed at any time by written notice from one party to the other.

14. *This agreement shall relate only to the (Program) specifically, and to no other effort undertaken either by XYZ or ABC, jointly or separately; and supersedes all prior oral and written agreements; communications and documents between the parties with respect to the subject matter thereof.*

XYZ INC.

By _____

Title _____

XYZ Inc. _____

ABC CORPORATION

By _____

Title _____

ABC Corporation Date _____

Appendix B to Chapter 4

Teaming Agreement Questionnaire

by Charles L. Eger *

---

* Used with permission of Mr. Eger

TEAMING AGREEMENT QUESTIONNAIRE

A.   *Identify the business form of the teaming arrangement:*
- *Prime-subcontract*
- *Partnership*
- *Joint Venture*
- *Other (describe)*

B.   *Identify all parties to the teaming arrangement. If applicable, identify who is the prime contractor and who is the subcontractor:*

C.   *Describe the product to be produced by the teaming arrangement:*

D.   *1. Does any team member currently produce this product? If yes, identify the team member.*
2. Does any team member currently produce a product involving similar technology? If yes, identify the team member and product(s).

E.   *Identify your competitors and your teammate's competitors for this business opportunity (including known competing teams for the bid):*
[Comment: Identification of the product market is essential. Questions B through E are intended to assist in the determination of the product market and in the determination of whether the agreement is a horizontal agreement between competitors or potential competitors. In addition, these questions establish whether the teaming companies compete.]

F.   *Describe what each teaming company is bringing to the arrangement:*

G.   *Identify all potential teammates:*
[Comment: Questions F and G are for the purposes of determining the business justification for the teaming arrangement.]

H.   *State your reasons for desiring to team: (Indicate all reasons, including cost savings.)*
[Comment: This question is designed to probe the business justification for the arrangement.]

I.   *Do you intend to use the Company's standard teaming agreement?___If your response is "no," what will this agreement prohibit?*

J. *Identify the intended duration of the arrangement:*
    - *Duration of the program:*
    - *Number of years:*
    - *Other:*

K. *If the agreement is for the life of the program, state why such a duration is necessary:*_____
    [Comment: Questions I through K are intended to probe for the degree of restrictiveness of the teaming arrangement.]

L. *Will highly sensitive technical data be disclosed from one teammate to another?*
    [Comment: Questions L goes to the issue of ancillary.]

M. *Are there any documents (e.g., an RFQ, correspondence, surveys, business development studies, etc.) that discuss, refer or relate to this teaming arrangement?*_____*If yes, attach copies of the documents to this questionnaire.*
    [Comment: The documents requested by Question M may help in the determination of whether there is an unlawful anticompetitive intent.]

N. *Have the parties to be bid been disclosed or intended to be disclosed by any party?*___*If yes, identify each party and describe:*
    (i) the nature of the disclosure;
    (ii) the reason such disclosure is necessary for the teaming arrangement.
    [Comment: Question N goes to the question of collusion. The answers are relevant both with regard to antitrust analysis and the signing of the required Certificate of Independent Price Determination.]

O. *If we are the prime contractor, did you conduct a "make or buy" analysis?*___*If yes, state the results:*
    [Comment: Question O goes to the issue of whether the vertical arrangement is intended to restrict a source of supply from competitors or whether it is the result of a legitimate need.]

Appendix C to Chapter 4

"Guidelines" for Establishing a (Vertical) Teaming Agreement

by James P. Gallatin, Jr. & Bruce S. Ramo [2]

2. James P. Gallatin, Jr., and Bruce S. Ramo, "Contractor Team Arrangements—Good Fences Make Good Neighbors," an article appearing in *Contract Management Magazine*, April 1986, pages 11 and 38.

"GUIDELINES" FOR ESTABLISHING
A (VERTICAL) TEAMING AGREEMENT

Certain basic issues should be covered in any company teaming agreement, particularly those which are of a vertical type, for example, a prime contractor to subcontractor(s) relationship. Two authorities on the subject of teaming have cited eight basic elements which should be present in all such contractor agreements. They are:

- *A statement of purpose for teaming, normally referring to the specific complementary technology or expertise of the respective team members and identifying a single acquisition to which the agreement is applicable.*

- *A provision identifying the team members which will respond to the government's solicitation as the prime contractor and describing the prime contractor's duties and rights concerning the submittal of the proposal and negotiations with the government.*

- *A provision defining the subcontractor's duties and obligations in support of the proposal.*

- *A provision stating the parties' intent to enter into a subcontract for work identified in a statement of work (SOW) incorporated into the agreement, provided the prime contractor is the successful offeror.*

- *An "exclusivity" provision, establishing that the prime contractor will not propose any other subcontractor for the work described in the SOW and that the subcontractor will not propose to the government or any other potential prime contractor the work described in the SOW.*

- *A provision listing the events which will cause the agreement to terminate, normally including 1) cancellation of the solicitation, 2) award of the prime contract to another contractor, 3) a substantial change in the government's requirements, and 4) the elapsing of 12 months from the date of the agreement.*

- *A provision clarifying that each party to the agreement is an independent contractor and that there shall be no joint control, joint property, joint liability for losses and expenses, or joint participation in profits or losses.*

- *A provision establishing procedures for the exchange of proprietary information and restrictions on the reproduction, disclosure, and use of such data.*

Appendix D to Chapter 4

A "Model Outline" for a Teaming Agreement

by an anonymous source

A *"MODEL OUTLINE" FOR A TEAMING AGREEMENT*

When undertaking a new endeavor, it is always beneficial to learn from the lessons of those who have done similar work before us. Such is certainly the case with something as complex and difficult as a company teaming agreement.

Shown below is an outline from a real teaming arrangement between two major prime contractors in the aerospace & defense industry. The titles for each section are presented in *italics*, and descriptive commentary is provided within [brackets].

Introduction to the Teaming Arrangement.
   [This provides information regarding the date of execution, where the document was executed, the intent of the parties for entering into the agreement, identifies the customer, etc.]

1. *Definitions used in the document.*
   [This identifies important terms used in the text by providing a definition of all "unique" terms used in the document, specifically those which may be capable of having multiple or ambiguous meanings. This section also provides the intended meaning of the parties for terms related to proprietary and technical information.]

2. *Nature of the teaming relationship.*
   [The parties should explain and elaborate upon their intent for entering into the teaming arrangement. This is especially important when the parties want to create a relationship that differs (e.g., expands or restricts) from the forms defined within the FAR, DCAA, or other industry definitions of teaming arrangements.]

3. *The relationship of the parties — by program phase.*
   [The members of the teaming arrangement may determine that the roles, relationships and responsibilities of each participant should change as the program moves from one programmatic phase to another. This is often beneficial due to the fact that the different programmatic phases will present differing types of issues and challenges for the team, each requiring a different mix of skills, and that the different members of the team often possess differing strengths and capabilities. The team will want to structure its relationship in a way that gives it the flexibility to adjust itself to match the strengths of its members with the changing demands of each respective programmatic phase.]

4. *Information interchange.*
   [This section will attempt to identify and protect the proprietary data rights of the respective team members. Ownership of the data should be clearly specified. In addition, procedures for sharing and protecting the data should be identified.]

5. *Security.*
   [This section will outline the security regulations imposed on this program by the United States government.]

6. *Standards of performance.*
   [The obligations of the parties with respect to the standards of performance for their effort is identified. These standards might be prescribed by common industry practice, by the purchasing customer, or by state law. It is important to highlight any "unique" standards to insure that all parties are aware of them.]

7. *Audits.*
   [This section discusses the ability of the respective parties to examine the records of each other. It is important to specify these rights, since in many cases, the team members will be "exercising" these audit rights when a "problem" has arisen, and this is often not a time when the parties are cooperative or understanding.]

8. *Disclosure of information to the public and publicity.*
   [This section should identify the rights of the respective team members to make program disclosures to the buying customer and to the public. In other words, this section identifies who speaks for what. Many programs will face sensitive political issues, and potential problems can be avoided when the team members discuss only their respective areas of expertise, as information can be easily misinterpreted.]

9. *Severability and reformation.*
   [This section identifies the intent of the parties to allow for continuance of their agreement in the event that portions of it are later found to be invalid or unenforceable. Their intent can range from a desire to terminate the entire arrangement, to continuing the relationship with all remaining sections that are deemed to be valid.]

10. *Applicable law.*
[The parties should identify and specify the state's law which will applied to the teaming agreement. This is important since the team members are often considered "citizens" of different states, and the laws of each state can vary considerably. Much time and energy can be wasted fighting over this issue should the parties fail to specify this information and a dispute later arise.]

11. *Amendment.*
[The ability of the parties to amend the agreement shall be stated (e.g., at the mutual assent of the parties, etc.). It is important for the parties to be able to adjust their agreement to respond to unforeseeable events that may arise. The mechanisms for making these amendments should be specified in advance so that when the time comes to make them, the parties can focus their energies on the best changes to make, rather than on how to make them. The titles and/or positions of those persons who can sign such amendments should be specified by name.]

12. *Entire agreement and headings.*

[This section contains the legal declaration that all documents which are intended to be a part of this agreement are a part of it, and that no other materials except those listed within the document are to be construed by others to be a part of the teaming document. The purpose of this section is to preclude parties from trying to introduce new or differing terms or conditions — especially those which were not intended by the team members at the time the agreement was executed — into the teaming arrangement.]

13. *Notices.*
[This section describes the procedure for each party to "give official notice" to the other party with regard to issues relating to the teaming agreement. The specific title(s) of the official(s) and their corresponding mailing address(es) should be called out, as well as the method of notice (e.g., registered mail, etc.), as well as provisions for the amount of time that can pass before the other party is presumed to have received notice (e.g., five working days after sending notice by registered mail).]

14. *Successors and assigns.*
[This section contains the legal statement that no assignment of this

agreement may be made by either party without written approval of the other party. The effect of this statement is to ensure that the team membership will not change (i.e., that the specific parties that signed the agreement will perform under it).]

15. *Time of the essence.*
[This section contains the legal statement that time is of the essence in this agreement. Unless such a statement is specifically called out in the agreement, it is considered not to be there. The effect of declaring that time is of the essence is that the failure of one of the parties to meet the due dates and/or delivery dates and/or milestone dates specified in the teaming arrangement constitutes a material breach of the contract, accompanied by the ramifications of a material breach. All parties will now take their performance commitments seriously.]

16. *Disputes.*
[This section should specify the policies for handling any disputes to the agreement, including the titles of the individuals who are to be involved in the process. This section should also outline the procedures for addressing situations where disputes cannot be worked out, such as setting time limits for dispute resolution, and the applicable state laws that will apply should legal redress be necessary.]

17. *Remedies.*
[This section will identify the types of legal remedies that may be sought by the parties, should they use the courts to resolve their disputes. The most common types of remedies sought are monetary damages and injunctive relief.]

18. *Term and termination and preservation of teaming arrangement.*
[This section identifies the time period for the agreement (i.e., how long the members intend it to last), as well as specifies the conditions under which the agreement will terminate (e.g., the team does not win the contract, the program is canceled, etc.).]

Appendices to the Teaming Agreement:

A. *Workshare split between parties.*
[This appendix will provide a detailed breakdown of the intended division

of labor among the members. This workshare division is often identified by section of the system, by functions, by phases, etc. Most importantly, the respective dollar values for each member's workshare is specified.]

B. *Protected technology.*
[This appendix will contain any additional procedures deemed necessary for protecting any special technologies and/or processes that the members might possess. This is often necessary because the team members possess differing strengths, often in the form of special manufacturing or technological processes, and are usually in competition with each other (with the exception of their collaboration under this teaming agreement). Members will not want to lose their rights to these technologies to their competitors because of their participation on the team.]

C. *Handling and marking of proprietary data.*
[This appendix outlines the specific procedures for handling the special proprietary data of the respective members. Unlike Section 4 in the agreement above (which focused on identifying the ownership rights of the data), this appendix focuses on the mechanisms for the day-to-day handling of the data, such as identifying the specific job titles of people assigned to handle such materials.]

D. *Procedure for disputes.*
[This appendix will provide the detailed procedure to be used for the treatment of disputes between the parties, including information about the time periods for steps in the process, the powers and qualifications of the referee (assuming arbitration will be used), definitions of materials, procedures for the discovery process, finality of the judgment, etc.]

E. *United States government approved foreign technology sources.*
[This appendix outlines any restrictions on the use of foreign technology transfers and sources. Also included in this appendix is information regarding any offset agreements or limitations, licensing agreements, etc.]

F. *Manufacturing plan interface.*
[This appendix provides a detailed flow diagram for the intended final manufacturing assembly plan.]

Glossary of Project Procurement Management Terms [1]

Advanced Material Release (AMR): A document sometimes used by organizations to initiate the purchase of long-lead time or time-critical materials prior to design completion or start of the project.

Agency: A relationship in which one person acts for another person, with or without their consent.

A Guide to the Project Management Body of Knowledge (PMBOK)®: An official publication of the Project Management Institute (PMI), a basic reference and the world's de facto standard for the project management profession.

Alternate Disputes Resolution (ADR): A process used primarily in the construction industry which attempts to settle claims and disputes without resorting to litigation. The two primary means of ADR are Arbitration and Mediation.

Arbitration: A method of ADR which attempts to settle claims and disputes in a more informal process than actual litigation. A professional arbitrator is brought in to act as a type of judge, and the findings by agreement can be binding on the parties, or merely recommendations.

Assignment: The transfer from a person(s) to another person(s) of the physical possession of property or the rights in property.

Authorized Un-priced Work: Any change of scope for which authorization to proceed has been given, but the estimated costs are not yet determined.

Authorized Work: Total authorized scope which includes work that has been definitized, plus any effort for which authorization has been given, but definitized contract costs have not been settled.

Award Fee Contracts: A type of cost reimbursable, or fixed price, or time and materials contract in which some portion of the seller's earned fee is based on the subjective determination of performance by the buyer. Such findings of the buyer are normally final, and not subject to further appeal.

Backcharge: Costs which are rightfully the responsibility of the seller typically to repair defective merchandise, but which by prior agreement will be incurred by the buyer and charged back to the seller.

Basis of Estimate (BOE): The justification or rationale supporting an

---

1. Notice: this Glossary is intended to provide an informal summary of project procurement terms. These are not legal definitions. Always employ competent legal counsel to interpret the precise meaning of all legal terms.

estimate of required costs, or request for time in a schedule.

Best and Final Offer (BAFO): A request from the buyer to the seller(s), typically at the end of some type of negotiation or clarification of issues, to submit one final revised best price.

Bidder's Conferences: An open meeting called by the buyer with all prospective sellers invited to answer and clarify any questions concerning a competitive procurement.

Bill of Materials (BOM): A complete listing of all parts and raw materials that go into an article showing the quantity of each item required to make the unit.

Bonds: A document provided by the seller to the buyer, ensuring settlement of an obligation of the seller by a third person, acting as guarantor or surety. While there are numerous bonds in use, the three most common types in procurement are bid, payment, and completion.

Bottom-Up Cost Estimate: A detailed cost estimate of the work and related burdens, usually made by the industrial engineering or price/cost estimating groups.

Brainstorming: A controlled process whereby a select group of individuals are requested to offer suggestions on a particular subject, where one suggestion is often expanded by another suggestion. Brainstorming is often employed to isolate and manage project risks.

Budget: A fiscal plan of operations for a given period.

Budget At Completion (BAC): The sum of all authorized budgets for a project or procurement. It is management's authorized commitment of resources for the project. The term BAC can have different meaning from organization to organization depending on what management have authorized for the project: direct labor hours only, direct labor dollars, other direct costs, burdens, profit, etc. The authorized BAC depends on management's expectations.

Budgeting: Time-phased financial requirements.

Burden: Overhead expenses distributed over appropriate direct labor and/or material base. See also Indirect Cost.

Buyer: An individual who typically has delegated authority by company management to issue legal contracts to another organization to procure something. Typically buyers are assigned to projects to procure scope for the project.

Note: in the year 2000 edition of the Project Management Institute's (PMI) publication *A Guide to the Project Management Body of Knowledge (PMBOK)*® the terms "buyer" and "seller" were standardized. A "buyer" is defined as someone who represents the project to procure scope for the project, and a "seller" is someone who provides the procured scope to the project.

Centralized Procurement: The practice of having all procurement authority centralized or consolidated in a single procurement organization, and buyers who have procurement authority are assigned to the projects to support their procurement needs. Likely, most organizations employ centralized procurement, as contrasted with decentralized procurement.

Changes: A departure from an approved baseline, with either the addition or deletion of scope. Changes once approved, result in a revised baseline.

Claims: A demand by one party to a contract or procurement to another party to their arrangement. Claims are made typically to seek an adjustment to a contractual arrangement, often in the form of more money or more time to perform.

Commercial Off The Shelf (COTS): Commodities which are readily available from sellers, typically stocked by the suppliers. COTS items may take the form of hardware, software, and standardized services.

Commitment: A binding financial obligation, often in the form of a purchase order.

Competition: The process of soliciting two or more responses from qualified but competing sellers for a single procurement.

Concurrent Engineering: The development of new products with the use of multi-functional teams working in unison from the initial concept until completion of the product. This process is sometimes called multi-functional teams, integrated product development teams, or simply project teams.

Configuration Change Board (CCB): A formal committee which may exist by many titles, whose purpose is to control changes to a baseline configuration. The CCB typically reviews each change for its impact on the costs, schedule, and configuration, and either approves or rejects the proposed change.

Constructive Changes: A potential change to a contract which is the result of some action, or a failure to take action, on the part of the buyer, but more often by anyone in the project's organization who may have some type of authority, real or implied, to act on behalf of the project. Often constructive changes will occur by interference with the seller's ability to perform.

Contract Administration: The management of procurements to ensure compliance with the requirements of the contract and to control changes to the baseline contract.

Note: the Project Management Institute's *A Guide to the Project Management Body of Knowledge (PMBOK)®* describes "Contract Administration" as representing the fifth of six distinct project procurement processes.

Contract Close Out: The final completion of all contractual issues dealing with project procurements, including in particular the settlement of all outstanding seller claims.

Note: the Project Management Institute's *A Guide to the Project*

Management Body of Knowledge (PMBOK) ® describes "Contract Close Out" as representing the last of the six distinct project procurement processes.

Contract Target Price: The negotiated estimated procurement costs plus seller's profit or fee.

Corporate Teaming Agreements: See Teaming Agreements

Cost Analysis: A through examination to test the reasonableness of all elements of proposed costs, including labor, other direct costs, burdens, profit, proposed by a seller supporting a cost reimbursable or time and materials type procurement. Cost analysis is typically not available on fixed-price procurements.

Cost Control: Any system of keeping costs within the bounds of authorized budgets or standards based upon work actually performed.

Cost Element: A unit of costs, typically in the form of direct labor, direct materials, other direct costs, and indirect rates or burden costs.

Cost Estimate: The expected costs to perform a task or to acquire an item. Cost estimates may be a single value or a range of values.

Cost Incurred: Costs identified through the use of an accrued method of accounting, or costs actually paid. Costs normally will include direct labor, direct materials, and all allowable indirect costs.

Cost Overrun: The amount by which a procurement contract exceeds or expects to exceed the estimated costs, and or the final limitation (the ceiling) of a contract.

Cost Reimbursement Type Contract: A category of contracts based on payments to a contractor for all allowable incurred costs, normally requiring only a "best efforts" performance standard from the seller. All risks for cost growth over the estimated value rests with the project.

Cost Variance (CV): On a cost reimbursable type contract the CV is the difference between the estimated costs and the actual costs incurred.

In an earned value management application a CV is the difference between the earned value accomplished less the actual costs incurred.

Critical Path: A series of dependent tasks in a network schedule representing the longest sequence for a project, thus the shortest time the project can be completed. Any slippage of tasks along the critical path increases the duration of a project.

Critical Seller, Subcontractor, Supplier: A contractor or supplier performing a decisive portion of a project which generally requires close oversight, control, and reporting. Critical sellers are often designated as a result of customer or management direction.

Damages: A legal term representing the monetary value of injury caused by the actions of another.

Decentralized Procurement: The

practice of allowing procurements to be made by individual projects, and or by functional departments. Newly formed organizations will often allow decentralized procurements, but as they mature typically move to centralized procurement arrangements.

Delegation of Authority (DOA): A process by which management gives specific authority to a subordinate to perform a certain action. In procurement management the DOA typically means the authority given to individuals to place orders with other companies up to a specified value.

Direct Costs: Those costs (including labor, material, and other direct costs) which can be accurately allocated to work performed on a particular project. Direct costs are best contrasted with indirect costs which cannot be identified to a specific project.

Discrete Milestone: A milestone which has a definite, scheduled occurrence in time, signaling the start and finish of an activity. Synonymous with the term "objective indicator."

Dispute: A disagreement between buyer and seller which has not been settled by negotiation, which may lead to some type of Alternate Disputes Resolution or even litigation.

Earned Hours: The time expressed in standard hours credited to work as a result of the completion of a given task or a group of tasks.

Earned Value Management (EVM) and Earned Value Project Management (EVPM): A project management technique which focuses on the completion of authorized work and its authorized budget, with the intent of predicting the final required costs and time necessary to finish the project.

E-Commerce or Electronic Commerce: The use of the Internet for conducting business-to-business and business-to-consumer transactions, including project procurements.

Enterprise Resource Planning (ERP): A total corporate computer application which seeks to integrate multiple business functions such as technical, manufacturing, financial, human resources, and procurement, most recently referred to as supply management. ERP is a more ambitious application than either its forerunners of MRP or MRP II systems.

Estimate At Completion (EAC): A forecasted value expressed in either dollars and/or hours, to represent the expected final required costs of work when completed. The EAC typically represents the actual costs incurred, plus the estimated costs for completing all the remaining work.

Estimate To Complete (ETC): The ETC can be expressed in either dollars or hours, developed to represent the value of the effort required to complete a task or group of tasks.

Estimating: The process of preparing a required value to complete a discrete segment of work.

Ethics: The standards and discipline of dealing with what is proper versus what is improper conduct in the management of projects. High ethical standards are particularly critical in the selection and award of project procurements.

Event: Something that happens at a point or moment in time. A significant event is often called a "milestone."

Expenditure: A charge against available funds, evidenced by a voucher, claim, or other documents. Expenditures represent the actual payment of funds.

Federal Acquisition Regulation (FAR): The United States Federal Government's detailed procurement system which must be applied to all Federally funded projects, including all resulting procurements.

Fixed Price Contracts: A generic category of contracts based on the establishment of firm legal commitments for the seller to complete the required work. The performing seller is legally obligated to finish the job, no matter how much it costs to complete. Risks of all cost growth thus rest on the performing contractor.

Force Majeure: A contractual term which gives the obligated parties an excuse to not perform or to delay their contractual obligations because of circumstances beyond their control such as "acts of God" including unusually bad weather, natural disasters, political uprisings, strikes, etc.

Front Loading: An attempt by a performing contractor to delay the acknowledgment of a cost overrun by providing adequate budgets for near-term work at the expense of the far-term effort which will be underfunded. Its purpose is to delay the acknowledgment of a potential cost overrun, in the hope that the contractor may "get well" through changes in the contractual statement of work. Front loading is often the result of inadequate or unrealistic negotiated contract target costs.

Funding Profile: A projection or forecast of funding requirements.

Gantt Chart: The most common scheduling display, graphically portraying planned tasks over time, frequently also called a "bar chart."

General and Administrative (G&A): A form of indirect expenses incurred for the administration of a company, often including senior executive expenses and corporate costs. Such expenses are usually spread over the total direct and indirect costs for all projects in the company.

Guarantor: Someone who is liable for an obligation, but in a secondary position to the principle. It is best contrasted with a surety who has a primary liability to that of the principle.

Incentive Fee Contracts: A type of cost reimbursable or fixed price contract provision in which all or some portion of the seller's fee is determined by achieving specific performance of work. The performance being measured may be based on costs, or other tangible and measurable achievements. Any seller disputes with fees allocated can be subject to litigation.

Independent Cost Analysis: An independent analysis of proposed project cost estimates conducted by an impartial group or outside consultant, not associated with the day to day management of the project.

Independent Cost Estimate: An independent estimate of proposed project costs prepared by someone responding to the solicitation document, the RFP, but without the knowledge of what other respondents may have estimated. These separate estimates are used by management to assess the reasonableness of respondent's costs during the source selection process.

Indirect Cost: Resources expended by an organization which cannot be directly identified to any specific contract, project, product or service. Thus they are allocated to projects et al based on some approved formula. They are sometimes also called overhead costs.

Inspection: The examination and sometimes testing of seller products and services to determine that they conform to the purchase specification and requirements.

Integrated Product Development Teams (IPDT): The development of new products with use of multi-functional teams, working in unison from the conceptual idea until completion of the product. IPDTs are sometimes also referred to as "concurrent engineering" or "project teams" and are best contrasted with the traditional form of sequential product development.

Joint Venture (JV): A legal entity taking any form intended by the participating parties, often with use of an association or partnership, conducted for a limited time or objective, to seek mutual gains or profits. JVs are often formed to capture and perform a new project.

Labor Rate Variances: Difference between budgeted labor rates and actual labor rates experienced.

Letter Contracts: A legally enforceable contract temporarily authoring a seller to begin performance immediately, but which lacks the specific details necessary to complete their agreement. Often the missing ingredient is the final statement of work or specification. Thus letter contracts are considered to be high risk, and something to avoid. Up to the point of final negotiation, letter contracts resemble "cost plus a percentage of costs fee contracts."

Liquidated Damages: A contract provision in which specific damages are cited in the contract at a stipulated value, and payable to the injured party in the event some milestone is not achieved, often a contractual delivery. Liquidated damages can only be compensatory damages, to make the injured party whole again. If found to be punitive, they will likely be held unenforceable.

Major Complexity Contracts: Any procurement which is critical for the success of the project, in which the seller is charged with producing something new, something not done before, to the specification of the project's buyer.

These procurements are typically high value, and often high risk.

Make or Buy Analysis: The classification of project scope as to whether it will be performed by the project's organization (Make work) or procured from an outside company (Buy work).

Manufacturing Resource Planning (MRP II): A method for the planning of all resources of a manufacturing company. It addresses operational planning, financial planning, and normally has a simulation capability to answer "what if" questions. MRP II is made up of a variety of linked functions: business planning, production planning, master production scheduling, material requirements planning (MRP), capacity requirements, and support systems for capacity and material control. Outputs from these systems would be integrated with financial reports such as the business plan, purchase commitment report, shipping budget, inventory projections, etc. Manufacturing Resource Planning (MRP II) is a direct outgrowth and extension of Material Requirements Planning (MRP) systems.

Master Project Schedule (MPS): The highest summary level schedule for a project, often also called the master schedule, depicting the overall time phasing of the project, and listing all major interfaces, milestones, and key objectives.

Material: Property which may be incorporated into an end item to be delivered for a project or which may be consumed or expended in the performance of a project.

Material Requirements Planning (MRP): An automated procurement system which uses the bill of material to define requirements, less actual inventory records, and the master project schedule to calculate purchasing requirements for materials.

Matrix Management: An organizational arrangement in which the responsibility for project performance is delegated to a project manager, but the actual project work is done by the functional departments, assigning people to work on the projects. The role of the project manager is to define the scope, and authorize the work, schedule, and budget. The role of the functional manager is to designate who will do the work, and to supervise how the work will be done.

Mediation: A method of ADR which attempts to settle claims and disputes in an informal negotiated method, avoiding more expensive arbitration and litigation. A professional mediator is brought in to attempt to reach a compromise from all parties, a negotiated settlement.

Milestone: An event, a point in time, usually of particular importance, a big or major event.

Minor Complexity Contracts: Procurement which are critical for the success of the project, often for a high value, but which exist with the seller, according to the seller's own product specification. Such procurements are always important, but typically not high risk since they exist with the seller.

Multi-functional Project Teams: See either "Concurrent Engineering" or "Integrated Product Development Teams."

Negotiated Contract Costs: The estimated costs negotiated in a Cost Plus-Fixed-Fee Contract, or the negotiated contract target costs in either a Cost Plus Incentive Fee Contract or a Fixed Price Incentive Fee Contract.

Negotiation: The discussion that takes place between the Buyer and Seller over a disputed matter(s) hopefully leading to a mutual agreement and settlement.

Non-Recurring Costs: Expenditures against specific tasks that are expected to occur only once on a given program. Examples are preliminary design effort, qualification testing, initial tooling and planning, etc. Most costs on projects are non-recurring.

Not-To-Exceed (NTE): Written notice from a buyer to a seller, typically occurring after the seller has provided a preliminary estimate of the costs associated with a change in scope, authorizing the seller to incur costs up to a given monetary ceiling, at some lesser percentage of the estimated costs.

Notice to Proceed: Written authorization from a buyer to a seller that they are permitted to proceed on a given project or procurement.

Novation: A legal term describing a substitution of a contract, debt, obligation, or parties to one agreement for another. By mutual agreement, a new contract replaces an earlier contract.

Offset Agreements: Typically resulting in foreign sales between nations, whereby corporate obligations are created by virtue of the international sales of commodities requiring the purchase or re-sale of goods. Example, one country sells airplanes to another country, and the individual company selling the product promises to buy or re-sell an equal amount commodities from that country in order to offset the international trade imbalance.

Option: A right embedded in a procurement which allows the buyer to order additional quantities of the same product(s) or services for a stipulated period of time. Sometimes options allow the buyer to unilaterally extend the performance period of the contract.

Order of Precedence: A provision which sets forth the ranking order of contractual documents contained in a solicitation or procurement in the event there are conflicts in the language of individual documents.

Other Direct Costs (ODC): Any category of cost elements which can be isolated to specific tasks or projects, other than labor and material. Included in ODC are such items as travel, computer time, and services.

Overhead: Costs incurred in the operation of a business which cannot be directly related to the individual projects, products or services being produced. See also "Indirect Cost."

Overrun: Costs actually incurred or projected to be incurred which are in excess of the original estimated and authorized costs. An overrun is that value of costs which are needed to complete a project or procurement, over that value originally authorized by management.

Partnership: A legal relationship between two or more persons or companies to pool their resources, typically to pursue new business ventures, with the understanding that they will share the risks, profits or losses from such ventures.

Performance Based Payments: A concept of making progress payments to sellers based on their achievement of physical work, as previously defined and agreed to by the buyer. The physical work is typically defined with use of milestones, with weighted values for each milestone, the sum of which will add up to the procurement value. It is a simple form of "earned value management."

Period of Performance: The time interval from start to finish of contractual performance that includes all effort required to satisfy the statement of work.

Price Analysis: The effort of evaluating seller proposed prices at the bottom-line price value, as compared with a detailed examination of individual cost elements. Comparisons of prices can be made between sellers in a competition, or with prior related work, published catalogue prices, etc.

Price Variance (PV): The difference between the budgeted costs for a purchased item and the actual costs.

Privity of Contract: A direct contractual relationship between two or more contracting parties. Buyers and sellers will have a privity of contract. Buyers and second or third tier sellers do not have a privity of contract relationship.

Procurement Management Plan: Such plans will sometimes relate to a single project, and sometimes to a number of projects within an organization. The Procurement Management Plan addresses the methodology of what will be bought, when, how, with what, for how much, the risks, and so forth.

Procurement Planning: The initial activity which starts at the inception of a new project, which addresses all project scope which will be procured from sources outside of the project's company.

Note: the Project Management Institute's *A Guide to the Project Management Body of Knowledge (PMBOK)®* describes "Procurement Planning" as representing the first of six distinct project procurement processes.

Progress Payments: A contract term authorizing payments made to a seller during the life of a fixed-price type contract, on the basis of some agreed-to methodology, for example, estimated physical percentage of work completed, performance based milestone payments, or simply costs incurred as used on many government type procurements.

Project: A one-time-only endeavor, to achieve specific objectives, with a precise start and completion date, and finite authorized resources to accomplish the goals.

Project Teams: See either "Concurrent Engineering" or "Integrated Product Development Teams."

Project Manager: An individual who has been assigned responsibility for accomplishing a specific unit of work. The project manager is typically responsible for the planning, implementing, controlling, and reporting of status on a given project.

Project Management Institute (PMI): The Project Management Institute, with over 100,000 members worldwide, is the leading non-profit professional association dealing in the discipline of the management of projects.

Purchase Order (PO): The official legal document issued by a buyer to a seller authorizing a procurement. Typically, only individuals who have delegated procurement authority may issue a Purchase Order for the organization, and most often this does not include the project manager.

Purchase Requisition (PR): A document which requests that a specific procurement be made on their behalf, defining the purchase, and authorizing budget for the effort. Typically projects issue Purchase Requisitions to the procurement organization requesting a particular buy.

Recurring Costs: Expenditures against specific tasks or items that would expect occur on a repetitive basis, often on a subsequent production run.

Request for Information (RFI): A request from buyer to sellers to seek information on the company or products for sale.

Request for Proposal (RFP): The Request for Proposal (RFP) is the most sophisticated of all procurement solicitation documents and will include everything needed by a seller to respond to a complex solicitation, including a statement of work, terms and conditions, etc. While the precise RFP format will vary by company, this document will be used for all major procurements.

Request for Qualifications (RFQ): Typically used to solicit information on prospective sellers past experience and competence in a particular area. It is used by buyers to screen out the unqualified, unsuitable sellers so that only qualified sellers are solicited with the formal RPF.

Request for Quotation (RFQ): Exact formats will vary by company, but the Request for Quotation is normally used to obtain price information on goods or services, which may or may not lead to a purchase.

Risk Management: The systematic process of identifying, analyzing, and responding to risks, and to bring all identified risks down to acceptable levels.

Schedule: A graphic display of planned work taking the form of activities, events, and relationships.

Scheduling: The act of preparing and/or implementing schedules.

Scope: A definition of the work to be

accomplished on a project or procurement.

Scope-Creep: The addition of work as a result of a poor or incomplete definition of project scope.

Seller: Sometimes also called a contractor, subcontractor, supplier, or vendor, it is an external organization which responds to a buyer's contract to provide a procured item.

Note: in the year 2000 edition of the Project Management Institute's (PMI) publication *A Guide to the Project Management Body of Knowledge (PMBOK)®* the terms "buyer" and "seller" were standardized. A "buyer" is defined as someone who represents the project to procure scope for the project, and a "seller" is someone who provides the procured scope to the project.

Single Source: A condition which occurs when there are multiple qualified sources for a given product, but the buyer or project elects to place an order from only one seller thus waiving the opportunity to hold a competition. Typically single source procurements must be authorized by senior management.

Small Business: Any business enterprise that is not dominant in its field. Dominance can be defined as the number of company employees, or sometimes gross sales of the firm. The placement of procurements with small businesses is a particularly important issue when dealing with government funded projects at all levels, federal, state, and local.

Sole Source: A condition which can exist when there is only one source for a given product and the buyer is thus forced to procure from only that source.

Solicitation: Is the process of requesting responses from sellers eventually resulting in a procurement.

Note: the Project Management Institute's *A Guide to the Project Management Body of Knowledge (PMBOK)®* describes "Solicitation" as representing the third of six distinct project procurement processes.

Solicitation Planning: Is the process of making plans leading to a solicitation of responses from sellers.

Note: the Project Management Institute's *A Guide to the Project Management Body of Knowledge (PMBOK)®* describes "Solicitation Planning" as representing the second of six distinct project procurement processes.

Source Selection: Is the process of evaluating seller's proposals leading to the award of a procurement.

Note: the Project Management Institute's *A Guide to the Project Management Body of Knowledge (PMBOK)®* describes "Source Selection" as representing the forth of six distinct project procurement processes.

Specification: A definition of the technical requirements for the item being procured, including the criteria to verify compliance. Generally there are three types of specifications in use: design, functional, and performance.

Standard: A formal document that describes the technical parameters of a product.

Standard Cost: The normal expected cost of an operation, process, or product including labor, material, and overhead charges, computed on the basis of past performance costs, estimates, or work measurement.

Standard Time: The amount of time allowed for the performance of a specific unit of work.

Statement of Work (SOW): A complete description of the work to be done and the requirements to be satisfied under a procurement.

Subcontract: A contractual document which legally defines the effort of providing services, data, or hardware from one firm to another.

Supply Management: The most recent popular term for the buying function, previously referred to as procurement, purchasing, material, materiel, etc.

Surety: Someone who is liable for an obligation in an equal position to that of the principle. It is best contrasted with a guarantor who has a secondary liability after the principle.

Task: Also called an activity, effort that takes place over a period of time, which generally consumes resources.

Teaming Agreements/Alliances/Arrangements: A legal contractual arrangement between two or more corporations typically to form a part-

nership or joint venture, but can be some other arrangement as defined by the parties. Usually these arrangements are formed to capture new business and the roles of each firm is specifically prescribed in their agreement. Whenever the new business opportunity ends, generally the teaming agreement also ends.

Teams: See either "Concurrent Engineering" or "Integrated Product Development Teams."

Termination of Contracts: The end of a contract, by satisfying all the contractual requirements, or by default, or convenience, or by mutual agreement of the parties.

Terms and Conditions (T&C): The supplemental, often standardized, requirements included in many contracts that form a critical part of the agreement of the parties. Example, progress payments provisions is a typical T & C in fixed price procurements.

Time and Materials (T & M) Contracts: A popular type of contractual arrangement in which the price (through profits) is stated at a fixed hourly value for each classification of worker engaged, and the materials are reimbursed at their actual cost, sometimes including handling fees and profits. T & M contracts are a sort of hybrid type between fixed unit price and cost reimbursable contracts.

Note: in the year 2000 edition of the Project Management Institute's (PMI) publication *A Guide to the Project Management Body of Knowledge (PMBOK)* ® the Time and Materials contract was defined as a third contract type, along with cost reimbursable and fixed price types.

Time is of the Essence: A contract clause in which schedule performance is considered to be strictly binding if the term "time is of the essence" is included in the contract. If included, failure to deliver performance as scheduled is considered to be a breach of the contract. If not included failure to deliver as scheduled will not breach the contract.

Uniform Commercial Code (UCC): An agreement adopted by all 50 states covering commercial laws, for the purpose of standardizing the interpretation and application of such laws in all states.

Unit Cost: Total labor, material, and overhead cost for one unit of production, i.e., one part, one gallon, one pound, etc.

Unpriced Changes: Authorized but un-negotiated changes to the contract.

Usage: The number of units of an item, expressed in either quantities or dollars, consumed over a specific period of time.

Usage Variance (UV): The difference between the budgeted quantity of materials and the actual quantity used.

Variable Cost: Costs that may change with the quantity of items consumed. Variable costs are best contrasted with fixed costs that do not change with quantities consumed.

Warranty: In a sale of goods, warranty can be either an express or an implied promise by a seller as to the condition, fitness, title, and use of goods being sold.

Virtual Teams: A group of individuals working on a common project, but who are not co-located with each other. Sometimes these projects can be disbursed around the world, with people who have never met, perhaps will never meet.

Work Breakdown Structure (WBS) The WBS is a product-oriented hierarchical family tree of hardware, software, services and project-unique tasks which organizes, defines, and graphically displays the project to be performed, as well as all work to be accomplished.

Work Breakdown Structure Dictionary: A narrative document which describes the effort to accomplish all work contained in each WBS element. The WBS Dictionary will often result in the project or procurement statement of work (SOW).

Work Breakdown Structure Element: A discrete portion of the WBS at any level. A WBS element may be an identifiable product, a set of data, a service, or any combination, and is often used to separate the make from buy tasks.

Wrap-Rates: Direct labor rates expressed at the bottom line, including all burdens and profit. Wrap rates are often used to set the hourly price for time and materials contracts.

About the Author: Quentin W. Fleming

Quentin Fleming is a professional business manager, author, lecturer, and management consultant in the field of project management. His particular expertise is in procurement management for projects and earned value project management systems.

He developed two new courses in the project management series for the University of California at Irvine: project procurement management and earned value project management.

He is the author of eight published management textbooks that are used by universities and consulting firms in their training seminars.

He has been an active member of the Project Management Institute (PMI), and served as president of his local Orange County Chapter in 1998. That same year he also served as the Technical Project Manager for the Project Management Institute's 1998 International Conference in Long Beach, California where over 265 professional papers were delivered.

During 1999-2000, he served on the eight person "core team" which updated the Project Management Institute's *A Guide to the Project Management Body of Knowledge (PMBOK Guide), Year 2000 Edition*. Quentin was responsible for all earned value management content, and also the chapter covering project procurement management.

Earlier in his career he was given a United States government appointment as the seventh and the last American Peace Corps Director in Iran. He and his wife and their three children were moved to Tehran, Iran where he managed the Peace Corps missions in both Iran and the small island nation of Bahrain.

His website is at http://www.QuentinF.com

Subject Index